BUSHCRAFT

Dedication

For all the students of bushcraft who have attended Woodlore courses. You have been the greatest teachers: watching you tackle this vast and complex subject has been inspiring to one who has walked this path so long.

BUSHCRAFT

Ray Mears

Illustrations by Ben McNutt

Hodder & Stoughton

First published in Great Britain in 2002 by Hodder and Stoughton
A division of Hodder Headline

A Hodder & Stoughton book

1 3 5 7 9 10 8 6 4 2

A CIP catalogue record for this title is available from the British Library

ISBN 0 340 79258 2

Typeset in Bembo
Designed by Ned Hoste/2H
Editorial: Patrick Cunningham, Caroline North, Hazel Orme, Ian Paten
Printed and bound in Great Britain by Butler & Tanner

Hodder and Stoughton
A division of Hodder Headline
338 Euston Road
London NW1 3BH

Contents

FREFACE

by Ewan MacGregor

There I was, standing in the rain trying to make a shelter in the middle of the Honduran jungle, when a thought came to me: why am I doing this? The answer: Ray Mears. When I was asked if I wanted to go and make a television programme about how I would cope with a week in the rainforest, my immediate reaction was 'No!' Then they told me who I would be going with, and I changed my answer to 'Well maybe'.

Like most of us, I only knew about Ray Mears from his television series where he makes fires and shelters as if by magic. Let me tell you that what you see on screen is only a tiny part of what Ray and Bushcraft are about. When you're with Ray you not only learn some amazing skills (and, yes, it is possible to do them on your own) but you also learn a lot about yourself. There was one moment while we were in Honduras when I just lost it. I was wet, I was freezing cold and I wanted to go home that minute.

I stormed off into the forest on my own, slashing at anything and everything with my panga.

When I came back, Ray just asked me if I'd found any of the twenty-odd varieties of seriously poisonous snake that live there and suggested that if I had been bitten that would have been it, because there was no way they could have got me out of the jungle before I died. Point taken, Ray, I just hadn't thought it through.

Only a few of us will ever be lucky enough to experience Ray's wonderfully enabling ideas and skills at first hand, so I'm very pleased that he's found the time to explore and explain some of them in this book. Whether you're going into the outback tomorrow or just fancy a weekend camping in the garden you'll learn from *Bushcraft*.

I just wish I'd had a copy before I went to Honduras.......

Ewan MacGregor, August 2001

INTRODUCTION

'We learned that one cannot defy nature, but must adapt and accommodate oneself to her. Nature will not change; it is man who must change, if he is to live in conditions where nature is dominant.'
Knut Haukelid Skis *Against the Atom*

Today no wilderness on our planet is more than four days' travel from our doorstep and, as a consequence we can as easily find ourselves hiking in a rainforest as upon the arctic tundra. But living as we do today in cities, we no longer rely to any degree upon our own abilities and knowledge of the land around us. Instead when visiting wild country we meet the challenges of the trail with a sophisticated array of specialised tools and a rucksack full of food. It can be argued that the modern approach enables us to go further and achieve more than our ancestors could. But we must remember our ancestors were not playing in the wild but were instead living there. Their challenge was to live tightly with nature's rhythm rather than try to overcome her.

Bushcraft is the term I employ to describe a deeper knowledge of the wild and of nature. It is a huge tree that branches out in many directions to botany, zoology, craft work, outdoors leadership and countless other divisions. At its root though is a reliance upon oneself and on nature. In the study of bushcraft we step beyond survival and learn the subtlety that makes outdoor life both certain and enjoyable. Every man, woman or child who visits wild places by whatever means will benefit from bushcraft knowledge. What could be more natural than to walk in wild places able to recognise the wild things around us, confidently able to find food, shelter, fire and water. And these are but the foundation stones of bushcraft.

I do not wish though to suggest that we should turn our backs on the skills and tools of today in pusuit of a romantic stone age ideal. Far from it – my hope is that we shall learn to use our modern tools more wisely by bolstering them with wisdom from our past. Bushcraft ties us closely to nature, at its core is respect for nature and all living things. A concern that can guide us in the employment of new technologies that tend so easily to blind us to the natural world.

But bushcraft is not necessarily easily learned – many of the skills will challenge us to dig deep inside ourselves and discover hidden toughness and resilience that our modern life rarely demands of us. Rising to these challenges develops determination and a powerful positive mental attitude that in turn gives birth to an increased liveliness of spirit. Overall students of bushcraft report that having become more alert to the land around them they enjoy an improved understanding and relationship with nature and themselves.

The great difficulty in writing about bushcraft is the sheer scale of the task. To write one volume that contains all would be prohibitively expensive. Reluctantly acceptant of this fact I have chosen to confine myself to what can be considered the fundamental skills of the subject. I have assumed that the reader is already interested in travelling in wilderness and can already navigate and is conversant with first aid techniques. I have not set out to describe every method for each section, far from it – my aim is to describe the most important skills or the most versatile.

Training in bushcraft can assist us to preserve the very freedom that it teaches us to value. Many of the indigenous peoples I have been fortunate to learn from survive today culturally, and in some cases as individuals, because their bushcraft skills have enabled them to exist in or escape to wild places beyond the reach of oppressive invaders, be they governmental or commercial or religious. Even closer to home examples of such value in bushcraft can be found. During the Nazi occupation of Norway 1940-45 the possession of tents, windproof clothing, boots, rucksacks, and blankets was prohibited under a penalty of three years' imprisonment or a very heavy fine. This was an attempt to prevent the free movement of resistance fighters in Norway's remote and difficult to police countryside. Whilst limited control was exercised over the equipment of the Norwegian people, their knowhow and mountain tested spirit could not be taken away. Despite harsh treatment Norwegian resistance used their knowledge of the mountains and forests to outwit and hinder their enemy, eventually training an army in the cover of their trees in readiness to cast their oppressors back whence they came.

Knowledge is invisible and weighs not at all. Be mindful that in times of crisis if you can find shelter in the forest, rub sticks for fire and know which wild plants around you can be eaten you cannot easily be denied access to a home, hearth and a meal. All that is necessary is that we preserve wild places and our knowledge of them.

OUTFIT

'I learned how much of what we think to be necessary is superfluous; I learned how few things are essential, and how essential those things really are.'
Bernard Ferguson, *Chindits, Burma 1943.*

When I first went camping I had no proper equipment at all. It was a memorable experience. I had only a reflective foil blanket, which I used as a tarp, an orange survival bag, a sleeping-bag, and a biscuit tin. Not surprisingly, I had no sleep that night: instead my colleague and I sat beside a fire intoxicated by the adventure. We didn't notice the hardship.

I gradually improved my outfit and today I have one outfit suitable for every environment on Earth. But those early experiences were vitally important because even today, with all the correct equipment, I am aware that things can go wrong, that on expeditions it's all too easy to be separated from your basic kit. At these times the knowledge that you can cope when you haven't got equipment helps you to realise that there's no drama really, just another adventure ahead.

As a novice camper you may find it daunting to put together an outfit, even if you have a list of equipment compiled by an expert. Many shops don't stock the items you really need, and sales assistants are sometimes unhelpful, ill-informed or both. It's not uncommon for people to go into a shop with a list of specific items and emerge with an outfit that they believe to be the correct one, only to discover in the wilderness that it is inappropriate. I have seen people come to the far north with two-season sleeping-bags, having been told that they were rated for four or five.

When putting together a suitable outfit for wilderness travel, the golden rule is K I S S - Keep It Simple, Stupid. You will not need anything elaborate, easily broken or complicated. Your outfit should be adaptable according to the climate and the nature of the activities you are to undertake.

Something to carry your outfit in

The type of rucksack you choose will depend on what you plan to do. For short overnight hikes, a large day sack of 35 litres volume will be adequate. For more extended journeys, a medium-sized pack of 55-60 litres volume will be large enough in hot climates where you will need less clothing and a lighter sleeping-bag. For colder weather a 100 litre rucksack or larger will be necessary.

At its most basic, this is what you will need:

something to carry your outfit in

something to sleep under

something to sleep in

something to sleep on

navigational equipment

something to cook over

something to cook in

something to carry water

a mug

eating utensils

food

medical kit

illumination at night

wash kit

odds and ends to make life comfortable – 'possibles'

clothing

35 litre day sack.

If you are canoeing you will need a day sack with a large canoe pack, which should be fitted with straps to enable you to carry it as if it were a rucksack. There are two choices: the traditional canvas Duluth sack, or the more modern dry bag with rucksack strap attachments. For canoeing I prefer the Duluth sack; for whitewater rafting, the dry bag.

I prefer rucksacks to have only one main compartment without any division: this reduces the zips and seams, making for a stronger rucksack which withstands the rigours of wild journeys. I like there to be several large outside pockets for the items needed constantly, such as water-bottles, water-purification equipment, first-aid kit, torch and lunch.

A rucksack should not ride too high above the shoulder line. Many are designed for moorland and mountain conditions where there are few overhanging obstructions for them to snag on so they are tall and slim. In woodland they can be hazardous when you have to duck beneath branches.

Most rucksacks today have internal frames, which make them more compact. However, this may cause your back to sweat, chafe and become sore, particularly in the tropics. For that reason many people still use external-frame rucksacks in wilderness and good ones are available, particularly those made by Norrøna of Norway.

55-60 litre pack.

100 litre rucksack.

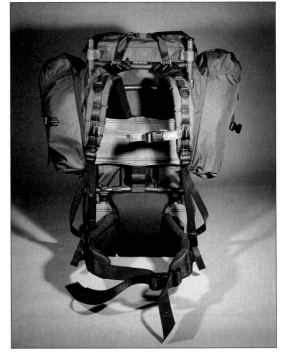

100 litre rucksack showing external frame.

Something to sleep under

The most versatile shelter is the simple tarp or fly-sheet, and I favour the Australian Army hoochi, which is well equipped with attachment points and made to a high standard. I pack my tarp up with guy lines and suspension lines attached, then fold it neatly so that when I come to put it up after dark there are no tangles (see photo above). When making a more fixed camp I use a larger canvas tarp set over a ridge pole or over a length of rope stretched tightly between two trees. The advantages of using a tarp in wet weather are that you have a dry space but are not cut off from the environment around you, and can enter and exit from any direction. The single entrance to a conventional tent soon becomes a muddy quagmire.

As the temperature drops, thermally efficient shelters are more appropriate, such as hiking or mountain tents. The Hilleberg, a Swedish-manufactured tent, is made to a high standard, with superb ventilation: the space between the inner and outer tents is larger than on most comparable tents, so condensation is not a problem inside.

A tent is also preferable in tropical conditions or where insects and/or snakes are hazardous, or where there are few trees to string a mosquito net or a fly-sheet the Australian Mozzie Dome has two flexible poles that cross to create a double hoop that stretches taut a fine mosquito net, which is sealed to an integral ground sheet. A lightweight fly-sheet can be attached over this with another pole. Classic wall tents are used in the far north with wood-burning stoves, often in conditions where poles need not be carried but can be cut from the forest.

Tarp shelters are airy and enable you to observe nature on all sides.

Hilleberg Keron 3GT – an excellent tent for two to three people.
(inset) Good ventilation reduces condensation problems.

Of tent designs my favourite is the Scandinavian tepee Kota or Laavu, as used in the far north of Scandinavia. Like the American plains tepee, the traditional tent had many poles, but now has only one. I use three varieties: a fairly large seven- or nine-man polycotton canvas tepee, within which I fit a wood-burning stove and chimney, or a two–four man lightweight nylon tepee with a folding firebox. The great advantage of tepees is that in winter or inclement weather you can stay warm and cook inside them and they are easily illuminated with candles.

One other excellent form of shelter is the parachute: in good conditions, it can make an awning capable of breaking strong rain and offers protection from sunlight too. Although not entirely waterproof, it provides sufficient cover for a large group. It can be strung in many ways, but perhaps the best is simply to attach a rope to the central portion of the parachute, throw the end over a high branch, pull up the parachute then spread out the gores, or panels.

Lightweight nylon tepee – light enough to be carried for solo camping, yet large enough to sleep in comfort.

Parachute shelters are ideal for training camps.

Something to sleep in

Your sleeping-bag is one of the most important items of your equipment so choose it carefully. Avoid sleeping-bags that have not been designed for specifically outdoor use. Thin caravan sleeping-bags are inadequate in all but tropical conditions.

Your sleeping-bag should fit you well: before you buy it, get into it and make sure that it is both long and wide enough, that you can move around in it freely, and that there is room for your clothes and boots if you are going to be in cold conditions, as it is normal practice to store them overnight in your sleeping-bag – otherwise they may freeze. Choose a sleeping-bag suitable for the temperature range you are likely to encounter. Remember that we all sleep at a different temperature: one sleeping-bag may not suit two people in the same party. Season ratings are unreliable as no universal standard applies. If you need a warm sleeping-bag, put it on the ground to see how thick it is when it is not in use. A sleeping-bag retains your body warmth by creating a lagging of insulative material around you, which must trap air: to be warm the bag must be thick. Take with you a sleeping-bag that is likely to be too warm, rather than the reverse: you can always undo the zip, if need be, and use it as a duvet.

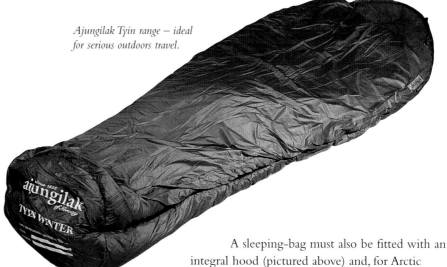

Ajungilak Tyin range – ideal for serious outdoors travel.

Ajungilak Kompakt Junior – specially designed for young teenagers.

A sleeping-bag must also be fitted with an integral hood (pictured above) and, for Arctic conditions, a baffle that closes around your shoulders and prevents you breathing moisture into the bag, which reduces insulation. Some manufacturers, such as Ajungilak, make children's sleeping-bags (pictured left). Teenagers can use adult sleeping-bags, but tie a belt around the bag to restrict the length to suit the occupant. As they grow the belt can be moved downwards.

In very hot climates I tend to use a poncho liner – a thin lightweight blanket used by the US military to insulate the military poncho, which is invaluable. It dries quickly and is ideal in the tropics.

In hot, arid climates, with vehicles, a swag or a bed roll is commonly used. This is a canvas case containing a 5-cm thick foam mattress, a small duvet and a pillow. It's excellent for sleeping out under the stars, ideal in the desert.

Sales assistants devote much time to discussing the relative merits of sleeping-bag stuffing materials. They usually argue that down is lightweight when it is packed but if it gets wet it stays wet and you get cold; synthetic materials are slightly heavier and bulkier, but retain warmth when damp. This argument is all true, but once any sleeping-bag is wet it ceases to provide adequate insulation. When I am in the high Arctic I prefer a

Ajungilak Little Viking for small children grows with the youngster and ensures they enjoy sleeping out.

down sleeping-bag because there is less risk that it will become moist, it packs up small, it weighs little and gives good warmth. When I am in temperate climates then I use a synthetic sleeping-bag because it is better in damp conditions, but I ensure that I keep it dry.

The efficiency of all sleeping-bags can be improved if used with a Gore-tex bivvy bag. Ex-military ones are ideal and the British Army bivvy bag is of high quality, providing extra warmth and protection for your bag. If you put a good-quality sleeping-bag with a sleeping mat inside a Gore-tex bivvy bag you have a lightweight bed roll. The bivvy bag protects you from draughts and breezes, so is particularly useful when sleeping under a tarp. In an emergency you can sleep out without a shelter if you have a bivvy bag and a good sleeping-bag. When you carry your sleeping-bag make sure it is protected from moisture. Even if you think your rucksack is waterproof the sleeping-bag must still be protected from moisture because few rucksacks are truly waterproof and those that claim to be rarely stay so for long because they have such a hard life. Either stuff your sleeping-bag into a dry bag, or pack it into a bin-liner, inside the stuff sack.

Poncho liners are light and versatile, and dry out quickly.

Something to sleep on

A sleeping mat is a vital item. While it is possible to improvise beds efficiently from natural materials it is far easier to use either a closed-cell foam mattress or Thermarest mat, which is an open-cell mattress within an impervious envelope, which can be inflated so it is a cross between an air-bed and a foam mattress. I use a three-quarter lightweight Thermarest, which folds up to almost nothing and is light, strong and durable. It blocks the transmission of heat from your body to the ground. Trying to sleep outdoors without ground insulation or one of these is misery.

In the far north, spruce boughs are still widely used under a foam mat to provide a good depth of insulation. Also in the far north reindeer or caribou skin is still in regular use: because each hair is hollow, these skins make a perfect sleeping mat – but the hairs shed: avoid this by putting the reindeer skin in a thin nylon case. Although these are bulky they make good insulation in snowy conditions.

Navigational equipment

The compass is the key to the wilderness, with your map, but you may also need other navigational equipment. Before your journey, your planning will tell you what maps you need and the nature of the terrain you will cross. Establishing suitable navigation equipment is fundamental to your planning.

Begin by ordering or purchasing maps in the most suitable scale for the area to which you are going, and allow plenty of time for these to arrive. Ideally the scale should be 1:50,000 or 1:25,000, but bear in mind that in some parts of the world the only maps available may be 1:500,000.

Your maps should be protected from moisture damage. Keep them well stashed inside your rucksack, wrapped in waterproof zip-lock bags. The map which is in current use should be protected inside a map case – the soft lightweight one I favour is made by a company called Ortlieb.

Your compass is a precision tool and must be carefully chosen and protected. For the wilderness sighting compasses are ideal. The Silva compass type 54 or type 15 TDCL is perhaps the most popular one in use today and for good reason: the type 54 provides a very accurate sighting of bearings using a lens system while the type 15 provides a sighting using a mirror and is rather more robust because the mirror cover folds to protect the needle housing. Regardless of which compass you choose to use it must be kept in a case. I keep mine in a top jacket pocket where it is readily available. When travelling by aircraft I ensure that my compass travels as hand luggage and thus is protected from pressure differences, which may cause a bubble to appear in the liquid-filled needle housing.

Remember that for navigation you will also need a waterproof-paper notebook and soft B pencil to record daily your route, the bearings on which you have marched and grid references. This is very important as it gives you the chance to check whether you have made a

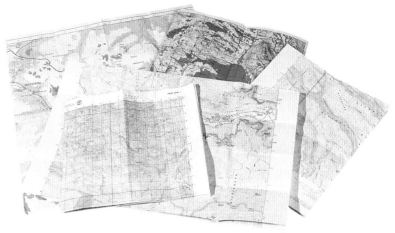

Survey maps for walking 1: 50,000/1:25,000.

mistake and, if so, retrace your route. This is crucial in wild country where there are few landmarks or features, especially in rainforest.

The global positioning system, or GPS, is having a major impact on outdoor pursuits. No bigger than a mobile phone, it can receive transmissions from a series of orbiting satellites and triangulate its position with great accuracy. The Garmin e-trex Summit also provides an electronic compass and altimeter, a wonderful tool, which enables you to predict weather trends, take sightings, locate yourself and plot your journey.

GPS has been resisted by some outdoors traditionalists, while others have hailed it as the successor to the compass. While it should certainly be used in the wilderness, it is not an alternative to a map and compass: any electronic device is prone to damage, battery failure or weather damage. It should be treated as an adjunct to the traditional map and compass.

Key to the wilderness - Silva Type 15TDCL compass.

Silva Type 54 compass.

Garmin e-Trex Vista Global Positioning System (GPS).

Cooking equipment

Depending on the nature of your journey, how light you wish to travel and the climate in which you are travelling, you will need to take with you suitable cooking equipment, and perhaps a stove: either a pocket-sized military tommy cooker, which burns solid fuel tablets made of hexamine, or a methylated-spirits-fired trangia, or perhaps a pressure petrol stove.

Mini Trangia spirit stove.

Optimus Nova – pressure petrol stove.

A range of different size pans is important, depending on the size of your party.

Water carriers, mugs, eating and food

A water carrier is not necessary in areas where there is a lot of water, but everywhere else it is of critical importance. I prefer the strong army canteen: I use two one-litre British Army water bottles, which are strong and reliable. These are made of black plastic and protect the water, which may have been purified with iodine, from degrading in sunlight. In addition, I often carry a two-quart collapsible water canteen, made by the US Army, which I can fill towards the end of the day. In deserts I increase the number of two-quart canteens to ensure I have a minimum of six litres of water contained in vessels with me.

NATO 1 litre flask, 2 quart US canteen, lightweight Ortlieb civilian water bag.

A drinking cup or mug is important: avoid plastic because it gets greasy and difficult to clean in the wild. Hand-carved wooden cups from the burl on the side of a tree are aesthetically pleasing but far more practical is a metal military mug or cup, particularly the stainless-steel ones which are graduated to enable you to judge liquid volumes when cooking. A stainless-steel mug can serve as a cooking pot in a very lightweight outfit. The lid will keep off flies and other insects, should you be disturbed and have to attend to the fire or whatever while you are eating. Obviously in this way you avoid unnecessary illness. All stainless-steel utensils can be heated over a stove or fire to sterilise them.

You will also need a spoon, but a fork is not essential. You can buy titanium or plastic spoons in any outdoors shop – or you could carve a beautiful piece of wood into one; see page 25.

Food for the trail must be carefully packed to protect it from the weather and damp. If you are travelling in bear country, pack it so that it can be suspended from a tree, out of the reach of marauding claws.

This stainless steel mug has become a trusty friend.

Medical kit

With any luck your medical kit will simply be a burden you
have to carry and never use. However, if you are planning a
wilderness trip and haven't already had any first aid-training
you should get some: in the wilderness, you may need to be
able to do more than a first-aider in an urban situation. If you
haven't done a course recently, you should attend one to update
yourself on current practice and refresh your memory. You may
be days from professional medical assistance and must be able to
deal with a wide range of problems and even make life-saving
decisions. You will almost certainly have to be able to treat and
manage wounds.

The contents of your medical kit will be bound by space and
weight restrictions and experience. It must, however, be
appropriate to the type of expedition you have planned.
Discuss with your GP the essentials for a long haul trip. You
will need all or some of the following items.

Tools To Control Infection

• surgical gloves
• some antiseptic hand wipes
• a CPR barrier of some description - pocket mask or shield

Tools

• EMT shears or small scissors
• tweezers for removing splinters
• water-purification tablets, either chlorine or iodine tablets for
  use when irrigating wounds.
• a sterile scalpel blade
• a needle for draining blisters
• a paper clip to reduce blood underneath a thumbnail
• a magnifying lens for removal of ticks or other insects from
  skin
• some gaffer tape to be wrapped around splints
• digital thermometer to read high and low temperatures

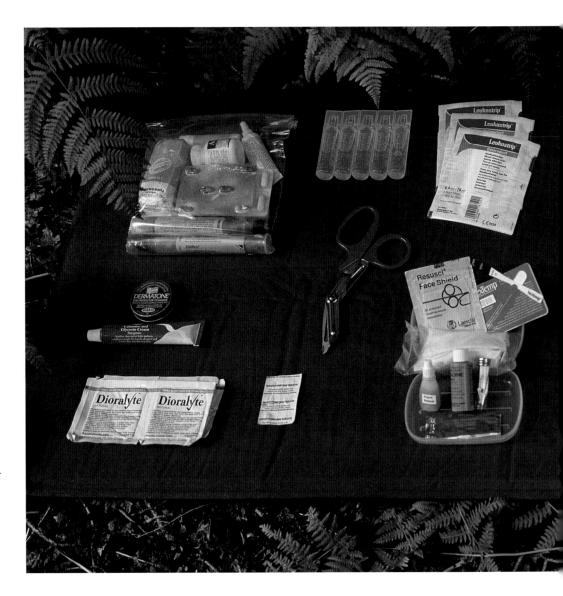

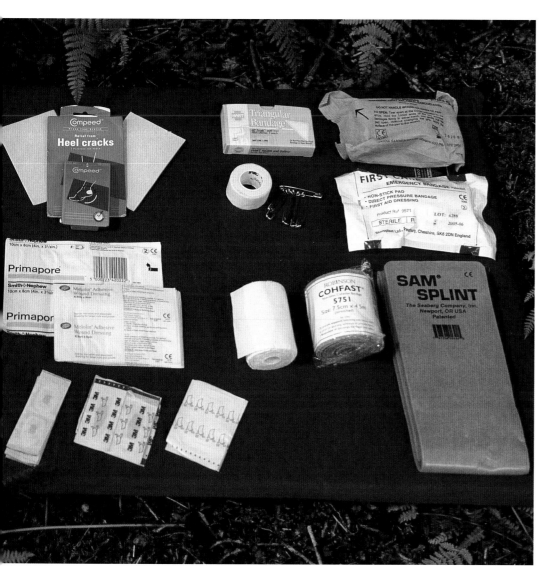

For long trips

- an emergency dental kit
- a notebook and pencil to record details of a condition, location and map reference, when sending someone for help
- forceps, for suturing, and sutures if qualified to use them
- a sam splint, in flexible aluminium
- a high-reading thermometer
- a low-reading thermometer, to check for hypothermia
- venom extractor and anti-venom, in areas with venomous snakes
- sterile liquids, for wound irrigation with a 20cc syringe with a green canula or steripod
- topical antiseptic such as Povidone Iodine in the form of Aqueous Betadene solution for bites, small lesions and minor cuts
- anti-microbial ointment for slow-healing wounds and ulcers
- aloe vera, for sunburn
- calamine lotion and hydrocortisone for burns

For blisters

- hydrocollide bandages for burst blisters – try Compeed bandages which are perfect for the job
- mole foam and mole skin to prevent the rubbing at a hot spot in a boot

Bandages

- an assortment of adhesive bandages, such as 3M nexcore active strips which stay on; Leukostrips, Cover strips or Steri Strips to close a clean wound
- 5cm or 10cm square non-adherent gauze pads, Meloin pads or similar, for wound treatment and covering
- self-adhesive gauze pads
- a sterile trauma pad to apply pressure and help staunch bleeding.
- an elastic bandage, either 7.5cm crêpe, or adhesive coban bandage, if preferred, for sprains
- safety pins

Illumination

Lighting is important for dealing with emergencies at night. There are several varieties of illumination. With my vehicle-portable camp, I carry pressure petrol lanterns which go into the vehicle last so that if I arrive at a campsite in the dark they are the first item to hand. Here self-igniting lanterns have an advantage over those that must be primed and lit. Take with you some spare mantels.

Candles are an old bush favourite and still useful, particularly in tents which protect them from breezes. In the rainforest, where breezes are unusual, they are used widely at night. Head torches are useful, such as the one made by Petzel, which incorporates LED lights, runs on three AAA batteries and has a very long life. It is ideal when sorting out a camp, or moving in and out of a tent.

I like a small LED light, which I can wear around my neck, and when the sun starts to go down I make sure I have it with me: if I put down a conventional torch in the dark I can always locate it again. I also like to have a small handheld flashlight with a powerful halogen bulb, which is useful in rescue situations or emergencies, and can be saved for that purpose alone.

Petzl Tikka head torch and spare batteries.

Wash kit

Personal hygiene is important in the field and especially in hot climates as a means of staying healthy. Keep your wash kit simple; avoid scented products, as they attract insects. I carry with me pine-tar soap, effective in removing parasite insects, an antibacterial antiperspirant and for removing pine resin from skin or clothing.

Travel towels fold up small, are absorbent and dry rapidly anywhere except the tropics, where they don't dry and smell mouldy. On my last journey in the rainforest my travel towel smelt so awful that I burned it and used a large cotton bandanna instead.

Clothing

In bushcraft we find ourselves outdoors in conditions that range from arid to Arctic. Dressing for the conditions in which you will be travelling is a key aspect of being comfortable and enjoying the experience. You will need to maintain a versatile clothing system, though, because conditions can change so rapidly. While scientists strive to find one garment that will adjust to any climate, I rely on the old principle of several garments carefully chosen for each climatic zone. Bear in mind that almost as soon as you start moving your body temperature will change and your clothes should allow excessive heat and moisture to vent out, preventing insulative layers becoming soaked and reducing their effectiveness.

Arid lands

Arid land is perhaps the easiest of all environments for which to dress. Wear woollen socks inside lightweight leather boots. Some of the best boots for these areas are to be found in Africa where comfortable flat-soled leather shoes are made for safari use, which are excellent for hiking through the bush. If these are not available, consider ex-military desert boots.

Underwear should be loose-fitting cotton. I like to wear shorts wherever possible, but you must have long trousers with you: to cover up against the sun and for protection in the evening from biting insects. The best way to avoid malaria and other diseases transmitted by insect bite, like dengue fever and scrub typhus, is to cover yourself in loose-fitting tightly woven fabrics.

As for tops, I wear a tightly woven cotton jacket/shirt, loose-fitting to vent moisture and give shade. Otherwise

Cool and comfortable – a long sleeved jacket and jersey are carried in day sack.

wear a T-shirt and a lightweight jacket, or simply wear a tightly woven cotton shirt. The jacket/shirt is harder wearing and survives longer in thorny country.

It is always a good idea to carry with you a pullover as it can be quite cold at night. You can wear it under a jacket/shirt for protection against wind. Bear in mind that in some areas, such as the North African desert, during winter temperatures can drop extremely low, and in these conditions I have taken a down jacket to keep warm at night.

One of the most important items of all is a hat to protect you from the sun: the stronger the sunlight the wider the brim is the old rule, so if you are in the Australian desert go for the broadest brim available – the sun's rays are much stronger there than in many other arid areas. I like the hats made by Akubra who produce a felted hat of superior quality.

Wear sunglasses to reduce the effect of glare, especially around saltpans, which can be white and cause discomfort to those with sensitive eyes. A head net kept in the top pocket of your shirt discourages insects after dark.

Lightweight leather safari boots.

Jungle

In the rainforest clothing has to withstand continuous wet. Sometimes you will be dry but usually you will be wet, either because it is raining or because it is humid and you are sweating profusely.

There is no better footwear than the US Army jungle boot: look for genuine boots in the modern version, which has Cordura uppers and leather soles with speedlacing. They are much more comfortable than the earlier models. They are supplied in width fittings, so choose carefully and ensure that yours are in the right size. New boots will stretch a little

after initial wearing. Inside I wear two pairs of wool socks. Wool doesn't go mouldy and unpleasant like cotton socks.

US Army jungle boots.

I prefer Lycra cycling shorts as underwear: they don't chafe between your legs.

Wear long trousers, not shorts – go for strong ones that dry fast. Again the best are often ex-military trousers. Try to avoid camouflage – in many countries you may be mistaken for a soldier and find yourself in trouble.

On top, a long-sleeved shirt or a jacket/shirt of tightly woven cotton gives good protection against insects and thorns. Make sure it has long sleeves which can be rolled down in the evening to cover up and avoid mosquito bites.

I tend not to wear a hat when I'm hiking through the rainforest as the brim impedes my vision, causing me to bang my head on low branches and vines, but on river journeys in canoes a classic short-brimmed cotton jungle hat is essential.

Long trousers and long-sleeved cotton clothing

Normally in the rainforest we have two sets of clothes: a dry set and a wet set. Your wet clothes are those you wear during the day. In the evening, after setting up camp, you change out of your wet clothes, wring them out and hang them up to dry as best they will, then put on your dry clothes, which are kept carefully in a dry bag. Powder your feet when you take off your boots and put on a pair of lightweight sneakers or hockey boots to wear in the evening around camp. Pack them carefully before setting out the next day, when you will put on your wet clothes again – unpleasant, but five minutes later you will feel as though you had never taken them off.

Temperate

This is perhaps the hardest of all areas to dress for because you can experience such a wide range of climatic conditions. With four distinct seasons your dress may vary between everything from Arctic and arid, particularly during the spring when you may experience summer and winter conditions all in one day. Here I like a good strong leather hiking boot that comes high up my leg. If you step into soft ground in short boots, they are swamped. I like a boot with a Gore-tex liner, but this is not essential as waterproof socks are available to prevent your feet becoming cold and moist. Further protection from rain is afforded by waterproof gaiters.

Waterproofs are a vital piece of your equipment – jacket, trousers and gaiters

Wear two pairs of good wool socks and ex-military trousers but nothing too expensive: you may have to push through thorns and briars and your trousers will take a battering. If you are going far out on the trail, consider taking some tightly woven windproof trousers, such as those made of Ventile fabric for added protection.

I prefer cotton underwear but in these circumstances others wear cycling shorts or even swimming trunks.

Conventional wisdom suggests that we should wear modern fibre thermal tops but I go for a cotton or wool thermal shirt rather than synthetic fibre ones. I find they do not pick up body odours so quickly and are more pleasant to wear in the long term. Over the top of this I tend to wear wool, either a tightly woven shirt or woollen thermals (see page 17). Over them a windproof jacket or a heavier wool shirt, depending on whether I am in woods or the open. If you are in the open go for the windproof jacket, the shirt in woods.

In this environment waterproof clothing is important so take jacket and trouser in either Gore-tex fabric or Triple Point: these fabrics breathe, allowing body vapours to pass out while keeping out the rain. Don't forget a hat; try to find one that is insulative, windproof and waterproof.

Lowa military boots.

Arctic

In the Arctic we are dressing against dry cold although on rare occasions it rains so protection from moisture is also important. When the temperature drops below zero, you will discover that the modern fabrics that worked well in temperate climates become as stiff as vinyl.

Footwear must be chosen to suit the activity you are to be engaged in; for cross-country skiing choose the appropriate cross-country ski boots, two sizes larger than normal to accommodate felt inner boots for extra insulation and plenty of room. If your footwear – in fact any of your clothing in the Arctic – is tight it will restrict your circulation and you will get cold. So extra room is necessary.

If you are going to be working with snowmobiles and skis, instead of a conventional cross-country ski boot consider taking a rubber boot adapted for cross-country skiers such as those made by Nokia. They give good protection from the moisture commonly encountered on a snowmobile when travelling over frozen lakes with a heavy snow pack on top. These boots also come with a felt inner liner.

In cold dry conditions when I am using snow-shoes, my favourite boots are mukluks, made from moose hide with a felt inner sole and plenty of room for the foot to move. The best are made by a company called Steger Mukluks. Inside them, I wear wool socks, a thin pair and a medium-thick pair relying for warmth on the felt liner. I don't want too much bulk in the socks which might press on my feet and reduce the circulation.

I normally use wool underwear in the Arctic and my middle layers are wool: I take two pairs of wool long johns in different increasing weights of wool density, and three woollen shirts, which can be worn over each other again in

Rubber boots with felt inners adapted for skiers.

Steger Mukluks for cold dry conditions.

You can never have too many clothes when travelling by snowmobile. Wear goggles over hood so you can easily turn round and look behind.

In extreme cold an extra skull cap beneath your hat can make all the difference to warmth.

Lovikka mittens with leather over mitts.

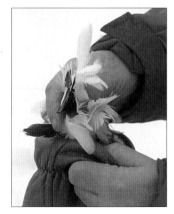

Ptarmigan feathers stuffed into gloves for extra warmth.

Ullfrote underwear in layers.

$200gm/m^2$ $400gm/m^2$ $600gm/m^2$ Windshell

three different weights of wool. Here I prefer Ullfrote fabrics, which are, without a doubt, the best for this environment; they come in $200g/m^2$ to $400g/m^2$ or $600g/m^2$ weights, which makes it possible to create a perfectly balanced layered clothing system. The manufacturers claim that as the wool is of the highest quality it can be worn next to the skin without causing itching. I cannot confirm this because my skin has never been irritated by wool, but the high quality of the product is undeniable.

Headgear is very important in the Arctic, and worn for most of the time. Here I like a hat that combines rabbit fur with fabric. This is not too warm on the crown so I don't overheat; and when the temperature drops I add either a wool skull-cap made by Ullfrote or, when I am travelling on a snowmobile, a full woollen balaclava.

I use two types of glove: British Army leather gloves with a Gore-tex liner are excellent for carrying out small, fiddly tasks in the cold; for using an axe, I wear woollen mittens produced in Lapland by the Sami people, called lovikka, with a leather Chopper mitt on top.

For emergencies, I also carry warm, windproof over-trousers and a down jacket for travelling in very cold conditions on snowmobiles or when I have to stand still for any length of time. It is also useful to have thickly woven woollen trousers, some windproof over-trousers or ski trousers and a waterproof jacket. My own windproof outer layers are made of Ventile - a single-layer fabric trouser and a double-layer anorak with a fur hood. In the North artificial fur does not work as effectively as a real fur, and a fur ruff is vitally important when travelling on snowmobiles for any distance.

CUTTING TOOLS

In bushcraft sharp, appropriate cutting tools make possible a wide range of improvisation and trail craft that enhance life in the wilderness. Here I shall present the tools I employ and the way I use them, based on my experience of wilderness travel on every continent except Antarctica and over eighteen years' teaching bushcraft. If you follow my advice, you will learn quickly to use your tools well. Bear in mind always that safety is the product of a mature outlook and presence of mind.

Four basic types of cutting tool are used in bushcraft; the knife, the saw, the axe, and the parang or machete. Each has applications to which they are uniquely suited. In addition, there are a few specialist tools for use in unique environments or to improve craft work and backcountry handicraft.

It is important to understand these tools: an inappropriately chosen cutting tool is inefficient and can be dangerous to the user. Also cutting tools are heavy, so choose wisely rather than burdening yourself unnecessarily. Learn how to use each tool safely: this will take time, humility and careful practice.

I have inflicted many scars on myself over the years: every one was the result of poor technique, haste or loss of concentration. I hope your road to skilful cutting will be bloodless as you learn from my mistakes rather than your own.

The knife

Once it was inconceivable for anyone to venture into wild lands without a sensible knife. Today, though, urban outdoors enthusiasts take with them a perception of the knife as a weapon and insist on carrying only folding-blade penknives. In bushcraft folding knives are virtually useless.

The knife is your number one tool, with which you can make almost anything you need, cut up food or craft beautiful objects. Once, on a difficult journey in Africa, I carved animals from pieces of firewood to give as gifts to people who offered assistance.

Choosing

All sorts of advice will be offered when you are trying to choose a knife, and there is no worse bore than the knife bore. Those skilled with a knife let their work speak for them – even with a poor knife they will still produce good work.

When I started teaching bushcraft, students struggled to acquire skills because their knives were blunt, too large or folding-blade designs. Experience taught

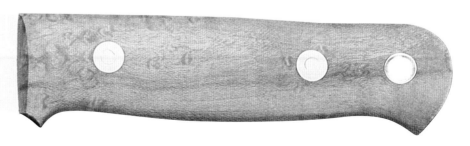

A knife is the most important survival tool. Frustrated at not being able to find the ideal knife for my work I ended up designing my own, which went into production in 1990.

that even locking folding-blade knives can collapse on a finger and that they do not encourage strong, confident cutting because they flex a little at the hinge. Lack of confidence leads to uncommitted carving and dangerous technique. Some sheath knives look workmanlike but break on simple tasks because they are too hard and brittle. When choosing a knife, take into account the following:

Size: Do not choose a knife with a large blade: we do not want to hack, but to carve. This is best achieved with a blade 8–12cm long.

Handle: It should be well designed for easy grip: avoid finger notches as they make it difficult to vary your grasp comfortably. Find one that is a comfortable shape and size for you to hold. My knife grip has a smooth finish but has never slipped from my grasp because of its shape. Never use a knife with a symmetrical grip: in poor light or when you are tired, you may mistake the edge for the blade back and cut yourself.

Avoid blades with this strong a curve.

Blade shape: It should have an edge on only one side: double edge blades are for fighting. A spear shaped blade is ideal, enabling the blade to be inverted and used to peel bark and skin. Avoid blades that are very round, where the belly rises to the tip, as the knife will tend to slip off the work-piece at the end of each cut. Avoid serrated blades: they hamper good carving; you will be learning

to sharpen your knife to a razor's edge, serrations will provide no appreciable advantage. The blade tang should ideally be full tang, i.e. extending the full length of the handle at full handle width. This is the strongest arrangement, although shortened or narrowed tangs are acceptable if well made.

Guard: A small guard just in front of the edge is useful but by no means essential as it can interfere with sharpening and carving.

Steel: Any good cutlery steel will do, either stainless or carbon, but it must be easily sharpened and not brittle. Unfortunately many knives made today are both difficult to sharpen and overly brittle because the purchaser demands a knife that will stay sharp as long as possible. This, of course, depends on what the blade is cutting, for how long and how well. Every knife dulls and needs to be sharpened. A well-tempered blade is easily sharpened, does not dull quickly and will not snap or shatter in a wide range of tasks. My personal preference is for high-carbon tool steel, which meets all these needs admirably; although prone to rust this is a minor drawback, easily avoided by keeping the blade dry and clean. If you are working predominantly in a salt-water environment, opt for stainless steel.

Edge shape: The way an edge is ground can have a significant impact on how a blade cuts. Generally the grind shape of the edge is chosen by the manufacturer for ease and cosmetic appeal. Having experimented with each type of grinding - hollow, convex, secondary bevel and flat bevel - I have found a fine flat bevel grind to be the most efficient for bushcraft. This type of grind is perfectly suited to cutting wood as it provides a sharp edge that slices efficiently and cleanly. It is prone to damage if you touch bone when skinning a large animal, but this can be avoided by modifying your butchery technique.

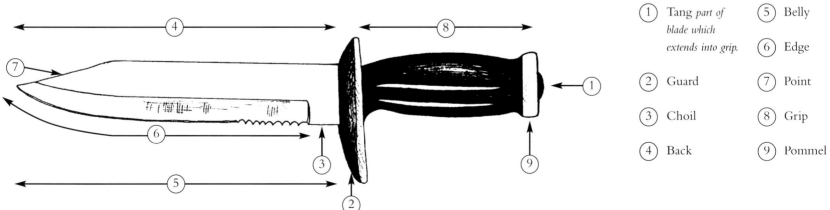

1. Tang *part of blade which extends into grip.*
2. Guard
3. Choil
4. Back
5. Belly
6. Edge
7. Point
8. Grip
9. Pommel

SAFETY

Before you even consider using your knife, think safety. Bear in mind that, once sharpened, your blade will be razor sharp.

Stow your knife in a strong sheath. If you are hiking in fairly civilised country it can be carried in your rucksack. However, when you venture into remote regions, attach it to your belt or hang it round your neck and shoulder on a strong cord. The latter method enables you to wear a rucksack waist strap in comfort or trousers without a belt and you'll know immediately where it is if you need it.

There will be times when you need to stow your knife safely for a few moments — tucking it under your armpit is a good method, but be careful not to slice yourself on withdrawal. Keep the edge facing downwards.

When the knife is not in use, even for a few moments, it must be put back into its sheath, which should be kept clean: clean your knife if it is dirty before sheathing it. If the sheath is dirty and you cut yourself, the wound is more likely to become infected.

An old-time rule of bushcraft is never to lend your knife: a damaged knife may result in a broken friendship. However, if you have to pass your knife do so like this as illustrated on the right.

This technique is intended for a single edged blade and will prevent injury if the knife is snatched from you.

Even if you are the best carver in the world you will cut yourself one day. Whenever you pick up your knife, pick up your first aid kit too.

Carve away from the outside of your body. A common error is to sit down and carve on a piece of wood between your legs. If the knife slips you may sever the femoral artery, which runs along the inside of your femur.

Train yourself always to keep your supporting hand behind the back of the blade, not in line with the cut or where a slip might slice into you.

①

②

③

Cutting technique

A knife being well used is a joy to behold: the transformation of a piece of wood into a tool is magical and the smooth cut marks are pure art. But to achieve such skill requires patience, practice and familiarity with fundamental safety techniques.

Every piece of wood has a grain structure that determines its strength and performance in a range of tasks. The structure varies from species to species: one wood might be suited to a task that requires flexibility, while another might be resistant to splitting. The grain structure will affect the ease or difficulty you will experience in carving the wood: in learning to understand its behaviour, you will become able to predict the wood's likely response to carving. Then you will carve more easily, the grain assisting you.

☛ Think of a piece of wood as a tightly compressed bundle of fibres laid parallel to each other.

☛ If you wish you can split the wood apart by forcing a blade or wedge down into it from the ends of the fibres.

☛ If you wish to cut through the fibres it will be most easily achieved by slicing at an angle so that the load of the cut is applied to one fibre at a time rather than the massed bundle.

☛ You can cut through the grain at 90° only when the bundle is thin and you can exert sufficient force.

☛ If you can stretch the fibres until they are taut, they are more easily cut – just as it is easier to cut a taut string than a slack one.

☛ When you wish to carve deeply into a piece of wood you may need to sever the fibres at the end of your intended cut to prevent them lifting and splitting ahead of the blade: such a 'stop cut' is a fundamental technique of wood carving and requires forethought and careful consideration of the grain.

☛ You can carve against the grain if you do so lightly with a strong slicing action.

GRIPS

Forehand grip.

Backhand grip.

Chestlever grip.

Reinforced grip 1.

Reinforced grip 2.

The Forehand Grip

This is the grip you will use most often: it provides strength and power as well as good control. Note that the thumb is not placed on the back of the blade. The cut is made with the strength of your arm and back. A safe follow-through is essential with this cut, be it clear space or a cutting block.

The Backhand Grip

This grip is rarely used, except for when cutting a taut cord being held by someone else. By turning the edge towards yourself you are taking control of the risk and ensuring that the blade does not slip through the work-piece to cut someone else. The cut is made with the arm.

The Chest-lever Grip or Side Grip

In this grip the blade is held with its edge towards your knuckle, enabling you to place your thumb on the face of the blade. The knife is held horizontally across your chest, edge facing outwards, thumb uppermost. The cut is effected with your arm and an intake of breath. In this way your chest acts as a pneumatic ram, generating tremendous force, enabling you to use your hand strength to control the angle of the cut.

The Reinforced Grips

Useful for fine work, the cut is effected with the thumb of the hand holding the work-piece pressing on the back of the blade.

CUTS

Breaking *Make a series of small cuts around the work piece to weaken it, then snap it in half.*

Shaving *Using a straight arm.*

Shaping *By pivoting around the thumb.*

Pointing *Using 3 clean cuts.*

Trimming *By cutting in the direction of branch growth, use power and follow through so that the cut ends beyond the branch to be trimmed*

Truncating *Using a wooden baton*

Draw knife

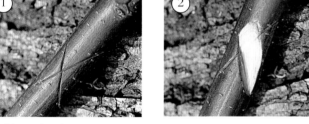

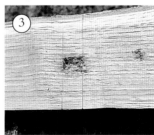

Making a hook *Slice in two crossing cuts.*

Chip out the wood from three quarters of the cross.

Deepen the beak of the hook formed.

Front view.

Side view.

Perforating *Scribe a rectangular hole.*

Chip out the wood on the first side

Scribe lines from front side around the edge to rear side.

Using lines and estimation repeat hole making, until holes meet in the middle

Clean out hole and make neat.

23

  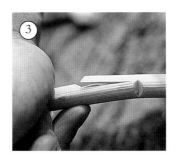  

Spear notch *The spear notch is an easy way to notch the end of a stick.*

How to sharpen a knife

It is said that a woodsman is only as sharp as his knife. To sharpen your knife you will need a set of abrasive stones ranging from coarse to fine. At home you can indulge yourself with a set of large bench stones, while in the field you will need a small lightweight alternative. Abrasive stones are manufactured from a wide range of materials. My preference is to use Japanese water stones which work fast and conveniently to give a razor edge. Use three grits 800 for coarse, 1200 for medium and 6000 for fine. In the field carry a combination 1200/6000 stone sawn in half.

To use these stones soak them in water before use. Only use the coarse stone if really necessary, when you have seriously blunted your knife or damaged it. Lay your knife on the stone and raise the back until the bevel of the blade lies flat on the stone and now push the blade away from you as if trying to cut a thin layer from the top of the stone. Do this eight times before turning the blade over and sharpening the opposite face towards you. Now make eight more strokes alternating the faces of the blade. As you do this a paste will form on the stone, do not wipe this away as it helps to speed up the process; keep the stone wet by splashing it with water throughout the process. Move on to a finer stone and repeat the process. The 6000 grit stone need not be soaked but only wetted; preferably create a slurry on the stone prior to use with a small nagura stone (these are specially made for the purpose and can be purchased with your stones).

After using the 6000 stone clean the blade and then strop it on the inside of a leather belt 50 times, alternating the blade face on each stroke. This will help to ensure a sharp and durable edge. To complete the process I run the blade very lightly down the finest ceramic sharpening rod to give the edge more bite. If you do not have a ceramic rod use the edge of a car window.

In the field we must employ a simpler approach, wet the small field stone and sharpen each side with a slicing action with pressure on the slicing stroke only. Do one face, then the other, then alternate as usual. If possible strop the blade; if a leather belt is not available a smooth piece of wood can also be used.

(1) *Eight strokes away.*

(2) *Eight strokes towards, the eight alternating*

(3) *Strop.*

(4) *Towards the blade tip you will need to lift the grip to accomodate the blade curvature.*

Ceramic sharpening rod.

Sharpening in the field.

How to carve a spoon

Hand carved spoons are both beautiful and functional, and bring memories of the place and company in which they were carved.

Split the billet.

Look for a section which has a natural spoon-like kink.

Carve in the shoulders of the bowl and flatten the sides of the handle.

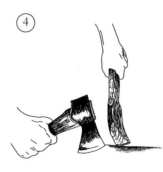

Point the tip of the bowl.

Flatten the underside of the bowl.

Shape the underside of the handle leaving thickness at narrow points and thinning at wide points.

Essentially the spoon is now blanked out, with clean top, bottom and side shaping. Complete the spoon by whittling these sides with your knife so that the spoon shapes blend naturally and with grace.

Lastly, hollow the bowl with a spoon gouge or crooked knife. Do not make the bowl too deep.

Bushcraft gadgets

An elegant way to suspend the lunch kettle.

Simple rustic pot hangers.

Note the use of the hook notch.

For the fixed or overnight camp, a pothanger with many hook notches gives flexibility and allows the heat control necessary for cooking breads and other outdoor fare.

The saw

Newcomers to bushcraft often underestimate the value of the saw – after all, the popular image of the backwoodsman shows him with an axe rather than a saw. In reality, of course, saws are efficient tools, enabling us to cut up wood with minimum wastage. They are safer to use than the axe, particularly in poor light or after dark, and can be entrusted to a complete beginner with only a few minutes' instruction. Saws also enable us to trim green wood neatly in a way that is less damaging to a tree, an important consideration.

The folding saw

The easiest saw to carry and use. It is the perfect companion to the small sheath knife. When choosing a folding saw, ensure that the blade locks securely in the open and closed positions.

To work efficiently a saw must cut a groove wider than the blade is thick. This is achieved in folding saws in one of two ways. The most common method is to have the blade hollow-ground behind the teeth: these blades cut well but are apt to snap in use, either at the tip or just in front of the handle, which means that they are not suited to wilderness travel where a saw will inevitably encounter rough usage. The alternative is a blade with teeth set wider than the blade: these are usually produced by welding very hard teeth on to a strong spring steel blade, and this is by far the strongest arrangement; the teeth stay sharp longer and cut a wider range of materials. In many years of issuing Sandvik Laplander saws to students, I have never had a blade break, because they have such strong blades. These saw blades cannot be re-sharpened; they are replaced when they become dull.

The bow or swede saw

This is an essential tool of a base camp where wood fires are employed. The bow can be fashioned from either a bent green branch, a carved frame or collapsible wooden frame; the best ones are oval tubular steel designs. Avoid saws that narrow at the forward end and saws that are excessively long. Ensure that it is equipped with its own mask; when not in use, mask the blade and hang it out of harm's way.

Blade intended for dead wood

Blade intended for green wood

A saw blade can be safely transported coiled in a billy-can, and the frame later improvised.

Generally speaking, hand saws are the safest of all cutting tools and injuries occur most when transporting a saw without its mask, or when the blade jumps at the start of a cut on to the back of your supporting hand. Obviously the saw should only be carried with the blade masked; if this is not possible consider removing the blade and coiling it inside a billy-can.

Safe cutting

When you initiate a saw cut, do so with your supporting hand passed through the bow of the saw; this will prevent the blade jumping and cutting you. Once the cut is slightly deeper than the depth of the blade, remove your hand and continue sawing with the thumb of your supporting hand pressed over the cut to lock the blade into it.

Start sawing like this to prevent the saw jumping out of the cut and on to the back of your hand.

Once established to a depth greater than the blade width, place your thumb over the cut.

Support

Before cutting any wood with your saw make sure that it is well supported to prevent movement: this will ensure that the energy you impart to the saw is fully transferred to the cut.

Although bow-saw blades are made narrow to reduce the likelihood of the blade binding in a cut that closes, this does happen frequently. To avoid it ensure that as the cut deepens, the wood is not supported in such a manner that the cut will close, gripping the blade. Not only is a trapped blade inconvenient, it will also be damaged: the kerf or set of the teeth will be narrowed. When felling a tree you can prevent the cut closing with a thin wedge driven in behind the saw blade.

Trimming a branch

When sawing down a heavy branch you must consider the force of tension within the limb. If you saw directly from the top surface of the branch the cut will open and eventually the branch will split free with unnecessary damage to the tree. Alternatively, if you cut upwards from underneath, you will avoid the problem of splitting but your saw will jam tight in the cut as it closes. Therefore cut a third of the way through the branch from the underside then cut down from above. By staggering the cuts we achieve a neat, stepped cut. With the main weight of the branch removed, you can now cut the branch cleanly near to the bole where it will heal correctly (see page 29).

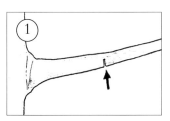

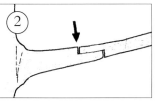

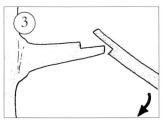

Splitting

To split wood, take a section of relatively straight wood free of knots and saw half-way through it at the centre. Now with the cut upwards strike the log on a rock or fallen tree a third of the way beyond the cut. The top half of that end of the log should split off. Reverse the log and repeat the process with the opposite end. Finally snap or saw the long half of wood in two.

Cutting up firewood

If you have to cut up a long piece of dead timber into shorter more convenient lengths, do not waste energy laboriously sawing through the wood. Instead cut half-way through it at intervals equal to your desired length of log. Then strike the log at these weak points on a nearby rock or log. Not only will you save energy, you will also extend the life of your saw.

Cutting green wood

When you cut green wood, do so only in a way that allows the tree to continue growing and remain healthy: for example, coppice broad-leaved saplings and remove only one branching tip from spruce boughs. If you need to remove a whole branch, cut it away cleanly with a saw at the bark scar where the branch joins the main stem. Done correctly the tree will heal itself, growing over to prevent infection by bacteria or fungi.

If you have to cut a sapling, do so in a place where there are several and choose one that is likely to be crowded by others. In this way you will be thinning the forest, allowing for healthier growth. Better still, look for a sucker from the base of a mature tree and cut it back close to the ground; several new shoots will spring from the old stump.

Fell a larger tree close to the ground in the tidy way of a professional forester.

The axe

In the world of woodcraft, the axe has long been accorded the same degree of affection as its cousin the canoe. Today, the knowledge of how to use it has been all but lost. Even some leading guides have only limited knowledge of the axe's use. It is rare to see a keen well-set-up blade: instead we commonly encounter the axe as a dull heavy wedge on the end of a stick rusting on a wood pile or collecting cobwebs in the corner of a barn. In bushcraft the axe still lives on, used mainly for cutting and splitting dead wood for the fire and in speeding up the carving of rustic tools. Traditionally, the type and size of axe depended on its intended purpose and the height of the user. Consequently there is a wide range of axe designs, from felling axes to axes for splitting and driving wedges. For wilderness travel your choice of axe will depend on the environment into which you are going. The further north that you travel, the more important the role of the axe becomes.

With a well-set-up axe we can make things of practical value and things of beauty quickly, from wood that might otherwise only be burned. You can split firewood so that it will burn more efficiently or fit inside your stove. You can also remove fallen trees, which may impede your travel, and fell dead standing firewood in winter.

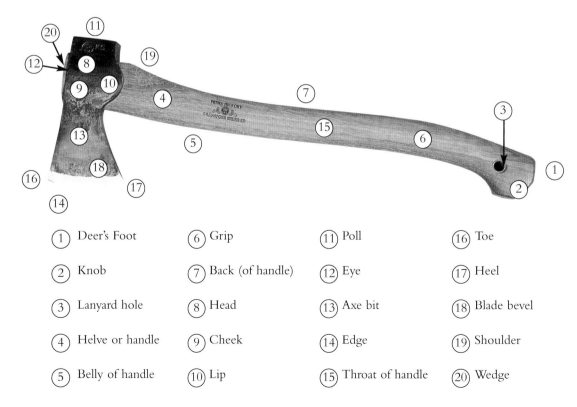

①	Deer's Foot	⑥	Grip	⑪	Poll	⑯	Toe
②	Knob	⑦	Back (of handle)	⑫	Eye	⑰	Heel
③	Lanyard hole	⑧	Head	⑬	Axe bit	⑱	Blade bevel
④	Helve or handle	⑨	Cheek	⑭	Edge	⑲	Shoulder
⑤	Belly of handle	⑩	Lip	⑮	Throat of handle	⑳	Wedge

The drawback is that the axe is a tool that requires training and experience to master. It must never be handed to a novice without expert supervision. It should only be used in good light, and must be stowed away from harm in camp.

The way to safely stow an unmasked double bit axe in the crotch of tree buttresses.

Make of axe

For wilderness use you will need an axe that is made with passion by perfectionists: Gränsfors of Sweden. Their axes are to be found deep in the bush wherever an axe is essential.

Types of axe

In the wilderness you will need an axe that can perform many tasks and which can be used in one hand as readily as two. Several options present themselves.

Forest axes.

Forest axes:

1. Double bit working axe.

2. American felling axe.

3. Scandinavian forest axe.★

4. Small forest axe.★

5. Wildlife hatchet/scout axe.★

6. Pocket axe.

★*most useful for wilderness travel.*

Crafting axes.

Crafting axes:

7. Splitting wedge (only hammer with maul or splitting maul).

8. Swedish broad axe.

9. Carpenter's axe.

10. Swedish carving axe.

11. Hunter's axe.

The Wildlife Hatchet/Scout Axe

This is the axe most commonly employed by beginners: it is the lightest axe at around 750 grams - heavy axes cause strain and tiredness in the inexperienced user, which can lead to accidents. With a length of 36cm it is easily portable but can only be used one-handed and is effective for chopping firewood, or light axe carving, provided it is sharp. Some words of caution: the short length of the helve means that the Scout axe has little counterbalance action when it is used with one hand: if you strike a springy branch the axe may bounce back towards you. Axes with a longer helve, held one-handed in the middle, provide a counterbalance effect that dampens rebound.

So long as this axe is used with care, and not used to tackle jobs that require a heavier axe, it is a first rate tool and a good partner to the bow saw for providing a fixed camp with plenty of sound firewood.

The Small Forest Axe

The number one choice for bushcraft. It weighs only 1 kilogram and its helve is 50cm long, so it can be used efficiently with one hand or pressed to bigger jobs with two.

The Scandinavian Forest Axe

A full sized two-handed axe, weighing 1.5 kilograms with a helve 64cm long. An experienced axe user will have sufficient strength to use it one-handed. I reserve this axe for use almost exclusively in boreal forest in winter where the demands of limbing (removing) snow-covered branches, and chopping into the tight grain of slow-growing timber present tough work This is a beautiful axe, to use with a pleasing weight and swing.

Safety Clothing

In forestry operations safety clothing and equipment have become the norm in recent years. In an ideal world we would use the axe only when wearing protective head-and footgear. However, in the bush you will not have protective clothing when you use this tool. Instead we must rely upon safe techniques and concentration.

Caring for your axe

- Prevent the head rusting by keeping it dry; in bad weather rub it over with the end of a wax candle.

- Occasionally apply boiled linseed oil to the helve.

- Never lend your axe to a novice.

- Do not leave your axe stuck into a log for any prolonged time or it will become blunt.

- Never hammer one axe against another, and never use your axe with or against anything harder than wood: to do so will damage the eye of the axe, loosening the handle.

- Try to avoid cutting into the ground as you may strike a stone that will damage the edge.

- Never chop on to rock or wood with nails driven into it.

- When using your axe in sub-zero conditions warm it with your hand to body heat first to make the steel less brittle.

- If you nick the edge of the axe, flatten the edge and resharpen it to the correct angle again.

- Never grind an axe on a dry or high-speed grinding wheel as you will spoil the temper of the blade. Do not sharpen the edge too thin – this often happens with a file – and unless it is intended to be so, do not hollow-grind the edge: the axe should have a flattish convex edge.

Use the edge of a bench stone for this. In the bush I have used a natural rock for this.

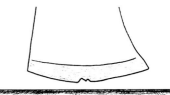

Remove nick.

Sharpen in normal way.

Basic axe safety

☛ Whenever the axe is not in use it should be masked with a strong case. At moments of rest during use it should be placed in safety either by setting it into a cutting block, the end of a log, or between the buttresses of a tree. Do not leave your axe set into a log for a prolonged period as the chemicals in the wood will attack the steel, blunting the axe.

☛ Avoid using an axe with a loose head.

☛ Keep children and animals such as sled dogs away from the axe.

☛ Be careful when walking with an axe in your hand: should you fall or trip, cast it away from your body. Always remain alert to the edge, the direction in which it is facing and the proximity of other people. While it is often recommended that the axe is carried cradled in the palm of your hand, in practice this is impractical: axes are most often carried grasped at the throat. As with any other cutting tool, when you carry an axe make certain you're also carrying a suitable first-aid kit.

☛ When you come to use the axe ensure before you begin work that your clothing will not impede the swing – scarves or cumbersome outdoor clothing and waterproofs may get in the way, and a poor swing may lead to an inaccurate blow. Next, make certain there are no branches, trees or other obstacles that may impede the swing: ideally you should be in a clear space large enough that you can reach out with the axe end so that it represents the radius of a circle within which there are no obstructions.

☛ Whenever you use an axe, it is imperative that you should have a safe follow-through: a block, log or the ground to act as a backstop to your cut so that should you miss the work-piece or the work-piece breaks unexpectedly the axe will not pass through and bury itself in any part of your body or anyone else's. Instead it should fall harmlessly on to the safe backstop. Do not cut into the roots or trunks of living trees as this will damage them.

☛ If you are tired, consider whether you should be using an axe at all. Perhaps the job can be more safely achieved with a saw, or left until you are less tired. In poor light, when standing on snow, or if you're new to the axe, do your chopping in a kneeling position. This will ensure that the ground acts as the safe backstop.

☛ When you use the axe one-handed, you risk chopping the hand that is supporting the work-piece. To prevent this, pay attention to the potential path that the blade of the axe will follow. When using an axe, we vary the angle, force and intensity of blows as demand requires. This means that the axe will swing from a variety of pivot points: at the wrist, the elbow, the shoulder or even the back. In good axe work, each blow of the axe is considered before it is made. In any swing of the axe, stay alert to the pivot point, as this will dictate the size of a sphere of danger, which has at its circumference the furthest tip or toe of the axe blade. It is absolutely imperative that any body part within this sphere has either a block between it and the axe blade, or is behind the axe while cutting.

☛ Allow the weight of the axe head to do the work. If you try to force it to come down on the work-piece harder, you will lose control over its direction. In good axe work the axe head is simply lifted and dropped on to the work-piece with arm strength used only to guide it accurately rather than to force it down. If you can learn to do this well, in time you will naturally develop the ability to increase the force of the axe blow while retaining accuracy. If the axe is not cutting, you are either placing the blows badly or it is blunt.

How to free a stuck axe

If your axe becomes stuck in the chopping block you can free it by a sharp, downward blow to the tip of the helve. Failing this, use gentle sharp tugs alternating between up and down until it works free. Never apply sideways force to the helve or excessive force up or down: if you do so you will inevitably snap the handle.

Felling

In bushcraft we do not fell trees very often; usually we work with already fallen dead timber. However, in boreal forests it can be necessary to fell living trees, for tent or shelter poles, and dead standing timber, for firewood. Bear in mind that in the far north green birch is important firewood. In tropical rainforest it may be necessary to fell trees to create an opening in the forest canopy for helicopter rescue in emergencies.

In Siberia, the Evenk people use a heavy axe to fell small saplings with just two diagonally opposing chops at ground level, demonstrating beautifully 'Maximum efficiency for minimum effort'. For larger trees, a more considered approach is necessary. However, before felling any tree, you must first study it carefully and look for any lean: it is easier to work with gravity than try to overcome it. Next, look for any dead branches trapped in the crown of the tree – the last thing you need is a dead branch, a widow-maker, landing on your head while you are chopping. Study the path that the falling tree will take, and try to avoid felling trees that will snag in standing trees.

Felling with the axe alone

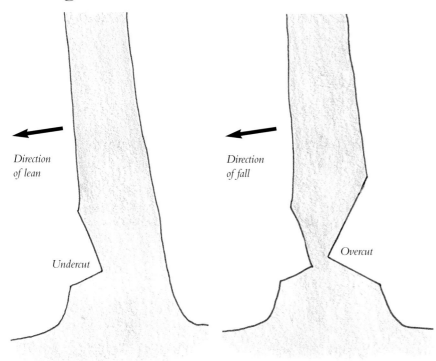

Direction of lean

Undercut

Direction of fall

Overcut

Felling with axe and saw

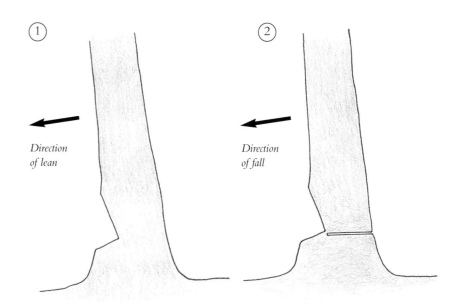

Direction of lean

Direction of fall

Limbing and Trimming

Having dropped your tree, you will need to trim the branches. Start near the base of the tree and trim towards the top, always keeping the trunk between yourself and the limb you are cutting. Thick limbs may need preparatory cuts to speed their removal.

Chopping

Cutting the tree into useful sections is achieved by sawing or chopping and the former is more efficient. However, you may have no option but to chop. This is a potentially hazardous activity. To chop through a log, you will need to cut out a V as wide at its opening as the log is thick. You will use an ambidextrous swing, changing your hand position to facilitate both left- and right-hand swings of the axe. Never attempt to bury the axe in the wood as it will stick. Instead, allow the axe to work at its own pace springing free nice sized chips of wood. Once you have chopped two-thirds of the way through the log move round to chop from the opposite side and finish the job.

Common mistakes are to chop too hard and become tired, to make too narrow a V cut, and not to pay proper regard to the way in which the log is lying: it may be easier if repositioned.

Splitting

This is perhaps the most common use of the axe in bushcraft. You must learn how to split a long piece of wood, and how to split short lengths for firewood. If you wish to split a tree into boards or splints for a specific purpose, you will need to cut wedges. Wedges made from wood are called gluts: they should be cut from strong wood types that will resist splitting when hammered. Never hammer a metal wedge with the back of your axe unless it is specially designed to do so: this damages the eye and loosens the head.

Splitting firewood on a chopping block is an essential axe skill. Ideally the block should be knee high, and the log to be chopped placed at the far side of the block to ensure a safe follow-through.

If you do not have a chopping block you can improvise one by using the crotch of a forked branch or by a swift blow to the raised end of a knot-free, chopped or preferably sawn log.

Another method of splitting small logs or quartered logs is to place the axe on the log and bring both down on to a block at the same moment; this is a good technique for a beginner to use as there is a safe swing and follow-through. Make sure that the thumb of your supporting hand is not trapped between the axe helve and the log on splitting or you will bruise if not break it.

Note that the wood being split is placed on the far side of the block and when the axe passes through, it lands safely on the block. Ideally the block would be level and knee high; however, this is not always possible.

Place the axe on the wood to be split and bring both down simultaneously on to the block. This method is useful when a stump or flattened chopping block is not available.

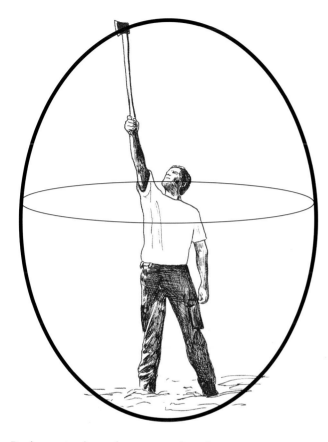

Reach up, out and around to ensure no obstructions.

My favourite method of splitting without a block using the small felling axe. Note the raised-forward edge of the log.

1. Raise forward end of log slightly and measure up – aim to strike as shown.

2. Strike with a committed blow – concentrate on accuracy.

3. Strike with a follow-through.

A chopping block can be improvised from split wood. But two pieces must be used to prevent the workpiece being spun upwards when struck.

Strike down on to the farthest log, bending your knees as the axe drops.

Flattening

To flatten a log, make a series of small chops an axe-blade length apart, then split out the wood between them.

Notching

Effort can be saved by weakening cuts to a long length of firewood, which can then be broken over a log or rock.

Hewing

Hewing is a technique to shape wood. You must cut down on to a block, and remember to keep your supporting hand out of harm's way: your fingers must stay on the opposite side of the work-piece to the axe blade and hew only below your supporting hand. If your hand tires, take a break.

Shaving

To shave feather sticks (see page 86) for kindling, grasp the axe head rather than the helve.

Slicing

Fine knife-work can be achieved by holding the axe head with the axe helve upwards out of the way.

Fitting a new handle

Should you break your helve you will need to carve and fit a new one. Do not burn out the old handle, even if the edge is buried in damp soil: this will destroy the temper of your blade and ruin it. Instead, chip out the old helve, or drill it out at home in your workshop.

Carve a replacement helve from seasoned wood, choosing hard wood such as hickory, ash, rowan or birch, depending on what is available. Carefully fit it to the eye of your axe, then split the top of the helve with your knife and a baton, and drive in a slender heart wood wedge – seasoned heart wood of oak is ideal. If you were able to salvage the metal staple that held the wedge in place, use this to further secure the new wedge.

A loose handle

If your helve becomes loose it will most likely need replacing. If you have just taken your axe to a drier, colder climate, however, you may find that allowing some linseed oil to soak into the eye rectifies the problem. In the bush, people often soak a loose axe head in water to make it swell and tighten. This is a short-term solution and the helve will eventually need replacing. An extra wedge is another short-term measure but, again, it only postpones the inevitable repair.

How to sharpen an axe

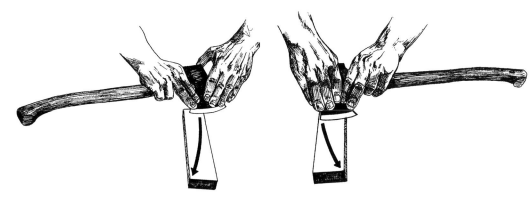

Sharpen you axe in a similar manner to your knife.   *Eight strokes away, eight towards, eight alternate.*

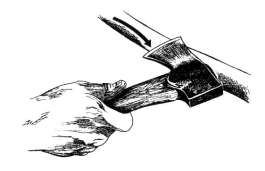

Strop on a leather belt.

In the field use a circular action on your cut down stone.

The parang or machete

The parang is the most dangerous cutting tool used in bushcraft. It has the longest edge, is used with a slashing action, which can be difficult to control, and is prone to deflection. For this reason we limit its use to tropical rainforest, or environments where similar materials need to be cut. Like all of the tools used in bushcraft, in the hands of an experienced craftsman the parang is fast and efficient. As with the axe, the secret is to allow the weight and speed of the blade to do the work.

There is perhaps more variety in quality in parangs than in any of the other cutting tools. When choosing a parang look for one that is not too long: 50 – 60cm is right for general-purpose use. You often encounter parangs with much longer blades than this in use by local people in tropical plantations, but their needs are somewhat different from those who hike through the forest, and they also have a lifetime's experience in using them. Try to avoid purchasing a parang with a springy, flexible blade: find one with a stiff, heavier blade, made from less springy steel. Look also at the method by which the handle is attached: parangs commonly have a narrow tang handle fitting, which may not be absolutely secure. I have seen the blade of a parang fly off the handle when in use and on one occasion only narrowly miss my toes. Look for handles with riveted plate grips attached and a full, or nearly full, tang attachment. Once again, whenever you carry a parang, you must carry a first-aid kit. Keep your parang in a sheath or hard wooden case. When drawing it out ensure that you are holding the faces of the case and not the edge in case the blade cuts through the rivets or stitching and cuts your hand.

Never let anyone or anything distract you while you are cutting with a parang. If you are being bothered by an insect or are interrupted by a question, stop what you are doing until the disturbance has passed. Also, avoid getting into a cutting frenzy: beginners with the parang tend to launch into tropical woods as

A parang must be strong and sharp to chop tropical hardwoods and to trim materials like bamboo, here having been flattened out for flooring.

though they are fighting a pirate army when, once again, considered blows are more effective and the norm. Also, assure yourself that you have a circle space around you the full length of your arm and blade within which to work.

Most of the work done with a parang requires a wrist action. It is important for efficient cutting that there is a clean follow-through, or space beyond the work-piece so that you can cut it and follow straight through beyond it. The best cuts made with a parang are done with a smooth, confident, swift action.

In pointing stakes a good parang will sever the pole at an angle of 30 degrees on the cutting block. It must be kept sharp, although chips in the blade are almost inevitable due to the rough and ready nature of the work to which it will be put.

As you make a cut ensure that no part of your body is in line with the parang's cutting edge and that other members of your party keep clear when parangs are in use: as I mentioned earlier toes, knees, fingers, hands and arms are all too vulnerable to the sharp edge of a parang.

Why carry such a dangerous tool at all? In tropical circumstances the parang is the master tool. Neither an axe – nor a saw – is as versatile as the parang, which can be used to fell poles, create clearings, and trim away lawyer vine, which will snag your clothing. The parang will also open up access to a wide array of tropical foodstuffs from coconuts to heart of palm.

The multi-tool

It has been said that a multi-tool is simply a collection of second rate tools, but its popularity speaks for itself. When we travel on off-road vehicles, snowmobiles, boats, motorbikes, or in helicopters we should of course ensure that we take a suitable tool-kit to effect repairs, but it always pays to have a multi-tool, equipped with needle-nose pliers and screw-drivers. I remember when a snow machine I had hired broke down, and its tool-kit was impossible to access because it was improperly stowed. I had to remove a spark plug, which fortunately I could do because my colleague had brought with him a Leatherman containing needle-nose pliers.

Special tools of bushcraft

The crooked knife functions as a one-handed drawknife-cum-gouge. In north-eastern America it was much used by the first nations of that region to fashion everything from canoe paddles to snowshoes.

A smaller, more specialist version is the spoon knife, which enables us to hollow out a bowl or the bowl of a spoon.

The multi-tool

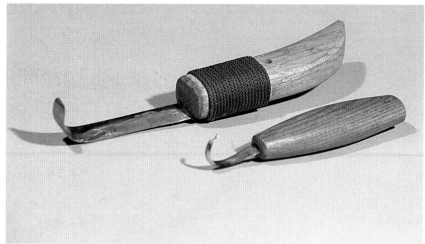

Crooked knife and spoon knife

Swedish army entrenching tool.

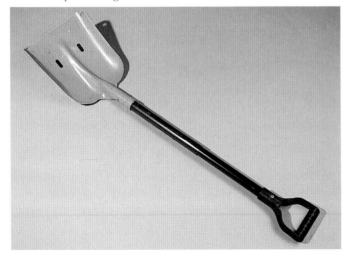

Snow shovel.

Digging tools

Occasionally you may need to dig a hole or excavate a root, and on the trail you can improvise a digging stick. In camp or if you are travelling by vehicle the best shovel is the Swedish Army entrenching tool: solidly made of steel, it is virtually indestructible. It can also be fitted with an attachment for digging snow.

The digging stick should be fashioned from hard wood with a tight grain. Find a log with a metre-long straight section, about 30–40mm in diameter, then carve one end either into a long, slender point for sandy conditions or into a chisel shape for hard clay. It can be made more durable by hardening the tip in the embers of a fire: scorch the wood slowly until it is about to turn brown and no further. In Aboriginal society the digging stick was essentially a woman's tool: desert peoples depict women in their paintings with digging sticks rather than throwing sticks and spears. In time of war it also served as the woman's weapon. Among the Bushmen of the Kalahari the digging stick is used by men as well as women. They rely on it to excavate edible and water-bearing tubers in times of drought and to locate the grubs that provide poison to tip their arrows.

Snow tools

The Snow Shovel

Perhaps the most important snow tool. First decide on your main requirements: if you are a mountaineer, you will look for lightweight compactness; if travelling in the Arctic, you will need it to shift soft powdery snow; in either case, your snow shovel should be portable. Look for telescopic aluminium handles: they are strong and versatile. A short-handled shovel may be easier to use in a confined space, when excavating a snow hole for example, but you will need a longer handle to dig a casualty out of an avalanche slide.

Avoid a round ball-grip handle on a shovel – it may be difficult to manoeuvre when your gloves are icy, particularly when digging out a snow cave or quinze. T- and L-grip handles suit mountaineers, who will probably be wearing gloves, but the best overall grip is the traditional D handle, which can be gripped easily by a mittened hand.

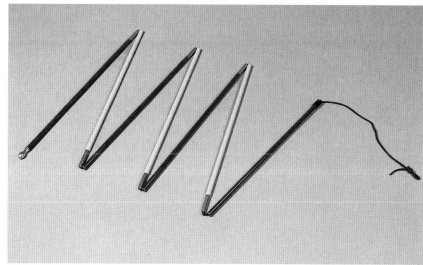

The snow saw

Useful in the mountains in winter as it will move snow quickly. It is an undervalued tool and not always easy to find. I prefer a solid, non-folding design, which, although bulkier, is stronger and more versatile than the folding kind. Failing this, you can use a small carpenter's saw which also provides the possibility of sawing wood for a shelter. Ensure that it is equipped with a mask.

The snow probe

A vital tool in avalanche areas. You should also wear avalanche transceivers to help rescuers locate you. A collapsible snow probe allows you to test the depth of snow and its hardness so that you can find a suitable place to construct a snow cave or trench. In an avalanche the snow probe will enable you to pinpoint a buried member of your party. Although you may hear stories of people surviving many hours in avalanche conditions, the truth is that the first three minutes are vital. Any party going into the mountains in winter must be prepared in terms of equipment and training to mount their own initial rescue.

WATER

Water is almost as important to humans as air, and in arid lands you must secure a source for yourself each day. This will dominate your route planning as your tracks join the blue dots on the map and you hope that each source will not have dried up. Never begrudge the weight of water in your rucksack: you must carry enough to last you on the way back to your previous source if the one ahead has vanished.

Some years ago I hiked such a trail. I had taken with me two one-litre army canteens and a large lightweight canteen made from nylon with a double-skinned polythene liner. My intended trip involved an extended hike into backcountry to a point where I would base myself, then go out on radial day-hike explorations, and this amount of water provided me with a healthy safety margin. The hike out was exhilarating, and after the second day my stride was smooth and relaxed. Also I was back in the desert habit of breathing with my mouth closed to reduce water loss, an old bush trick that takes time to get used to. The water sources to which I hiked were small but reliable, streams fed by late-spring upland that were clear and cold, but still requiring sterilisation to kill *Giardia lamblia*, a waterborne parasite. My base camp was cosy, and on the next two days I explored some nearby canyons and rocky outcrops. I went as light as possible on these hikes, with some essential items in my pockets and the lightweight canteen worn around my waist like a belt. On the third day out, pushing deeper into the backcountry, I was climbing up a steep slope to investigate an unusual plant when I slipped down the friable rocky slope.

I managed to stay on my feet as I glissaded down to a solid rock. But when I stepped on to it, it teetered and I fell on to a rocky ledge, narrowly missing a cholla cactus. I stood up, to discover that I had fallen on to a Yucca, aptly named Spanish bayonet, which had burst the bladder of my lightweight canteen. As the last of the water dripped away my hike was over. With midday still ahead I had to take care. I found a narrow, shady canyon where I spent the middle of the day sitting in the shade sipping water from a tiny rock seepage. At around three o'clock I set out back to my base camp, walking slowly and calmly. I reached it just after sunset with a raging thirst. That taught me the importance of having a strong water bottle. Since then I have found myself several times with little water, and without doubt, the ability to find safe water in wild lands is an essential skill. Familiarise yourself with as many ways of finding water as you can until they are second nature, and ensure that you know how to make water safe.

The importance of water

In a temperate environment humans require between 3 and 5 litres of water per day, depending on clothing and level of exertion, rising to 10 litres or more in hotter climates. Water enables us to keep warm in cold weather and cool in heat. It aids digestion and transports oxygen and energy to the muscles and eliminates waste. When we are correctly hydrated, we should produce approximately a litre of light straw-coloured urine per day.

Dehydration

The effects of water loss are felt relatively quickly. Even under normal wilderness circumstances we can become dehydrated when water is available by failing to drink enough. Surprisingly dehydration happens more frequently in a colder environment than in a hot one. Arctic conditions sap the body of moisture because the air is dry and the body needs more water to keep warm. Learn to recognise the symptoms of dehydration, and remember that it is easier to stay hydrated than to try to correct the effects of dehydration.

Symptoms of dehydration

The first and most obvious is thirst. Then you will experience discomfort that has been likened to the onset of flu, which may be accompanied by muscular aches and pains. Nausea sets in when you exert yourself and vomiting increases water loss. The nervous system is affected, leading to light-headedness or dizziness. Headaches, similar to a hangover, and tingling in the limbs are common, with irritability and reduced ability to make good decisions. Our saliva and urine outputs are greatly reduced and the lips crack. The urine becomes darker. Gradually you will become disoriented, hearing may be reduced, and you may experience serious cramps and joint stiffness. The eyesight fails, coma ensues and then death.

People who live and work in hot climates are frequently in a state of minor dehydration, the clearest sign of which is infrequent urination and dark urine. While this may go unnoticed for long periods, the ultimate consequence may be the production of kidney stones.

Namib desert: the trees in the ravine show the presence of water even during the dry season.

Preventing dehydration

In theory it is easy to prevent dehydration by drinking plenty of water, but in practice it is not always easy to achieve. Many beverages, such as tea and coffee, are diuretic, which reduces their benefit as a source of water. In extreme heat you may have to make a conscious decision to keep drinking, which is made difficult by the time and effort required to find and purify your water.

I ensure that I always carry sufficient water with me and a reliable means of purifying it. Each morning before the start of the day's activity I drink as much as I can, which makes it easy to maintain hydration throughout the rest of the day. Experience has shown me that it is easier to drink from a mug than a bottle, and if possible, I take with me a fruit flavouring for the water and use it well diluted. As the day progresses I drink frequently, and if an opportunity presents itself to refill my water bottles I take it.

Finding water
Reading a landscape

Even the most experienced travellers may be caught out by dwindling water supplies or the distance between watering places stretching out. In arid regions there may be unexpected drought – humans are not the only creatures to search for water. When it is scarce, competition intensifies and pressure on reliable water holes increases, so that they are dry when we arrive. Often when we do find water there is no clear pool fed by a shimmering waterfall, but a small muddy oasis surrounded by animal remains and dung. This poses the question of how to make it potable.

Learning to find water in a wilderness teaches us to read the landscape in great detail, noticing land forms, vegetation, animal and insect life. It is a skill few people practise, perhaps because of the 'It'll never happen to me' attitude. Anticipate the day when you need to find water and spend a couple of hiking days focusing your attention on the skills and information that follow.

Water Sources

Water sources are many and varied: some, like rivers and streams, are easily recognisable while others are all but invisible. To be proficient water collectors, we need to know how to locate sources, how to access them and how to use them. We need also to keep an open mind: some of the most important water sources are the most off-putting to use. To locate water we must be able to track it across a landscape and understand its elusive nature.

From the moment a snowflake settles on a mountain top it begins a relentless journey down towards the sea. Water seeks the path of least resistance, seeping through cracks in the earth until it meets a layer of bedrock where it is forced by water behind to make its way upwards to the surface at a spring. As it flows across the land it gathers greater volume: the giggling spring becomes a stream then eventually a river and at last it reaches an ocean.

Along its journey water gathers and discards pollutants, debris, viruses – in fact, all types of vegetable and mineral matter. Many potentially life-threatening waterborne pollutants are invisible to the naked eye, so we must endeavour to collect water from the most unpolluted source: the stream before the river, the spring before the stream.

Good places to search for water are:
- the base of cliffs
- narrow canyons
- tight bends in dry river beds
- rock kettles (depressions in rocks) on sandstone outcrops
- places where differing geological formations meet, where animal trails to water holes converge, becoming busier and more distinct, often a clear indication of a water hole.
  Remain alert to signs that may indicate fouled water, such as dead animals.

A rock kettle in Namibia.

Indicators of water

Experienced arid-land travellers develop a keen sense of the presence of plants, animals and insects that may indicate water in an otherwise barren landscape. Some vegetation, animals and insects can survive either on tiny amounts of moisture or obtain enough from dew. It is of great value to be able to differentiate between those that need plenty of water and those that do not.

Vegetation indicating water

- reeds
- palms, particularly the fan and doum palms
- willows
- alders
- ground ferns such as hart's-tongue
- figs
- casuarina trees
- wild sugar cane
- reedmace

Insects that indicate water

- bees
- wasps

Animals dependent on water holes

- wildebeest
- elephants - drink 100 litres at once and may go several days without drinking
- baboons
- monkeys – unreliable when edible fruits are available
- impala
- waterbuck
- bushbuck
- buffalo
- warthog
- hippo
- bush pig
- roan antelope
- red lechwe
- sitatunga
- burchells zebra
- mountain zebra – can go for up to three days without, and have been known to dig for water
- rhino - a less reliable indicator
- lion – a less reliable indicator, as they have been seen obtaining water from tsama melons
- leopard – a less reliable indicator
- kangaroo – will sometimes dig for water

Animals that are not dependent on water holes

- eland
- giraffe
- kudu
- red hartebeest
- gemsbok
- steenbok

Birds that indicate water

- finches – sometimes found at water holes or bore-holes in thousands, visible and audible from a distance
- pigeons and doves – drink mainly in the early morning and early evening
- grouse, particularly sand grouse
- guinea fowl
- herons

Zebra finch at a bore-hole.

In extremes

In really desperate circumstances people have shot larger herbivores, for example elephants, and drunk the liquid from the stomach. To do this collect the foul-looking green mass from the stomach, wrap it in a cloth and express the moisture by wringing it tightly. The disgusting liquid that results is drinkable but should be left to clarify first. You can speed up this process with the addition of a small piece of liver. Only consume liquid from herbivorous animals; omnivores and carnivores may harbour harmful bacteria.

Collecting water

Mopping

In an emergency dew is an abundant water source and we can emulate the desert beetles that specialise in collecting it. Early in the morning, take an item of absorbent clothing, like a cotton T-shirt, and brush it across dew-covered vegetation. When it is saturated, wring out the moisture into a container. You'll be surprised by how easy it is to collect a large quantity of water. Be aware that while dew is perfectly clean the surface on which it condenses may not be. So, always sterilise water collected like this before you drink it. *Do not collect dew from the surface of toxic plants.*

Drinking straws

On its journey downhill water may become trapped in naturally occurring bowls such as hollow logs or sumps formed in impermeable rock. Aboriginal peoples sometimes fashioned such receptacles by enlarging rock depressions and fitting them with a rock cap to shade the sump and prevent the water from evaporating. If you cannot access this water by mopping, improvise a drinking straw from an available grass stalk or other non-poisonous hollow-stemmed shrub. Use your mouth as a pump to suck up the water and then feed it into a container. If possible, sterilise the water before drinking it. Avoid water trapped in the trunks of poisonous trees or tea-coloured water that has become badly stained by tannins leaching out of bark.

Improvised wells

Sometimes you may only be able to find pools of stagnant water or a patch of moist ground with no visible water. In these circumstances you can make a well. Several varieties are described below – why not try one, just for practice?

Gypsy well

This technique is a way of obtaining water from saturated ground. Dug in saturated ground several metres from a stagnant pool, it can provide a way to obtain cleaner water than could be obtained from the pool itself.

1. Dig a round hole 60–80cm in diameter, until the bottom is 30cm below the depth at which you strike saturated ground. 2. Let it fill with water, which will be muddy. 3 and 4. Bail it out without disturbing the sides of the hole, then let the hole fill again. The water will be cleaner, especially if it is allowed to settle.

Frequently, this water is safe to drink as it is but if in doubt purify it. If you are intending to use the well for several days cover it with sticks or bark to prevent animals drinking from it and thereby contaminating the water.

In Australia I have seen this technique employed by desert Aborigines. Relying on knowledge of the desert landscape passed down through oral tradition, they located where water might be found, by probing the ground with a digging stick until damp soil adhered to its tip, thus pinpointing where to dig; 1.5 metres down they found a trickle of muddy water, which they filtered through a bundle of grass.

On the coast a gypsy well can be dug behind sand dunes. Although most of the water that fills it will be brackish or salty, the topmost layer is rainwater or run-off, trapped behind the dunes. It is usually fresh, or fresh enough, for consumption.

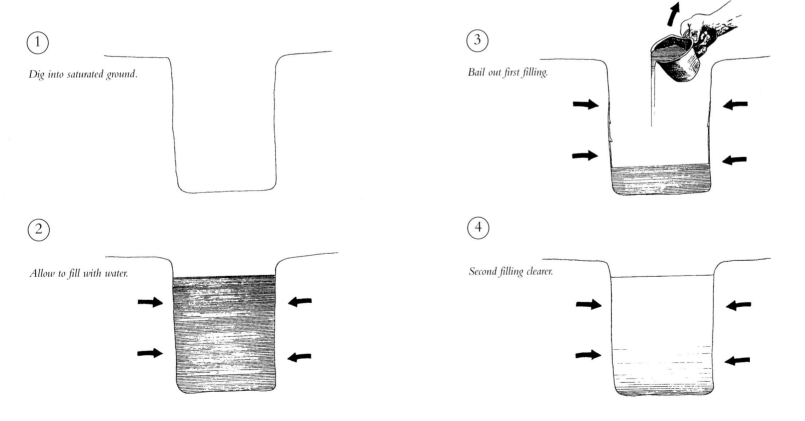

① *Dig into saturated ground.*

② *Allow to fill with water.*

③ *Bail out first filling.*

④ *Second filling clearer.*

Sip well

This technique is employed by Bushmen of the Kalahari. In arid lands water is sometimes trapped by rock under sandy ground, but digging will not release it. Excavate a hole to the diameter of a small fist in moist ground, and in the base place a small bundle of non-poisonous fibrous material, like grass leaves. Next put an improvised drinking straw – a strong grass stem with the node walls pierced through with a small stick – into the hole, resting it lightly on the bundle of grass. Now fill the hole, packing it tightly, but leaving the top end of the drinking straw exposed. Carefully pull the straw up about 1cm and begin to suck. You will eventually draw moisture from the soil into it, and, after considerable exertion on your part, water will gurgle to the top of the straw. This technique is not easy but it does work: to succeed the first time you must be patient and determined. Having succeeded once, you will find the process easier the next time as you will know what to expect.

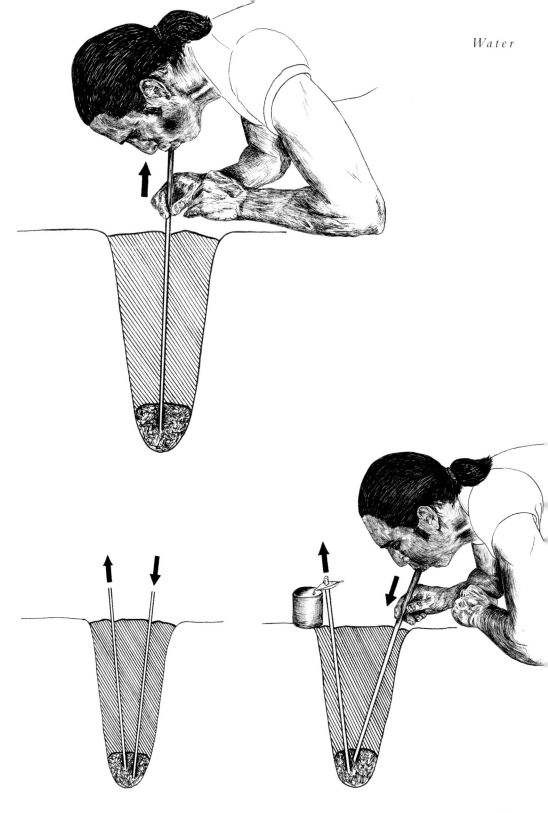

Fixed sip well

The fixed sip well is a cross between the sip well and the gypsy well, and is employed where it is possible to dig down into saturated ground. Dig a similar hole to that made for the sip well, fill the base with a grass filter and insert two drinking straws. Then back fill the hole. If you are confident that the water will be safe to drink, sip it through one straw – the other allows air into the hole to make the sucking easier. If you are in any doubt of the water's purity, blow into one of the straws, which will force water up the other. Place a piece of bark or a broad leaf over the second straw to create a water fountain, which will run into a container. When not in use, the water straws can be plugged with small wooden pegs or twisted grass stoppers.

Reed well

Make a gypsy well (see page 48) and fill it
with a bundle of reeds tightly bound with a
withy. Cut off the bottom of the bundle
and then cut out a bowl-shaped depression.
The bundle helps to filter out soil from the
water.

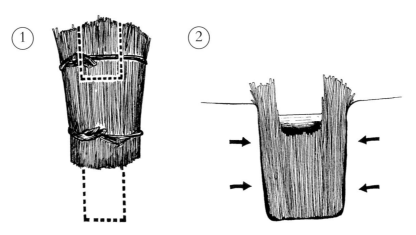

① ② ③

Rain traps

These may be fashioned from any large surface that can be
arranged to feed the rain that lands on it into a suitable
container. Avoid canvas tarpaulins or tent fly-sheets that have
been treated against decay or may be tainted. A lightweight fly-
sheet is ideal: if it is very strong it can even be used as the
receptacle as it may be capable of holding several gallons. Large
tropical leaves can be used as makeshift rain traps. Like dew,
rainwater is safe to drink but it may be tainted by dirt from the
collecting surface. On a recent jungle journey I was forced by
bad weather to set up camp on a ridge away from a river. I set
extra guy lines in the middle of the edges of my tarp to
improvise a rain trap for water to wash and cook with.

Dew traps

For water collection in the desert. Before sunset dig a pit
40–60cm deep and line it with an impermeable fabric such as
polythene or a lightweight fly-sheet. Fill this with large smooth
stones, as clean as possible. Leave it overnight, and moisture
will condense on the stones. Collect it before sunrise. Only
small quantities of water can be collected from dew traps, and
their performance will vary from season to season. Abandoned
vehicles may also act as dew traps – again try to exploit this
resource before sunrise. Dew traps make good homes for
scorpions so be careful when using them.

Dew trap.

Water from vegetation

Water trapped in pitcher plants has been used as an emergency water source.

In emergency sufficient water may, perhaps, be obtained from
your surrounding vegetation to take you on to the next reliable
watering point. Here are some ideas.

Vines

Many varieties of tropical vine, lianas and lawyer canes – such
as *Ampelocissus martini, Entada phaseloides, Tetrastagma lanceoloria,
Columella mollissima* – may contain liquid, but remember that
plants may suffer from drought just as we do. Chop out a 2-
metre section of vine, making the first cut high up. As soon as
you make the second cut low down, the capillary action
holding water within the vine will be broken and
water will flow freely from the lowest end. You can
slow it by holding the vine horizontally. Test the
liquid for potability: it should be clear, not red, yellow
or milky, and should not discolour when dripped into
your palm. Next taste a drip: it should not cause a
burning sensation in your mouth, or be bitter, or seem
to dry your mouth. Vine liquid is refreshing with
either no flavour or a mild, woody raw-potato taste. If
only small vines are available you can make a rack to
collect water from vines simultaneously. In the
Central African Republic a Mbayaka pygmy showed
me how a large vine can provide enough water to
shower with.

A rack improvised from a split bamboo to collect water from many vines.

Completely at home in the jungle, this pygmy girl taught me my first lesson in the use of the water vine.

51

Bamboo (left)

Large-sectioned bamboo sometimes holds water, which can be located by tapping the stems with the back of a parang and listening for a lower tone and sloshing. Cut a small hole into the section to tap the water, which is usually safe to drink, cool and refreshing. Large quantities can usually be collected quickly.

Trees

Trees may also contain large amounts of water, particularly through the growing season.

Although not strictly a tree, a banana plant can be easily felled at about 30cm above the ground. Cut out the central portion of the stump, and the resulting depression will gradually fill with water. Let the depression fill completely before use: the first water is sweet and sticky, usually very rich in tannin, which may stain your hands blue-black. It may be a good idea to discard the first filling as the second will contain a lower concentration of tannin.

Fig trees can be tapped, giving many gallons. Water flows only at night. Do not allow toxic milky sap to contaminate the water.

A simple bamboo tube pushed into a banana plant gives a quick but limited supply of water.

Birch trees can be tapped during the early spring, often yielding many gallons of sap, which can be used in an emergency as water but not in the long term. At other times of the year, this fluid can be obtained only by felling a tree so that the lower part of the trunk is higher than the crown. Chop through the top of the trunk, and fluid will gradually leak out. This is a drastic means of obtaining water, and only for true emergencies – it is unlikely that you will need to employ it, for where birch trees grow water is usually available. However, this technique has been employed with saplings in more arid parts of the world, including Australia.

Banana well – hollow out the base of a freshly felled banana plant.

Overnight this fills with water.

Cut a 1m section from banana stem.

Peel off a layer and slice off a narrow strip to expose cells.

Fold along the removed strip.

Tilt to collect water.

Roots

One of the principles of bushcraft is learning to recognise the means by which other living organisms survive extreme conditions. For example, some desert plants store water underground in their roots. The Bushmen of the Kalahari exploit these underground caches. They dig up water-root, Kghoa, *Fockea angustifolia,* split open its leathery skin on one side with the tip of a digging stick, mash the pulp at the blunt end, then squeeze the juice into their mouths. The flesh can also be eaten raw after peeling. Other roots used by Bushmen include *Ipomoea verbascoides,* treated in the same way as Kghoa, and *Raphionacme burkei,* which is shaved finely with a sharp-edged stick then squeezed.

Fockea angustifolia.

The leaf of desert kurrajong, an Australian source of water in arid lands.

Raphionacme burkei.

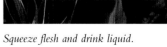

Scraped tuber flesh.

Squeeze flesh and drink liquid.

In central Australia the root of the desert kurrajong, *Brachychiton gregorii*, gives water. Examine the ground around the base of the tree for cracks radiating out from the tree, which indicate the location of a swollen root. It may be over a metre down, requiring considerable excavation. Once unearthed, peel off a short section of bark then shave it finely and squeeze it. Keep the remainder of the root, its bark intact, for future use. The swollen roots of young plants can be roasted and eaten after their bark has been removed, as can the large grubs sometimes found inside them.

In northern Australia the swollen root under a young red flowered kurrajong, *Brachychiton megaphyllus*, can also be used as a source of emergency water.

Red flowered kurrajong (Brachychiton gregorii) *has distinctive seed pods.*

Extracting water from desert kurrajong.

Fishook barrel cactus.

Cacti

The barrel cactus is often mentioned as an emergency water source, but in fact only the fish-hook barrel cactus can be used: other varieties contain oxalic acid. Cut the top off the cactus, scoop out the pulp and squeeze it in a bandana or other cloth until the liquid is released. Use these cacti only as a last resort: they make take hundreds of years to grow. *DANGER*: Do not confuse euphorbias with cacti. They look similar with their leathery exterior and spines, but unlike cacti, with their clear sap and bright emerald-green interior, euphorbias exude a white latex-like milky sap which is highly poisonous and will blister skin. People have died after eating meat cooked over a fire made with dead euphorbia stems.

The poisonous euphorbia (left and above right). Right: graves of travellers who died after eating meat cooked over a fire of euphorbia in Namibia.

Water by transpiration

Water is transpired from the leaves of plants. In arid areas where there is sufficient vegetation you can collect it in a clear polythene bag. Place the bag over a suitable leafy bough and tie it tightly to make an airtight seal. Sunlight on the leaves will cause condensation to form inside the bag, which pools at its lowest corner. If you constrict the corner of the bag, you will prevent the leaves soaking in the water and contaminating it by leaching of chemicals from the leaves. As this is a reliable technique, some armies issue transpiration bags as survival equipment.

Water from ice and snow

The word 'desert' conjures up images of camels and sand dunes, but is just as applicable to cold wilderness. How do you find fresh drinking water in the Arctic in winter when all the moisture is frozen?

To eat snow or not

Don't melt snow in your mouth or hand: the amount of energy you lose will outweigh the benefit of the water gained.

Inuit iceberg technique

In the high Arctic the Inuit find an iceberg with a gently sloping surface of freshwater ice – identifiable by its deep blue colour and willingness to shatter. They scoop out a small bowl-shaped depression at the top of the slope, then prop over it a block of freshwater ice. Below the depression, they create a cascade of similar depressions, connected together with a finger-wide channel that they fill with soft snow. They light a fire with seal blubber and sticks cut from a sled board. As the fire melts the ice block, the water trickles under the seal-blubber fire and down through the cascade of depressions. At first the water is stained by fat and soot but is gradually filtered by the snow in the channel between the depressions. The water collects in a depression free from pollutants for drinking.

Another technique is employed by Inuit hunters when they are butchering a caribou. They empty out the contents of its stomach, turn it inside out, fill it with snow and tie it shut with a length of intestine, then they tuck it back inside the body cavity while the animal is skinned. When they have finished, the snow in the stomach has melted in the heat given off by the animal's body. The bag is opened very carefully and the water is sucked through a block of snow, which filters out impurities.

The Inuit iceberg technique.

Finnish marshmallow

In Arctic conditions, cut a block of snow, push a large 'marshmallow' of it on to a stick, and hold it over a container placed to the side of a fire. The warm air slowly melts the 'marshmallow', generating a trickle of water.

Water-generating bag

When snow is too cold to make snowballs improvise a sack from an item of clothing or a mosquito headnet, fill it with snow and suspend it to melt over a container placed beside a fire.

Melting in a billy-can

If you have a metal cooking pot do not pack it tight with snow. Snow is a good insulator; many a billy-can has been ruined by the fire working against the metal rather than melting the snow. Instead tilt the pot slightly on its side and heat it only gently as you melt very small quantities in the bottom, making certain that any steam produced can escape and will not become trapped by tightly packed snow. Be patient, adding snow until you have a depth of water into which snow can be gradually added.

The solar still

One of the most frequently described emergency means of obtaining water. Dig a sloping, rounded trench in saturated soil, place a container at the lower end, then drape over the entire trench a clear polythene sheet. Seal it around the edges and weight it in the middle. Moisture will condense on the underside of the polythene and run down it to drip into a container. Note: although this technique works it rarely provides sufficient water to sustain life, and is only useful on sun-baked shorelines in super-saturated soil, or in riverbeds of arid lands where flash floods occur and the river sand is saturated.

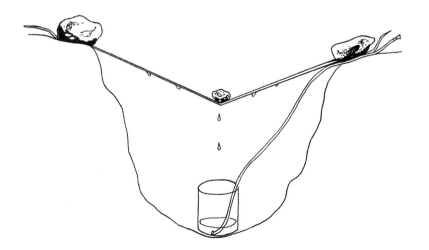

Making water safe to drink

Safe water is a rare commodity: the World Health Organisation has estimated that two thirds of the Earth's fresh water is unfit for human consumption. The United Nations has suggested that 80% of all diseases are water-related and the UNO that 25,000 people die *every day* after drinking contaminated water. While water contamination is most prevalent near areas of dense population, there are also waterborne contaminants which exist in wild country.

The majority of waterborne contaminants are microscopic, impart no odour or flavour to water and are not necessarily affected by extreme temperatures. This means that without access to a laboratory we cannot know whether untreated water is safe to drink or not. Water is commonly drunk straight from the source – a fast-flowing Canadian river, Scandinavian lake or an African spring – but whenever we drink untreated water we are taking a risk. When you are evaluating the likely safety of water, think less of the probability of contamination and focus on the likely consequences of drinking bad water. At best you may suffer from mild diarrhoea, at worst a viral infection. In either case discomfort, misery and incapacity will be the result.

Water purification

There are five basic contaminants: turbidity, parasitic worms, bacteria, viruses, and chemicals. Unfortunately no single method of water treatment will provide satisfactory treatment for all of these contaminants. So a combination of two or more should be employed. First, get to know the enemy.

Turbidity: this is dirty water which contains minerals, or particulate and organic matter that may make it cloudy or muddy. The fine gritty glacial debris that turns mountain streams milky may irritate the digestive system. Minerals and organic matter may also shield infectious micro-organisms from the effect of chemical sterilising agents. So, we should remove organic and particulate matter from the water before employing other sterilisation methods.

To reduce the turbidity, look for the clearest water source and try to collect it from where it runs over rocks and is well oxygenated. If this is not possible, we must filter it by passing it through finely woven cloth, clean sand or, best of all, activated charcoal.

Parasitic worms and protozoa: these include embryonic roundworms, tapeworms, and protozoa such as amoebae (dysentery) and *Giardia lamblia* (beaver fever). Some of these organisms are relatively large and can be eliminated with a mechanical filtration device, or boiling. Chemical treatments are also effective if allowed sufficient time to work. However, cryptosporidium, which can cause life threatening illness among the elderly, the very young and the sick, is resistant to iodine and chlorine and so brings into question the value of chemical-only water treatments. Fortunately it can be removed easily by filtration or boiling.

Bacteria: some of the most lethal water contaminants, they may be responsible for diarrhoea, dysentery, campylobacteriosis and E-coli. Because of their small size it is impractical to remove them by filtration but they can be destroyed by boiling or chemicals.

Viruses: the smallest health threatening micro-organisms, they can cause diseases such as hepatitis A & E and polio. They are destroyed by boiling or chemical disinfection.

Chemicals: pesticides, herbicides, fertilisers and heavy metals run off agricultural land, but are usually extremely diluted. I have not heard of an illness resulting from drinking such contaminated water. Heavy metals are difficult to remove, but chemicals can be greatly reduced by passing the water through a carbon filter.

A strategy for water purification

Whatever purification methods we employ, our system must
☛ be effective at neutralising all the prime health threats
☛ be quick and easy to use
☛ be conveniently portable.

Filtration

Muddy water: in circumstances where clear running water cannot be found we may have to resort to muddy puddles for our water. As already discussed turbid water can harbour and shield micro-organisms from chemical disinfection agents. It will also cause mechanical water filters and purifiers to clog prematurely. This being the case a means must be found to clarify the water as much as possible. Mud can be effectively filtered clear using tightly woven cloth, perhaps improvised from clothing. This can be made more effective by filling the filter with layers of sand and charcoal. Charcoal particularly will help to reduce

off-putting odours and taste. The British military have used a cloth filter bag, the 'Millbank Bag', for many years to very effectively remove mud from water. This lightweight reusable item of equipment can easily be carried as a standard item of your duffle. In use it must first be soaked. It is then filled with the dirty water and suspended; water seeps through the bag. To begin with this water is allowed to flow away to help cleanse the outside of the bag; once the water content has dropped by 10cm the resulting filtrate is collected. It is noticeably clearer but must now be sterilised before drinking. After use the bag should be turned inside out, washed and dried.

The 'Millbank Bag'.

Clear water: micro-organisms can be neutralised by boiling – usually the preferred option. Otherwise micro-filter it through either a ceramic or an activated carbon filter to remove parasites and some larger bacteria. Then treat the water chemically to ensure neutralisation of smaller bacteria and viruses.

Chemical treatment of clear water alone can prove effective but is less reliable than when employed in conjunction with micro-filtration.

NOTE: When purchasing a pump-action water-treatment device, be sure to establish whether it is a filter or a purifier. Purifiers filter the water and chemically disinfect it, killing all parasites, protozoa, bacteria and viruses. Filters alone cannot remove viruses and rely on a second stage of purification, either boiling or chemical disinfection.

Boiling

Boiling is a reliable method of sterilising water. Simply bringing water to the boil has been found to be sufficient to kill viruses, bacteria and parasitic cysts, even allowing for the lower temperature at which water boils at high altitude. It is not necessary to boil water for 30 minutes as is often misstated, but it is necessary to bring the water to the boiling point, at which the water bubbles furiously. In camp, kettles are often left simmering over the fire; to be absolutely thorough when putting river water over the fire make it camp policy to ensure that it has been at the rolling boil for three minutes before being left to simmer. When boiling water a cooking pot fitted with a lid will boil faster than without, using less fuel and causing less water to be lost as steam.

In regions where you are concerned about chemical pollution, try to always empty the kettle before filling to prevent a build up of a more concentrated solution.

Chemical disinfection

When it is inconvenient to use heat to sterilise our water we must rely upon chemical methods. There are only two chemicals that are in wide usage for water purification; they are iodine and chlorine. The great difficulty when employing either of these chemicals is achieving an accurate dosage, our aim being to destroy infectious micro-organisms by adding the least possible chemical disinfectant. Only use forms of these chemicals specifically intended for water purification and ensure that you follow the manufacturer's instructions for their use.

Bear in mind that:

Temperature affects the speed with which chemicals destroy micro-organisms. Both chlorine and iodine act more slowly in cold water, which will require you to increase the contact time. That is the time the chemical has to sterilise the water before either its use or subsequent removal or neutralisation of the chemical disinfectant.

Turbid water can shield infectious micro-organisms from the chemical disinfectant. In cloudy or discoloured water the dosage of chemicals must be increased to effect a certain kill. In such circumstances most manufacturers provide guidelines on the bottle or packet for increasing the dosage.

Chlorine

Most usually administered as either tablets or droplets. It is an effective treatment, but moderately alkaline water in chalky/limestone regions inhibits its ability to destroy micro-organisms so contact time must be increased. It is not suitable to be used without filtration in water containing organic detritus. Also it generally requires a longer contact time than iodine, which may be a significant drawback in extreme conditions. It can be used safely by those who may have an allergy to iodine or a thyroid condition.

Iodine

Usually administered as droplets, tablets or by passing the water through iodine resin beads. It should be avoided by people with thyroid complaints, allergy to iodine, or pregnant women, depending on the strength and delivery method of dosage. Generally iodine has fewer drawbacks than chlorine: it remains active in alkaline water, is less affected by organic matter and is faster-acting.

Employing chemical purification

As always with water we should aim to find the cleanest water that we can. If it is very muddy clean it first by passing it through a filter as described above.

This water can be treated in one of three ways:

Treated directly with either iodine or chlorine drops or tablets. This is the most commonly encountered method of chemical purification. The drawback is that it requires us to use a strong enough dose and contact time to treat protozoa like cryptosporidium which has proven to be more resistant to chemical purification. Water treated in this way also develops an unpleasant taste. (see below).

Passing it through a micro filter such as a ceramic filter and then treating with either iodine or chlorine drops or tablets to kill smaller bacteria and viruses is more reliable as the water has been cleaned of parasitic cysts, that can be resistant to chemicals, and larger bacteria prior to disinfection. More time consuming, it is a very reliable method of water treatment that mirrors municipal water treatment.

Passing it through a purifier that combines filtration with iodine resin disinfection has the advantage that the water is both filtered and purified in one operation. Also by passing the water through the iodine resin beads the dose is more accurately controlled, negative charged iodine molecules being attracted to the positive charged micro-organisms as they pass by.

Here there are two options:

Purifiers that leave a residual presence of iodine in the water. This iodine is detectable by taste but not unpleasantly so and ensures that the water does not become reinfected after leaving the purifier, for example from decanting it into a dirty cup or water canteen. It is also an excellent wound wash. These are features that greatly recommend this process.

Purifiers which remove the iodine as the purified water leaves the device. These are a good choice for people who are unable to consume iodine, although in use the operator must be scrupulous about keeping the exit port free of contaminated water (not always easy) and ensure that the water canteen or receptacle is kept clean.

Pumping river water through a purifier in the rainforest, Mosquito Coast, Honduras – a daily chore worth the effort.

Improving the taste of chemically treated water

Both chlorine and iodine impart a strong flavour to water. This can be rectified by three processes:
☞ neutralising the chemical with another, such as sodium thiosulfate or ascorbic acid (vitamin C)
☞ removing the chemical after purification by passing the water through a carbon filter
☞ leaving the water in a clear canteen in strong sunlight.

While these processes improve the flavour of the water, they also halt any anti-microbial action.

Water strategy

Now you may be confused by all the options! Here's my water strategy:

I observe a strict protocol in water treatment and handling. I keep my drinking cup and water canteens clean.

I carry only purified water in my water bottles.

Where possible, I always collect the visibly cleanest water available, from the healthiest-looking source.

I always suspect that water provided from sources I cannot see – for example taps in hotel rooms in the third world – is contaminated.

If water is cloudy I filter it through a Millbank bag or, if camped overnight, employ a gypsy well (see page 48).

My first-choice method of purification is boiling.

When I cannot boil water, I use a mechanical purifier that leaves residual iodine in the water.

If I flavour my drinking water I do so in my mug and *not* in the canteen.

Whenever I fill my canteen with purified water I flood the canteen threads to ensure purification of the bottle.

No water container is left uncapped in camp, and hands are never washed at the spout of any water container.

Sea water and brackish water

Dealing with salt or brackish water poses a different set of problems. Humans cannot drink water with a high salt content and deep inland water may be salty as well as coastal water. In arid countries water available from boreholes may contain as much salt as sea water itself.

There are only two practicable solutions for the removal of salt from water: one, to distill the water, or two, use a reverse osmosis pump to mechanically remove the salt.

Distillation

This can be difficult in the wilderness, and you will need suitable materials to improvise a still. In theory a still seems straightforward to operate but in practice it is an inefficient means of producing sufficient water for arid conditions. Take a jerry can and fit a pipe either to its opening, or better still, to its spout and attach it to a piercing in the can itself. This pipe is then fed either through a cooling tank of salt water into a receptacle or into a suspended plastic bag where steam can condense. The jerry can is filled with salt water to about half its capacity and then heat is applied beneath it from a fire or stove. The great difficulty is that a huge volume of water needs to be distilled to produce a relatively small quantity of drinking water.

Reverse osmosis pumps are expensive, slow to operate and prone to mechanical failure, which places them beyond practical use except at sea.

FIRE

I often wonder who it was who first learned to conjure fire at will. Certainly he could never have realised what an important discovery he had made. Until the flames from our campfires flickered in the wilds, each twilight brought the ever-present threat from predators equipped with senses that gave them the edge in darkness. But once people were able to relax by the fire, evening naturally became the time to talk, to tell stories and to develop ideas. Incurably inquisitive, our fireside ancestors were scientists without white coats. Throwing all kinds of objects into the flames, they found that fire could change the nature of things; it could harden the tip of a wooden digging stick and transform plants that could not be eaten raw into palatable, nourishing meals. And eventually, of course, it was in the ashes of fire that metals were discovered. The rest is history.

Few moments in life are as good as those when, at the end of a hiking day, with the tarp pitched, the meal eaten and the cooking things put away, we relax in good company beside the campfire. I like to watch as the lengthening shadows link arms and draw their dark blanket around us. Sitting close to the glow of the fire, our tiny outpost of humanity must look to the owls calling overhead just as it has for at least a million years. Hypnotised by the embers and flickering flames, our voices lower and time seems to stand still while clocks and watches outside the spell of this ancient magic race forwards. As sparks from a settling log rise into the night sky, they carry with them the atmosphere of a human experience that transcends cultural and linguistic differences, an experience so profound that even in the twenty-first century we carry it within us as a race memory.

Even hikers who prefer to cook on trail stoves must be able to make a fire quickly and efficiently. More than just a source of comfort, fire is a basic necessity for surviving in the wilderness. And it is not just a matter of knowing how to create a fire: we must understand how to manage it to meet our needs and also appreciate that we have a responsibility to ourselves, to other lovers of the outdoors and to nature herself to use it with wisdom and care, leaving as little trace of our passing as possible.

Early in the development of my own outdoor skills, I set out to learn every conceivable way of starting a fire, from striking a match successfully on a windy day to rubbing sticks together in a snowstorm. Searching out different anthropological accounts, I worked through various firestarting methods, in many cases having to experiment with British woods and tinders which were quite different from those being described. It was a slow, frustrating process, because few of the accounts provided enough detail for me to be sure of replicating them exactly. Since those days, however, I have been able to travel the world in search of peoples who still retain ancient firemaking wisdom and to acquire a broader understanding of the significance of fire to different cultures. For example, among the bushmen of the Kalahari, fire is in itself sacred, the product of the union between the male fire-drill and the female hearth-stick. More than just a stage for storytelling, it is the community's heart, a social focus for trance dances, other religious rites and healing. To these bushmen, to be without fire is almost to be without life itself. Its importance is clearly reflected in the contents of their hunting bags. It's a belt-and-braces approach we'd all do well to bear in mind. The land they inhabit may be arid, but they still carry three different means of firestarting: hand-drill sets, flint and steel and matches. The Mbayaka Pygmy of the Central African Republic take their fire with them wherever they go, wrapping up precious embers in leaves that resist combustion and transporting them in a burden basket or simply carrying along a glowing brand by hand. Travelling in single file, a group of pygmy look like a human steam engine, trailing a plume of smoke behind them. I asked them, through an interpreter, how they would start a fire in the forest if the old one went out. They immediately burst out laughing. 'We don't let our fire go out,' they declared. For the most part this is true, but as anyone who knows the bush, particularly the rainforest, will tell you, it's a valid question. So I repeated it. Again it was greeted with hilarity. 'Our fire never goes out. It is the oldest fire in the world,' they insisted.

Undeterred, I put the question a third time. On this occasion, one of the older men pre-empted the peals of laughter and made direct eye contact with me. He threw up his arms to indicate that he understood. 'Wait, wait, I'll show you,' he said. He ran over to a small, dome-shaped hut covered in brown, wilted leaves and disappeared inside. 'He knows, he'll show you,' the crowd reassured me as we all sat there expectantly. When the old man returned he brought with him a small leather pouch from which he produced a strip of steel that looked like a piece of old machete blade bent into a 'u' shape, a bit of stone and some palm fibres. With great care, he then demonstrated how you could strike sparks from the flint and steel onto the palm fibres, where they could be coaxed into a flame. I was entranced: for me the magic tricks of firelighting never lose any of their wonder.

Interestingly, the same kind of technology seems to have been in use in Europe during the Stone Age. When a 5,000 year old body was found preserved in glacial ice the equipment buried with him included horse's hoof fungus and the remains of some sparking material, along with a birch-bark box that contained grass and some fresh Norway maple leaves, which had been used to insulate burning embers.

Today, across the countless millennia separating us from the first person to kindle a fire, we can share that original thrill by training ourselves to make fire in a traditional way. More importantly, by so doing we can break our bond of dependence on modern firelighting gadgetry. Anyone who has travelled in wild places will already know that nature has a way of exposing our weaknesses, usually at times of greatest need. Bearing in mind that in difficult circumstances even the best-equipped backwoodsmen can find themselves embarrassed, we shall concentrate here on only the most reliable methods of firelighting. We'll look first at the most common and modern firelighting methods, and, once we've got these fires going, we'll move on to the traditional firelighting techniques and ways of managing a fire. With practice these methods should enable you to conquer even the conditions that you might encounter on the coastline of north-west Scotland in winter, where the cold and teeming rain conspire with a driving wind to thwart attempts to make a fire.

Producing a flame

There are many ways to light a fire, from using the obvious tools, like matches, to improvising with some very unlikely raw materials. As with all bushcraft, the secret to consistent success is to be found in the detail. So, take nothing for granted.

Matches

Introduced in 1827, the friction match is simple to use and has no mechanical components to fail, so it is not surprising that it remains the most popular means of producing a flame. In our daily lives we strike matches without a second thought, and in the wilderness, too, they are a very reliable means of firestarting, even in the worst weather. But here matches must be treated as a finite resource and protected from their biggest enemy, moisture. A matchbox can be swiftly emptied to no avail, particularly if your hands are cold or you are under stress. People have died of hypothermia because they have been unable to strike a match correctly.

There are several types of match available, and such a huge range of brands around the world that the quality can vary enormously. In some countries they are made from woods that do not ignite very easily, so it is a good idea to experiment before making a choice. Check that the head burns smoothly and the stick catches light easily.

Strike-anywhere match.

Strike-anywhere matches

These old-fashioned, simple matches are my first choice for wilderness travel. Nowadays they are less popular for everyday use for safety reasons – if they are bounced about overenthusiastically or exposed to a sudden shock that generates enough friction between the heads they have been known to catch light. In the wilderness, however, their versatility is a great advantage, as they can be struck against any rough surface, from a zip to a rock. They are also the easiest type to look after as only the matches themselves, and not the box bearing the striking surface, need to be kept dry.

Safety matches

Basic safety matches

These are the most common matches, the kind that need to be struck against the special surface on the side of the box to produce a flame. Both the matches and the striking surface need to be protected against moisture, a precaution which can prove inconvenient.

Waterproof matches

The heads of waterproof matches have a coating of lacquer which guards against moisture damage. However, the striking surface still needs to be protected; it also tends to wear out more quickly because the layer of lacquer on the match heads makes them harder.

Water- and wind-proof matches.

Protecting your matches from moisture

Stow your match supply in several waterproof containers distributed throughout your kit. If you must carry matches in your pocket ensure that the match surface is airtight to prevent your sweat from dampening them and remember never to touch them with wet hands. You can insulate matches against moisture by dipping their heads into lacquer or candlewax, which will also aid combustion. An old trick is to set them head to tail into wax in the matchbox. This is an excellent idea for an emergency supply, particularly on waterborne expeditions. (In Lapland, Sami trappers stash their matchboxes in their coffee sacks to keep them dry.)

Stormproof matches

Stormproof matches are prey to the same complications as the waterproof variety. The difference between them is that the stormproof match continues to burn even in windy conditions. The problem with them is that they often don't produce a flame until the head has finished burning, by which time the matchstick has become very short.

Making a matchbox from a used shotgun shell

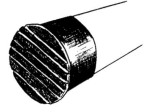

Take two used shotgun shells and heat the brass end of one until it can be pulled free of the plastic case. This becomes the cap. At the base of the second shell, saw in striking grooves. Trim away the folded end, wax slightly and fit cap.

Barbeque matches.

Barbecue matches

These burn long and hot and can be an excellent emergency lighter. Some lightweight hikers even carry them to use as a convenient fuel for brewing a drink.

Making a matchbox from birch bark

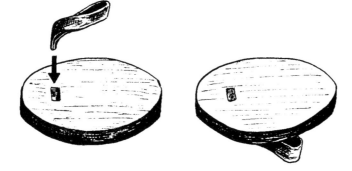

Cut a strip of bark as shown. Fit tabs through triangular holes.

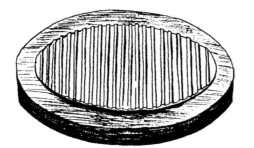

Carve wooden lid and fit with a leather or bark tab.

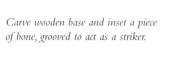

Carve wooden base and inset a piece of bone, grooved to act as a striker.

Birch bark matchbox.

Drying matches

One ploy to restore damp match heads that sometimes works is to pass the match through your hair a couple of times. Matches that have become totally soaked can sometimes be saved as long as the heads have not dissolved. There is no guarantee of success, but it is certainly worth trying. Lay them carefully out to dry in the sunlight or in the dry, warm air of a cabin (not beside a fire or stove, obviously). A useful tip is to lay the matches on a dry rucksack, tucking the sticks under a strap to stop them being blown away.

Striking a match correctly

Preparation is the key to all firelighting. Before striking a match ensure that you have to hand a mass of dry kindling, a candle or another means of extending the life of the flame.

Hold the match between your thumb and index finger, supporting the head against the striking surface with your middle finger. At an angle of 20 degrees sweep the match on to the surface so that the pressure is applied along the length of the stick. If you strike it at, say, 90 degrees, the side of the matchstick will absorb the force of the action which might cause it to break. Once you have struck the match, remove the supporting finger to avoid burning it and cup the match in your hand against the wind, allowing the stick to ignite with a strong flame before transferring it to your tinder. Remember not to drop the matchbox – it might get lost or wet. Hold the match below your tinder so that the flame just licks into life. If you hold it too close the tinder is liable to extinguish the flame.

Northland etiquette demands that you leave the cabin as you would hope to find it.

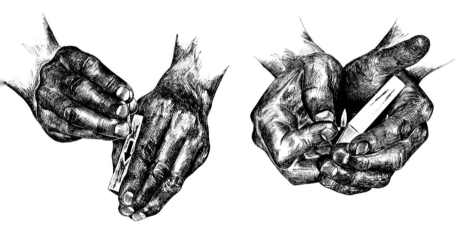

Leaving matches in cabins

All across the forested northlands there are cabins used by fishermen, hunters and trappers, glory holes of the unique northern lifestyle. They come in all shapes, sizes and states of renovation but they all have one thing in common. In extreme cold temperatures they are lifesaving palaces. It has often been said that the rough edged folk of the wilderness are the true masters of chivalry, and in my experience this is true. Despite the arrival of brash, urban types, rainbow clad in hydrocarbon clothing, bush etiquette is still employed by the indigenous people and longstanding professional guides.

One of the golden rules of the north is to leave the cabin as you would like to find it, complete with everything the next visitor will need. Ideally this should be a small stack of feather sticks, some split kindling and firewood. If the cabin is sound and dry, leave a box of matches with the ends of the matchsticks protruding from it. This small courtesy has saved lives when travellers in difficulty have finally made it to a cabin with hands so severely frostbitten that it has been impossible for them to open a matchbox.

Blue flame liquid butane lighter.

Lighters

Today the trusty match is falling into disuse as cheap reliable lighters become available in the most remote places. It is hard to appreciate the revolutionary impact a lighter can have on the lives of people accustomed to producing fire by friction.

If you are travelling in cold, wet weather it is wise to carry a lighter with you. Light and versatile, they take up little room in your outfit. The lighter best suited to wilderness travel is the type which burns liquid butane gas like a blowtorch and which has an integral cap to keep the working parts dry. If you can't get one with a cap, store your lighter in a small, dry bag or in a smoker's oilskin with some tinder.

Tinders and spills

Directly igniting kindling with your lighter will waste fuel. Instead put the flame of the lighter to some tinder, which can in turn be used to light the kindling.

Birch bark (right)

Birch bark curls inwards on itself as it gets hot, making it both difficult to handle and inclined to snuff itself out. To prevent this fold the bark like a paper fan to stiffen it, which will stop it curling.

Rubber tyre

When travelling in rainforests I carry my lighter in a smoker's oilskin along with some small strips of rubber, about 3 or 4cm by 1cm and 0.5cm thick, cut from an old car tyre. This is a first-rate and very cheap emergency firestarting outfit for anyone traversing very wet terrain or involved in wilderness-based water

Birch bark spill, folded to prevent curling.

activities. It resists all forms of moisture from sweat and general humidity to a thorough soaking when you are wading across deep rivers. When ignited these strips of rubber burn long and reliably, and two or three of them will create a good heart to your fire.

Camera film

In an emergency, ordinary camera film can be used as tinder. Tear off five or six 15cm lengths and fold each lengthways three times, concertina fashion. Holding them bunched together, light the ends and use them as a torch to ignite your kindling. Take care not to inhale the fumes they give off.

Sparks

Modern spark-generating devices. Probably the most versatile of all firestarters are lighter flints made from a pyrophoric alloy. When scraped against a hard edge, these produce a shower of white-hot sparks. Sixty years ago, outdoor adventurers had to make their own sparkers by setting lighter flints into pieces of perspex or bonding them to the edge of a piece of wood. Today spark-generators are available in a wide range of shapes and designs, from complex devices with the flint spring-loaded against an abrasive wheel to more simple versions activated with an edged tool. Some even come attached to a block of magnesium that can be scraped to produce shavings which can then be ignited with the sparks.

My personal preference is for a simple but thick, strong sparking stick which you scrape hard to produce a shower of large, white-hot sparks – sparks of such brilliant intensity that these fire-sticks have been used as a short-range night signal as well as a firestarter. Not only does this device work the best, it also lasts longer, sometimes for years. Its longevity, added to the wide range of materials which can be lit with the excellent sparks it provides, makes this tool without a shadow of a doubt the number one wilderness firelighter. It can even be used to shower sparks into the vapour from a hike stove, allowing you to light it from a safe distance. It will even ignite chemical firestarters, such as wet-start firelighters, hexamine fuel tablets partially crushed into powder.

But its biggest advantage is the almost endless variety of natural tinders it can ignite. Here are just a few examples:
- birch-bark peelings (peel only natural shedding bark)
- feather sticks of willow, spruce, and cedar, by dropping the spark under the last shaved curl
- all plant downs
- dry grasses
- shredded bark
- any fungi that can be used as tinder (see page 75)
- finely powdered oil-bearing shale
- tissue paper, teased thin
- candles with the wick teased out finely
- dry powdered herbivore dung
- red cedar bark scraped to a down

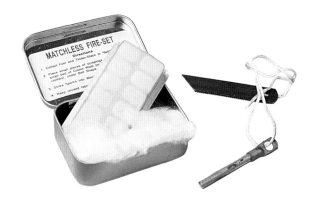

The NATO matchless fire-set.

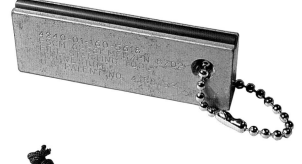

Magnesium block with artificial flint striker.

Strike force artificial flint striker. Emergency tinder can be contained in the box section.

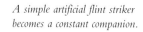

A simple artificial flint striker becomes a constant companion.

Scrape up a mass of fine bark shavings from a sheet of bark.

Place fire stick near to the shavings.

Use back of knife to shave sparks, pulling stick against blade.

Sparks falling on shavings will ignite the bark.

One of the most useful applications of the sparking stick is reigniting a burned 'fire dog' – a stick left with its ends partially burned after a fire has gone out. Strike the sparks on to the white ash-like area behind the charcoal end. When they take, blow on them to coax them into life and bring another ember alongside the new one to encourage it to grow larger. Once three sticks are aglow, fire should follow swiftly.

The main drawback to this kind of firestarter is, once again, its susceptibility to damp, which can eventually reduce it to a useless powder. This is less of a problem with the thicker sticks, and one which usually occurs when they are left in storage. On the trail they will be in daily use, which means that they won't be exposed to moisture for prolonged periods, but take care not to keep them in a damp pocket for any length of time.

Traditional flint and steels

The original flint-and-steel firestarter was made from iron pyrites and flint. Widely used in the Neolithic era, if not earlier, these sets were accompanied by horse's hoof fungus, *Fomes fomentarius*, by the tools required to turn it into tinder, and sometimes by a freshwater mollusc shell to hold the tinder during ignition.

In the Neolithic period this was a typical fire set – flint blades, bone awl, freshwater mussel shell, nodule of iron pyrites, flint strikers, fomes *tinder fungus.*

The tinder was prepared by breaking open the fungus or slicing it with a flint blade to expose the trama, the leathery layer beneath the cuticle, the horny outer surface. This layer was then scraped with the edge of a flint blade to provide a mass of fine, downy shavings, which were collected in the mollusc shell, on a leaf or on a piece of dry bark. The iron pyrites also needed to be scraped to remove the rusty oxide layer.

The technique used to create the sparks is very easy, although it produces fewer of them, and they are not as hot as those produced by other methods. Small sparks are struck from the iron pyrites with the edge of a flint blade on the tinder. Sometimes these blades were very small and mounted in the end of a piece of deer antler with tree-resin glue. Once a good spark lands on a fine fibre of tinder it catches and the tinder can be coaxed until it can be transferred to a bundle of finely teased grass or other inflammable vegetable fibre and blown into flames.

Horse's hoof fungus (Fomes formentarius)

Flint-and-steel.

When steel became available an improved flint-and-steel firestarter was made from carbon steel. The steel would be struck against the edge of a shard of flint, causing tiny, red-hot steel shavings to be cast off as sparks. If you want to try this method, assuming that you have access to a piece of flint, chert or similar hard, glassy rock, the difficulty will be finding a suitable piece of steel. It needs to have a high carbon content and to be tempered to the correct density. The steels used to make modern knife blades rarely give sparks, but some old-style carbon steel knives have blades that do so, as will old metal files or the tops of some axe heads. If you can get hold of a piece of high-carbon steel you can make your own fire steel by heating the metal to a cherry-red colour and quenching it in water to around 40 degrees Centigrade.

Striking sparks into a mass of char cloth.

Hunters can open shotgun shells to obtain tinder easily ignited with sparks.

Tinders for use with sparks

Tinders for use with a traditional flint and steel need to be very fine and to take a spark easily. Many of the tinders that will ignite from a pyrophoric alloy steel just won't work with more traditional techniques. In the past, when the flint was a principal means of firestarting, many of the tinders were impregnated with a solution of saltpetre to improve their combustibility. Saltpetre, or potassium nitrate, does occur naturally as a white, salt-like deposit and can sometimes be on the walls of caves and cellars, but to find it is so difficult in the field that it is beyond our reach for all practical purposes.

Cedar bark being shaved up for tinder.

Plants

Some plants produce downy seed heads that can be used to take a spark. These include:

- Rosebay willowherb. Collect the downy seed-heads, clean them of the remains of the seed-head cases and scorch the edges to take fine sparks.
- Cotton grass. Used by the Inuit as tinder.
- Poplar. Soak the down and dry it under compression. The edges need to be charred for use with fine sparks.
- Cat-tail. Treat in the same way as poplar down.
- Thistle. Difficult to use with all but modern sparks unless treated with saltpetre.
- Clematis down. Also best used with modern sparks unless treated with saltpetre.
- Kapok. Tropical tinder used with sparks. There are many types.

Clematis.

Kapok.

Traditionally, even those downs that do not of themselves accept a fine spark were pressed into service for firestarting. They could be added to the tinder to increase the size of the ember.

(The partial scorching required by many down tinders to make them capable of taking a spark is best carried out with a flame, although if necessary it can be achieved in the field by laborious repeated striking with sparks.)

Cramp ball fungus.

Fungus

The trusty cramp ball, *Daldinia concentrica*, is such good tinder material that it can even be used in place of charcoal to cook over. It does need to be totally dry to ignite successfully. Choose a fungus that is very dark brown in colour and which, when broken open, reveals silvery-grey concentric rings. Strike the sparks on to these rings and the fungus will glow and smoulder. Blow gently on to it to increase the glow until the fungus is burning like a charcoal briquette. Unfortunately, while it is common in the UK, usually it is rare in the rest of the world. The only other place I have seen it is in the rainforest of Zaire, though I have heard that it can be located in the rainforest of Thailand close to the Mekong River.

The classic tinder fungus, the horse's hoof fungus *Fomes fomentarius,* can still be found growing on dead birch trees in northern latitudes or on dead beech in southern Europe. The fungi are best collected when they are young, when the apex of the hoof-shaped body can be easily depressed with the thumb. Slice off

Horse's hoof fungus.

the horny outer surface (cuticle), and carve away the underside which resembles thousands of tiny tubes (the pores). You are left with the trama, the leathery brown layer that can be used for tinder. Rather than scraping the trama to produce a fibrous, downy tinder as our Neolithic ancestors did, you can place the

fungus on a smooth, wooden surface and immerse it in water, bring it to the boil and simmer it for twenty-four hours. Then gently pound it into a large, flat sheet using a wooden hammer. To improve the sparking quality either boil again for another twenty-four hours in a concentrated solution of hardwood ash and water, or rub hardwood ash into the fungus and massage it until it is dry. Commercially this tinder was produced and treated with saltpetre and sold under the name of amadou.

Several other species of fungi can be prepared in the same way to produce tinder. These are not as well known as the horse's hoof fungus because their smaller trama layers made them less of a commercial proposition. However, it is highly likely that they were used in ancient times. They include:

- ☞ true tinder fungus (*Phellinus igniarius*)
- ☞ artist's fungus (*Ganoderma applanatum*)
- ☞ *Ganoderma adspersum*
- ☞ maze-gill fungus (*Daedelia quercina*)
- ☞ blushing bracket (*Daedalopsis confragosa*)
- ☞ *Fomiotopsis pinicola*

Take some time to familiarise yourself with one of these types of fungi and investigate its trama layer. Then, should you find yourself in need of tinder in a strange land, you may be able to find a similar fungus that will do the job for you.

Char cloth

Char cloth is one of the most easily produced tinders for use with the flint-and-steel. It is simply cloth that has been burned until it turns very dark brown or black. Obviously you need to use a natural fabric, such as cotton, linen or silk. The quickest way to make it is to set light to a small piece of cloth and then stamp the fire out when it has burned to the required colour. A more efficient method is to tightly pack the cloth into an airtight tin and pierce a small hole in it. Put the tin into a fire. As the cloth inside chars, you will see smoke escaping from the hole. When smoke is no longer produced remove the tin from the fire and seal the hole. After the tin has cooled down you should have a container of perfectly charred cloth.

Wood punk

Dead, dry, soft decaying wood can sometimes be crumbled and used as spark tinder. Resinous wood punk, such as spruce, ignites well from sparks produced from modern sparking tools, while willow can be slightly charred to accept a spark from traditional flint-and-steels.

Fire by friction

If you have never created a fire by friction you might well be wondering what possible point there is in learning to do so in a world of matches and lighters. Well, apart from the immense satisfaction and sense of achievement to be gained from summoning this fundamental element for yourself, being able to perform every step of the firelighting process to perfection will make you a better all-round firelighter. When you can make fire in this way, your success in creating it with more modern tools should be an absolute certainty. But more than that, underlying all these techniques, bushcraft is the study of self-reliance. If we can produce fire directly, with nature's aid, we break our dependency on processes beyond our individual control to provide what is our most important resource. Besides, friction techniques not only work, but with practice and good preparation they are just as trustworthy as any other technique.

Drill and Bow

Of all the friction techniques, the drill-and-bow method is the most efficient and reliable, even in the worst weather. It can also be used in any environment where we may need to create fire. Oddly enough, given its dependability, I have never encountered it among any indigenous peoples who produce fire by friction, although several communities who use the hand drill have observed without prompting that their method could be improved with a bow. It may be that the technique has vanished because it was practised mainly in cold, damp regions where it has been replaced by the more user-friendly and portable matches and sparks.

The bow-and-drill method involves drilling one piece of wood into another at 90 degrees to the grain. The drill is pressed against the hearth by means of a bearing block and is rotated by means of a string secured tightly in a bow, for single-handed operation, or fitted with toggles for a team effort. The advantage of this technique is that considerable force can be applied to the fire set in both rotation and downward pressure. This means that a greater variety of woods can be used than is the case with other friction methods, which in turn makes it more suitable for a wider range of conditions and

environments. The material available for the string is a limiting factor. Strong cordage such as rawhide or nylon cord, being more resistant to abrasion, can cope with many different kinds of wood, whereas plant-fibre cords, which are less resilient, reduce the choice of wood. While the driest dead wood is ideal for this technique, the fact that I have several times managed to produce fire from green wood is a clear indication of its versatility.

As with all bushcraft skills, it pays to practise before you really need to depend on it. Many people are astonished to discover just how much there is to learn about what most take for granted as a simple and obvious process. Again attention to detail is vital. The key to successful bow-drill firestarting is choosing the correct wood for the drill and hearth. Early observers of friction firelighting maintained with Victorian scientific zeal that the most important factor was having a drill harder than the hearth board. This assertion has since been handed down as gospel, to the extent that people talking in a pub will say, 'Of course, the secret to rubbing sticks

To use the bow drill efficiently you must have the correct posture and form to provide stability, and allow an easy drilling action with one arm whilst the other maintains a steady downward pressure.

Making a bow drill

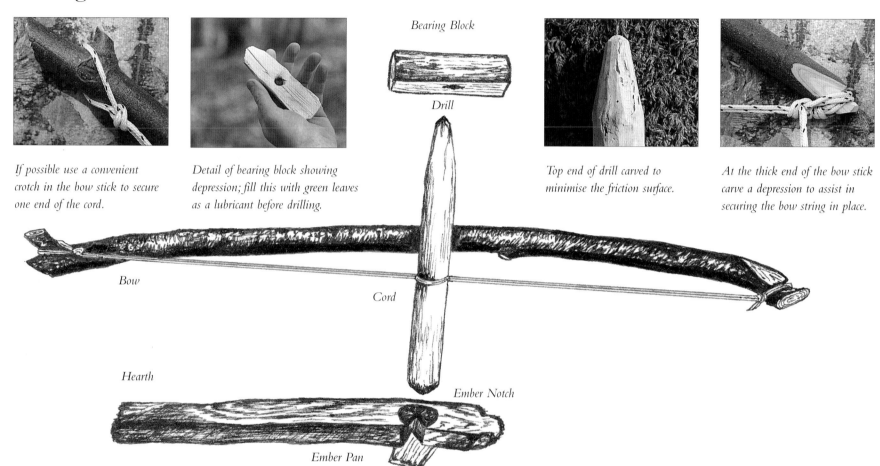

Bearing Block

Drill

Bow

Cord

Hearth

Ember Notch

Ember Pan

If possible use a convenient crotch in the bow stick to secure one end of the cord.

Detail of bearing block showing depression; fill this with green leaves as a lubricant before drilling.

Top end of drill carved to minimise the friction surface.

At the thick end of the bow stick carve a depression to assist in securing the bow string in place.

Bottom end of drill carved to maximise the friction surface.

Drill into the hearth until you have seated the drill into a depression the same diameter as the drill.

Detail of the ember notch, a ¹/8 segment removed from the hearth to allow friction dust to collect and form an ember.

The ember pan – bark, a shaving or a knife blade – is placed under the notch to collect the ember and protect it from the cold, damp ground.

The bow cord is wrapped around the drill so that the drill is on the outside of the bow.

together to make fire is having one stick harder than the other.' In the case of the hand drill this advice has some validity but with the bow drill it can be safely ignored.

True, some hard-soft combinations will work, but more often the harder wood simply consumes the softer variety without generating an ember, and when it does, the resultant erosion gives a shorter life span to the fire set. A more reliable principle is to select the same wood preferably from the same branch – for both drill and hearth, using pieces as near as possible to the right size to minimise the amount of carving you need to do. This way the drill and hearth consume each other at a more even rate and you reduce the amount of experimentation necessary with unfamiliar wood. You will need wood that is dead, still standing and as dry as you can find. It should be only just possible to dent the surface of the wood with your thumbnail. In extremely wet weather you may have to whittle the drill and hearth from the dry centre of a large timber. Once on the coast of British Columbia I was forced to resort to using a branch of a cedar tree that was submerged each day by a rising tide. Although the outer 6mm of the branch was saturated, the wood at its core was dry enough to generate fire.

The crucial dimension of the bow-and-drill set is the drill diameter. This can vary from wood to wood. Generally smaller diameters suit harder woods and warmer climates, and larger diameters softer woods or colder, damper conditions. An average diameter of 25 to 30mm will work with the widest range of woods. Make the drill 220mm long and absolutely straight, carving the top to reduce friction and the bottom to maximise it. Then fashion the hearth board, ensuring that it is wide enough to comfortably accept your drill. The bow should be 70cm long and inflexible. For the bearing block, use a wood harder than the one you choose for the drill and carve a small recess into it to accept the top of the drill. All you need for the ember pan is a shaving of wood or small piece of dry bark.

When you have all the components ready, make a slight depression in the hearth board to accept the drill. Drill down until the drill has seated itself in and has scorched its working end to its full diameter. Now carve away an eighth segment from the hearth. Fill the recess in the bearing block with green leaf material as lubricant.

When using the bow-and-drill, aim for stability. Pin the hearth firmly to the ground. Twisting the drill tightly into the bow cord, so that it is outside the bow, place its lower end into the hearth depression and hold it there by means of the bearing block. The bearing block must be securely anchored against your shinbone to prevent wobble. Drill smoothly and firmly, starting slowly and gradually increasing speed and pressure. When the hearth begins to smoke furiously, keep drilling for at least twenty more full strokes with the bow. Now gently lift the drill and bow out of the way. The notch in the hearth board should be full of a dark brown, smoking powder that clings tightly to the edge of the ember notch. Very

carefully, position a small stick on top of the ember as you rotate the hearth away. The ember should be self-supporting and smoking. Fan it gently with your hand to encourage it to coalesce before lifting the ember pan and transferring it to a tinder bundle, where it can be blown into flames. The bundle must be tightly packed. A common mistake is to leave the fibres too open, which makes it difficult for the ember to grow. Place the ember into the finest part of the tinder and gently pinch it with the fibres, ensuring that you don't crush it. Holding the tinder 20cm from your face, blow softly into the bundle, watching for a glowing ember and developing smoke. Each time you take a breath, sweep the bundle away and down from your face, drawing it back up in time with your breaths. As the ember gradually spreads in the bundle the smoke increases. When it becomes thick and white, pause briefly to check that your kindling is ready to take the burning tinder. Just before the bundle bursts into flames the smoke will darken and turn greenish. When you see this happening, puff into the bundle to produce flames.

Bushcraft is about skill, and skill is not developed overnight. So, if at first you don't succeed, keep trying. Determination is a natural byproduct of learning how to use the bow drill. If you consistently fail to produce an ember, ask a friend to assist you on the other end of the bow. Usually, once you have cracked it in tandem, solo success is not far behind. When you have got the hang of this technique you may want to experiment with other types of wood, or even try making a bow-and-drill in foreign climes. If you are working with unfamiliar woods, bear in mind that there are three main variables: the diameter of the drill, the speed with which the drill rotates and the amount of downward pressure you apply. Narrower drills tend to cause problems unless the wood is very hard or the conditions very dry. You are likely to achieve the best results if you keep your drill as thick as your thumb at its knuckle.

Bow-drill woods

Alder	Elm	Oak
Aspen	Fir (Balsam)	Pine
Baobab	Hazel	Poplar
Birch	Hibiscus	Wild rose
Cedar (red and	Horse chestnut	Saguaro rib
yellow)	*Ivy	*Sotol
Cherry root	Juniper	Spruce
Clematis	*Lime	*Sycamore
Cottonwood	Field maple	*Willow
Cypress	Norway maple	Yucca
Elder	Marula	*best woods

Hadza man in Tanzania using fire drill – note long drill.

Drill and hand

The hand drill is the world's most widespread friction firestarting method. It is without doubt my favourite firestarter: I find its elegant simplicity intoxicating. However, speaking practically it must be said that it has a limited range. In the north of the temperate zone, where the weather can be cold and is predominatly wet, this tool is less dependable and disappears from the anthropological record. This is not to say that it cannot be used in such regions at all – in fact, working in tandem with a colleague, I once created an ember on top of a block of ice in a blizzard in the depth of the Arctic winter to prove that it could work. But the fact remains that the further north you go, the more the bow-and-drill becomes the most reliable method of firestarting.

Hand drills can be produced in the field, but are more often carefully prepared before the traveller heads out on the trail. They can be made from a wide range of woods, including many shrubs that will not withstand the more vigorous action of the bow drill. To make a special hand drill set in advance, select a suitable wood, such as elder, with as little pith as possible. The

Arnhemland, Australia – virtually identical technique.

base of secondary-growth elder sticks is thick-walled, as is the whole of a primary shoot. Shave off the bark, smooth the stick and straighten it gently while it dries. If you have a fire, use this to hasten the drying process.

If you need to make a drill on the trail look for dead, dry drill wood, for example white willow, mullein, teasel, dog-rose stem or even a dead, dry burdock stem. In aboriginal Arnhemland, a red-flowered kurrajong stem killed by a previous season's burn is ideal. The drill will need to be 50 to 70cm long and as straight as possible. Smooth the stick with a sharp edge so that it is as smooth as a dowel rod. Any bumps left on the stick are apt to produce blisters. If you cannot find a long, straight drill of the right kind of wood, you can fit a short section of the correct wood to a long, straight piece of another variety. Carve the end of the drill in the same way as for the bow drill. For the hearth, you can use the same wood as you've chosen for the drill, or other good hearth woods such as sycamore, willow, clematis, acacia, juniper or cedar. Twirl the drill between your palms to establish a depression in the hearth and carve a notch into it in exactly the same way as you would for the bow drill.

To make fire, place an ember pan under the notch, secure the hearth board to the ground with your foot and begin drilling by rotating the drill between your palms with a steady downward pressure. As you do so your hands will travel down the drill. When you reach the end keep the drill in place as you reposition your hands at the top to begin again. Spitting into your palms and rubbing them together will help your grip. Try not to press your hands together too hard, as this will cause blisters. Concentrate instead on an easy movement for a smooth, fast drilling action. At first, as you warm the drill up, go slowly; then steadily increase your speed and downward pressure. Watch the hearth notch as it fills with powder. The hand drill produces an ember in the same way as the bow drill from which point onwards the process of making a fire is identical. When you have an ember, smoke will begin to rise from beneath the powder which will darken to black.

Hand-drill woods	Hearth woods
Alder	Alder
Aspen	Aspen
Baobab	Baobab
Bamboo	Blackboy
Blackboy	Burdock
Buddleia	Cedar
Burdock	Clematis
Cat-tail	Common corkwood
Common corkwood	Confetti tree
Cottonwood	Cottonwood
Confetti tree	Elder
Elder	False sandpaper raisin
False sandpaper raisin	Field maple
Grewip	Grewip
Hibiscus	Hibiscus
Horse chestnut	Horse chestnut
Knobbly compretum	Knobbly combretum
Large fever-berry	Large fever-berry
Marula	Marula
Mangetti	Mullein
Mullein	Norway maple
Pine	Pine
Red flowered kurrajong	Red flowered kurrajong
Sage brush	Saguaro rib
Saguaro rib	Sotol
Sotol	Sycamore
Sycamore	Sycamore fig
Sycamore fig	Trumpet thorn
Teasel	Willow
Trumpet thorn	
Willow	

Drill and pump

A more complicated method for effecting a drilling action is the pump drill which incorporates a fly wheel attached to the drill and a cord wrapped around the drill to achieve a clockwise – counter clockwise drill rotation with a falling and rising pump board. The only practical use I have heard of for this method is ceremonial with a drill over a metre in length. However, it can be fun for youth groups to try the skill.

Saw and flexible sawing thongs

With this firestarter the friction is produced by a wooden saw or thin creeper against a hearth board of 90 degrees to the grain. These fire sets, usually made from bamboo, are a remarkably quick and efficient means of creating fire in the tropics. The best is the saw used in the Philippines and Indonesia. The beauty of it is that all you need is a parang and some suitable bamboo, and you can even produce fire in the rain under your poncho. Choose a piece of dead bamboo over 5cm in diameter with a reasonably thick wall. Cut out a section bearing two nodes and about half of each of the straight sections above and below them. Split this in half and break a third one off one of the halves. Make a narrow notch in the outside of the shorter stick at 90 degrees to the grain and carve into it until you have a small hole about 3 or 4mm long and 1mm wide, through the bamboo. On the inside carve a shallow groove in line with the grain. This will be the hearth.

Spear thrower being used as fire saw, made from Marula wood.

Using bamboo fire saw in Costa Rica rainforest.

Taking the longer piece of bamboo, carve one edge like a knife blade for the saw. Then, using your parang, scrape off the shiny outer coating of the wood in a back-and-forth action so that you finish up with two bundles of shavings, one at either end. When these are approaching the size of a hen's egg remove them and put one on each side of the hole on the inside of the hearth. Hold them in place by skewering them through the hole with small sections of green bamboo.

Supporting the saw as fast as you can by leaning on it, or by pinning it to the ground, position the hearth on the saw's edge and rub it up and down. When you notice smoke starting to rise, rub and apply greater force. In tropical rainforest you will by now be sweating profusely. Try not to let your perspiration fall on to the working parts of the saw. If you have prepared everything and have pitched the intensity of your effort at the right level you should be able to stop sawing after about thirty seconds. Try blowing through the hearth hole. If you have managed to light the shavings you should see a plume of smoke streaming from the other side of the hearth. Keep blowing until the tinder bundles have begun to glow. It might be necessary to loosen the ember from the hole with a small pick of bamboo. Once the tinder bundles are glowing, remove them and blow them to life.

A variation on the fire saw is made using a piece of dead wood split at one end and holding the split open with a small wedge. A second saw board is sawed back and forth on top to create an ember in the split. I have seen this technique in action in the central Australian desert. There a piece of dead mulga wood with a natural crack about 4mm wide, created by the desiccating climate, served as the hearth. Very dry, powdered kangaroo droppings were fed into this tinder and a 'miru' spear-thrower sawed back and forth to create the ember. Compared to the previously mentioned techniques this fire saw is less reliable, but proves useful in very arid areas with hard sun-baked woods which are less suited to drilling.

The flexible sawing thong relies on hearth boards made either along the lines of the bamboo fire saw or according to the split-stick method described above, but the saw itself is made from a thin, flexible strip of bamboo or rattan. Frankly, though, while reliable, it requires such a refined technique and such carefully chosen materials that it falls beyond the range of fundamental bushcraft.

Fire plough

The fire plough is found along the Congo River and in Polynesia. The technique, which involves rubbing one dry stick against another in line with the grain, puzzled me for many years, because it seems so inefficient compared to the drilling methods. It was only when I saw it in operation at first hand on the banks of the Congo that I began to understand its relevance to that environment. The tool produces an ember the same size as that yielded by a bow drill, and doesn't need a cord. Here hand-drill materials are more prone to termite attack, whereas wood of the right type and suitable dimensions for the fire plough – they use one measuring about 25 by 30 by 400mm – is readily available.

In Western Samoa a fire plough made from dead, dry coastal hibiscus wood is still commonly used to conjure a fire in only a few seconds.

To construct a fire plough, start by carving a flat surface on the hearth stick. Shave up a curl of wood and then begin ploughing, very slowly at first, gradually increasing your speed and rotating the plough slightly on each stroke. The action will form a longitudinal groove and produce a fibrous, dark powder against the curled shaving. Be careful not to break apart the pile of powder that forms as you plough; this will become the ember.

Transfer the ember into the fibres in a half dry coconut husk, which will act as your tinder bundle.

Fire plough in use on the banks of the Congo.

Western Samoan fire plough.

Tinders for friction firestarting

All of the friction firestarting techniques produce a small ember of fine, scorched wood dust. To convert this ember to flame you need to nurture it in a bundle of tinder. This can be any flammable, dry, fibrous material to hand: dry grass, dry barks, inner and outer; dry lichens, coconut husks, webbing material from the base of palm fronds, fine wood shavings. Rub the tinder vigorously between your hands to make it as fine as possible. If you can, improve the bundle by placing even finer combustible material, such as plant downs, in its core. A good tinder bundle will be about the size of a grapefruit when tightly compressed. Good tinders for friction firestarters include:

 plant downs (as for sparks – see page 74)
 fungi (as for sparks – see page 75)
 grasses (most fibrous grass leaves)
 outer bark: clematis, cinquefoil, honeysuckle, red cedar, juniper, willowherb
 inner bark: lime, sweet chestnut, oak, willow (dried and beaten)
 hairs from mature ivy stem

Clematis bark being buffed to make it soft and fine.

Completed tinder bundle ready to go; store this in a warm dry place (for example tucked inside your clothing).

Fire by air compression

One of the strangest methods of producing fire is by compressing tinder in a tight piston. This method relies on the same principle as the diesel engine. A wooden piston with a thread seal greased in animal fat is fitted to a wooden barrel. Tinder is placed in a small depression at the end of the piston. You can use palm fibre, kapok, hoof fungus or cramp ball. The piston is struck smartly, with sufficient force to ignite the tinder in the barrel. Almost as soon as the piston has been depressed it is pulled out to reveal the smouldering tinder, which must be coaxed to life in a tinder bundle. Although it is a neat, compact device, it has to be said that it is difficult to operate successfully – virtually impossible to construct in the field. So it is more a matter of interest than a system of practical value. It also reduces reliability in monsoon conditions

Fire by chemical means

Fire can be started by various chemicals, of which perhaps only one combination is ever likely to be available to you in the wild. If you have a glycol-based antifreeze and some potassium permanganate, you can easily produce fire. Add a tablespoon of the antifreeze to a bundle of tinder, then sprinkle a teaspoon of potassium permanganate on to this, compress the bundle and put it down very quickly – on a warm day you may get a very fast reaction. The two chemicals will generate enough heat to set the bundle glowing. If the reaction is occurring slowly, don't be tempted either to pick up the bundle or to walk away and leave it. Treat it as if it were a live firework. An old-time favourite disinfectant of overland travellers – it can be diluted in water to disinfect wounds and suspect salad ingredients – potassium permanganate can also be mixed with sugar, nine parts chemical to one part sugar, and rubbed vigorously between two rocks to create sparks.

Fire by electrical means

If you have either a head torch with a fresh battery or a car battery you can create sparks to start a fire.

To use a head torch, you will need some wire wool from a vehicle repair kit. Lace this with plant downs and other fibrous tinder material and place this bundle against the battery terminals of the torch. It will glow sufficiently for you to blow on it to ignite the tinder.

To use a vehicle battery, disconnect it and connect jump leads to the terminals. Prepare some tinder, perhaps teased-apart field dressing from the car's first-aid kit. Taking care to hold the crocodile clips by their insulators to avoid an unwelcome shock, touch them together. This will bring forth bright sparks which will ignite the field dressing, and indeed most spark tinders.

Flame to fire

Having conjured a flame, we next need to know how to turn it into a fire. Perhaps because we no longer light fires on a daily basis, or perhaps simply because it has always been a tricky operation, firelighting is a skill which has to be learned and takes practice. Even many seasoned backcountry hikers get their fires going more by luck than judgement. We'll look at five techniques that will enable us to cope with a wide range of weather and environmental conditions.

To burn properly, a fire needs three components: HEAT, FUEL and OXYGEN

HEAT

Whichever firelighting technique you are using, the more heat you start with, the more certain you will be of success. Hence the great value of a blazing tinder bundle over the flickering flame of a match. In warm weather fires start fairly easily, whereas in conditions of extreme cold you may have to warm your tinder inside your clothing even to produce the initial flame.

FUEL

Fuel needs to be carefully selected and graded by size. All kindling should be from the driest wood you can find, ideally small sticks caught in branches a safe distance away from the dampening effects of the ground. As the fire starts fuel must be added gradually, small, thin kindling to start with, and then thicker wood. If you add bulky wood too soon the fire will fail to spread and then die.

Make sure that you pack the fuel closely enough to allow the flame to pass from one stick to another, otherwise the fire will burn out in the middle, leaving the top layers of fuel unscorched.

OXYGEN

Oxygen is, of course, ever present but it can be accidentally occluded if you pack the fuel too tightly.

Fire prefers to grow upwards, so flat piles of fuel burn more slowly and tend to smoulder. But avoid going too far the other way and ending up with something that looks like a tepee. As a general rule, build your fire from the bottom up, arranging the sticks in a criss-cross formation which will leave the necessary air spaces between them and at the same time allow gravity to ensure that they are fed into the flames.

Firelighting

Small sticks

Using small sticks is the most common method of building a fire. Begin by laying down a small platform of dry, dead wood about the thickness of your thumb. This will keep the tinder and kindling off the damp ground, insulate it in extreme cold and help it to burn quickly to provide your fire with a strong heart of embers. Lay two generous handfuls of small kindling crosswise on top of this

How to lay a fire – note platform and length of small sticks.

platform. These should be no thicker than a match and about 30cm long. Do not be tempted to break them in half to cut down the time it takes to create thick bundles. Place your tinder under the sticks where they cross and ignite it.

As the fire get under way, adjust the position of the stick bundles so that they cross directly over the flames and then leave them alone. All being well, you will see a rapidly accelerating plume of smoke rise from your fire, followed shortly by flames reaching through the bundles. At this point add a handful of pencil-thick fuel. When the flames appear through this progress to finger-thick and kindling and continue to increase the size of the fuel until you are burning wood of the desired thickness.

In very damp weather, or when it is raining, you may find your fire takes a little while to get going, but try not to interfere with it: many a fire is stifled by too much attention. Keep an eye on the smoke. If it is accelerating, leave the fire to develop at its own pace. If, however, the smoke is petering out, you will need to take action. You may be able to adjust the fuel and increase the oxygen supply, but the likelihood is that you will have to start again. If you can develop the habit of making your preparations carefully the first time, you should see your fire roar to life in no time.

Feather sticks

After prolonged rainfall, or in an unfamiliar environment, it may be quickest to light your fire with feather sticks. Search for a suitable piece of dead, standing wood that can be split down and shaved into feather sticks as described on page 36. As with a small-stick fire, lay a platform and using a thumb-thick piece of fuel wood, prop up the feather sticks so that their shavings face towards you, leaving a small space at their base to insert a match.

Poor feather stick.

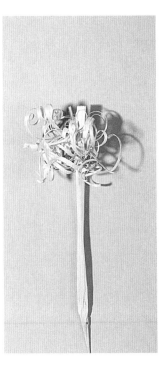

OK feather stick.

Good feather stick – mass of tight curls.

Split wood and birch bark

In regions where birch bark is abundant it can be used to ignite split wood. Prepare a platform and then lay two split sticks in an upside down, 'V' shape, crossing one stick above the other where they meet. Fill the centre of the 'V' with birch-bark strips, ignite them and criss-cross small sticks across the top.

Dry grass

This is an African variation. Collect a good handful of long, dry grass stems and bind them together into a giant spill. This can be used to light quite large sticks and get your fire under way.

Old fire dogs

The sticks left with partially burned ends after a fire has gone out can often easily be reignited with sparks, a friction-produced ember or any small flame. As long as they are dry, fire dogs can be relit months after they were last burned. Once one fire dog begins to glow it can be encouraged by blowing and the ember can be spread from one dog to another laid alongside it. Once you have three on the go you can usually start your fire anew. Incidentally, this is also a good means of starting a fire from another. Take three logs that are burning well and combine them with a bundle of fine kindling to light the second fire.

Choosing your fuel

There is a sound that can sometimes be heard in the woods very late at night that indicates the presence of novice backwoodsmen. It is the sound of sticks being broken for firewood. The proficient practitioner of bushcraft anticipates his or her needs before it gets dark. Choose the type of firewood you collect carefully, because different woods burn at different speeds and provide varying quantities of heat output.

Firewood must in general be dead, dry wood. Avoid whenever possible picking up firewood from the ground. The best is wood that has fallen, but has been caught up in other branches before reaching the ground. The more vertical its position, the drier it will be. Damp wood will burn poorly and produce too much smoke for a comfortable camp. It will also burn cold, as much of the fire's energy will be expended on drying out the fuel.

Bear in mind what you will be using your fire for and how long you will need it. For warmth and most campfire cookery you'll require fuel that burns slowly and gives out a lot of heat, whereas for a quick fire to boil the kettle and one which will burn to ashes rapidly, look for a wood that burns swiftly. The old adage, 'soft woods for boiling, hard woods for broiling' – broiling being the old-fashioned word for grilling or barbecuing – still holds true.

Hard woods for roasting
Apple
Ash
Beech
Birch
Sweet chestnut
Hazel
Holly
Hornbeam
Larch
Oak
Willow

Soft woods for boiling
Alder
Aspen
Cedar
Hawthorn
Horse chestnut
Lime
Pine
Poplar
Spruce
Sycamore

In days gone by children would be taught poems to help them remember which were the best firewoods. This is one of them:

Logs to burn! Logs to burn!
Logs to save the coal a turn!
Here's a word to make you wise
When you hear the woodsman's cries.

Beechwood fires burn bright and clear,
Hornbeam blazes too,
If the logs are kept a year
And seasoned through and through.

Oak logs will warm you well
If they're old and dry,
Larch logs of pinewood smell
But the sparks will fly.

Pine is good and so is yew
For warmth through wintry days
But poplar and willow, too
Take long to dry and blaze.

Birch logs will burn too fast,
Alder scarce at all.
Chestnut logs are good to last
If cut in the fall.

Holly logs will burn like wax,
You should burn them green,
Elm logs like smouldering flax,
No flame is seen.

Pear logs and apple logs,
They will scent your room.
Cherry logs across the dogs
Smell like flowers in bloom.

But ash logs, all smooth and grey,
Burn them green or old,
Buy up all that come your way,
They're worth their weight in gold.

Pine for kindling

Pine is one of the best natural kindlings. The stumps of old, dead pines are often very rich in resin. Known as fat pine, or ocote in Central America, they can be chopped into splints which ignite readily and burn well. Similar to this are pine knots, the bases of branches that can be struck from old pine logs with the poll of your axe or a heavy stick. These can be used as fuel or saved to add to the fire when more firelight is called for.

Dung

In treeless lands, nomadic peoples often use dung from their herbivorous livestock dried in the sun as their main fuel. It is quite possible to find naturally dried dung for fuel in such countries. But beware the scorpions which often rest under it.

Lighting pine kindling with a liquid butane lighter.

Managing a fire

Fire can be our most valuable resource, but given its capacity for destruction if it is allowed to get out of control, it can also be our greatest enemy, scarring landscapes and decimating forests. So it is important that we manage fire correctly and safely.

Except in cases of emergency, where a fire may be essential to survival, the first question we should ask ourselves is whether or not it is appropriate to light one at all. The campfire in particular is a matter of fierce debate. One view is that hike stoves should be carried into the wilderness and used instead, because they leave behind far fewer traces of our presence – and certainly far less damage than the fire scars left by the campfires of ignorant and lazy campers. On the other side are the back-to-nature campers, who maintain that sitting by a campfire brings them closer to nature in a spiritual way that is impossible with a hike stove. They also argue that burning fossil fuels in a machine which is expensive to produce in terms of the Earth's finite resources is in its own way just as bad for the environment.

Having spent the greater part of my life travelling in the Earth's wilderness regions from national parks to areas so remote as to be beyond the reach of regulations, my own feeling is that an unnecessary amount of hot air has been generated by this question, and that it all depends on where you are. It is certainly true that there are areas where the use of a campfire is inappropriate: places where it may trigger a forest fire, where fuel is not sufficiently plentiful, or where fires have never been lit before. In these regions a hike stove is a sensible option as it safeguards the environment we have set out to enjoy. But at the same time there are many other places where the flames do not threaten the forest, where fuel is abundant and where, with the proper management, a campfire need not leave any unwelcome after-effects.

To deny that a campfire has a spiritual dimension shows little understanding of the real issue. It not only brings us closer to nature but can encourage greater empathy with fellow hikers in the wilderness. Indeed, the crux of the problem is that fire and humankind go together. While the enlightened adventurer may be right to curse the sight of a fire scar, the truth is that the person who left was probably innocently responding to a deep-seated instinct. There will always be a small percentage of idiot firelighters, of course, but the majority of such offenders are potentially good bushmen and women who simply need educating. In my experience, once they are shown how to clear away a fire, most people rally to the cause and take great pride in leaving no sign that they have ever set up camp.

The blanket fire bans imposed without a clear and sensible reason in national parks rob us of the opportunity to explain why fires must be prohibited in some situations, let alone to educate the fire-user in the ways of managing a fire safely and without causing damage. As a result, the rules are sometimes ignored and fire scars continue to mar the landscape.

The best answer to the fire debate is the example of the indigenous peoples who live permanently in the wild. They are not troubled by urban idealism: fire is their most important resource, and they easily manage to use it on a daily basis without setting their habitats ablaze – unless, of course, they do so deliberately for a good reason. They often leave their fire circles behind; in fact the idea of clearing them is, in some cases, considered crazy as the fire site will indicate to the keen eyes of a tracker how many people have been camped, for how long and how recently – information that can be important to someone seeking help.

As far as non-indigenous peoples are concerned, I'd recommend aiming to travel through a landscape like a shadow, leaving as little trace of yourself and your activities as possible, and to use either a campfire or a stove as your location and circumstances dictate.

Siting and clearing away a fire

When you want to build a fire, give some thought to the place to do it. Don't make a rush to the first site. Don't choose an obvious beauty spot – a scenic riverside meadow, for example. Search out instead a quiet, concealed area that will give you some privacy and where you and your fire won't impinge on others. Avoid combustible vegetation, peaty soil and deep pine needles. What you need is a clear area with mineral soil that can easily be revealed by brushing back the humus, the kind of place frequently found under the dark canopy of broad-leafed woodland. It should provide shelter from wind and rain and an abundant supply of dead wood or dry dung for fuel. Always build your fuel on level ground, without digging a fire pit unless absolutely necessary; in a survival situation, you may need to make a shallow, bowl-shaped pit where you can keep a supply of ember so that you don't have to constantly relight your fire. Never place the fire on top of exposed roots or against a tree, rock or cliff face. Keep the fire itself as small as possible, using it only as required. You can use fire dogs to reignite if necessary. There is no point in surrounding it with rocks: this won't do anything other than blacken the rocks.

Bear in mind when you intend to break camp so that by the time you leave you have fed all the ends of your fire dogs into the fire and burned them to ash, which is the most easily cleared byproduct of a fire. If this isn't possible, open the embers of your fire to allow them to cool and move the remaining firewood outwards, isolating each stick from its neighbour. The embers should then go out. This process can be hastened by pouring water over the embers and mixing it with a stick until there is no more steam or smoke rising. Ensure that any charred sticks are well doused. If the coal and ashes are cold you will be able to pick them up by hand. Put them into your cookpot, remove them to a good distance and scatter them widely. You should now be left with just mineral earth. Use a light, dead-stick brush to spread the original humus over this so that the site blends in with the surroundings as you go. Have a last check for any litter that may have escaped your notice.

Underground roots can catch light and smoulder like a fuse, eventually surfacing to cause a forest fire. So, if you are in an area with soft soil, perforate the earth with a sharpened stick and pour in copious quantities of water. Coniferous trees, especially larches, are particularly susceptible to this problem. If you have set up camp on grassland it is best not to light a fire, but if circumstances leave you no alternative you can minimise its impact by carefully lifting some turf and digging down underneath it to the mineral soil. Make your fire pit much larger than your fire to avoid scorching the grass at the pit edge. I usually turn over smaller pieces of turf at the rim and form a soil border around the pit, which I keep well watered. Keep the lifted turf in a shady place and water it morning and evening. When you have finished with your fire, extinguish it, remove all of the ash and embers and rake the ground to soften it. Search around for some well-weathered animal dung and place this in the pit, watering it into a slurry, and replace the turf. Water the site of the fire as well. The ground should then recover quickly from the effects of the fire.

In forests carpeted with mossy peats fires are a particular risk, because the forest floor is itself combustible. In Scandinavia, where such conditions predominate, fires are built in a special way that minimises the danger. But even using this method, you should still lay a fire only if plenty of water is available and the weather hasn't been dry for a long time. Lift the moss to a depth that will create a fire circle larger than the fire you will be setting. Put the moss in a shady place and keep it watered. Saturate the ground in your fire circle with water, and then line the pit with rocks. Lots of small rocks are better than one large one as they provide better air flow at the fire base. Don't use rocks from a riverbed; if they are saturated they will explode when heated, as the moisture they contain expands, so choose the driest ones you can find. Light your fire on top of the rock platform which, once hot, will warm and improve the fire's performance. When breaking camp allow time for the fire to cool. Soak the site and lift the cold ashes and embers by hand for dispersal. Remove the cold rocks and scatter them well.

Ensure that the ground is not alight as peat fires are especially prone to smouldering underground along roots for weeks before eventually surfacing and igniting the forest. Take a sharpened stick and poke it into the ground to a depth of 30cm in and around the fire site, and pour generous quantities of water into the holes so that it penetrates deep into the peat layers, extinguishing any burning. Once you are satisfied that the fire is well and truly out, and there is no steam or smoke rising from any of the holes, replace the peat and moss that you originally moved.

Adapting your fire to your requirements

Once the fire is alight, the formation can be adjusted to suit the conditions and the uses to which you want to put it. The following are just a few examples.

Criss-cross fire lay

Built upwards like a low matchstick tower enclosing a base platform, tinder bundle and kindling with layers of fuel criss-crossed at 90 degrees above them. The fire burns well and settles efficiently to provide a deep bed of embers for cooking. It also throws out a good deal of heat, so it is a good design to lay in advance if you are going to need your fire to keep warm.

Criss-cross fire lay.

Indians' fire, Sanema, Venezuela.

Siberian fire lay – split wood and birch bark.

The leaning criss-cross fire lay

This is the method I usually choose to enlarge my fire. Laying layers of firewood so that their lower ends are on the ground and their top halves criss-cross in layers above the fire. It is a very stable arrangement that allows gravity to feed the fuel into the fire, leaving ends protruding so that the fire can easily be converted into a convenient arrangement.

The Indians' fire

The most useful of all designs, this simple fire is ideal for backcountry travellers. Lay the wood so that it points into the fire heart in a star shape. As the fire consumes the sticks they are gradually fed into the centre. It is easily modified, enlarged and extinguished – all you need to do is to open out the star. It is particularly well suited to use with a pot-hanger (see page 26).

The star fire

This variation on the Indians' fire comprises three, or more usually four, thick logs of equal diameter. Because the logs are uniform, a pot can be supported on the burning ends meeting in the middle. This is a good fire for maintaining a supply of water in a fixed camp.

The long-log fire

The traditional fire for open fronted bivouacs in cold weather. Using long logs supported by smaller ones, you can build a fire that stretches the length of your body to provide enough heat to keep you warm in the coldest weather. It will burn very efficiently and requires minimal tending. The little supporting logs can be green wood. In the far north in winter, birch trees have such a low moisture content that once a fire has a good ember bed they can be burned green, producing a slow-burning fire with an excellent output of heat. It is said that a log as thick as a capercaillie will last throughout Michaelmas night.

The star fire.

The long log fire.

Tepee fire lay

As the name suggests this is a design that is tepee-shaped; the lay most often shown in illustrations of campfires. It is not, however, one I ever use. It burns quickly, giving plenty of light, but tends to be unstable. It can also fail to feed itself by becoming lodged so that the middle burns out without igniting the upper layers.

Tepee fire.

To effect rescue, signal fires must have two parts: 1. A quick-burning, heat-generating section. 2. A smoke generator of green boughs.

Special circumstances

There may be times when you need to make some key modifications to your fire to cope with unusual conditions or circumstances.

Windy weather

Wind can be a great problem. In hot weather, a strong gust can blow flames, sparks and even embers into surrounding vegetation. So, unless there is no risk of starting a catastrophic conflagration, avoid lighting a fire in hot weather. Strong winds in cold climates will make your fire burn quickly. In these conditions double or even treble the amount of kindling when building your fire to ensure a lasting bed of embers forms. Then add fuel – select slow burning fuel whenever possible – placing it on the downwind side of the fire.

Wet weather

Just before bad weather the smoke from your fire may be seen clinging to the ground rather than rising into the sky. In wet weather you will need to use extra kindling. In very wet conditions, all the fuel you collect will carry some moisture. To counteract the effects of this, build a larger fire than you would in dry weather to keep yourself warm, and dry out the firewood you are adding at the same time. A normal-sized fire will tend to go cold every time you add more fuel as the fire's warmth diverts into drying it out. Splitting firewood will greatly improve its combustion.

Extreme cold

Extreme cold will slow down your fire and make it smoky. It will be working much harder to combat these conditions, so make sure that it has excellent ventilation and that you maintain a good bed of embers. The extra clothing we wear in this weather can insulate us from the warmth of the fire as well as from the cold, so take care not to scorch or melt it without realising by standing or sitting too close to the campfire.

On snow

Always clear the snow away down to the ground, even if this means digging a trench in several metres of the stuff. Clear enough space to give you room to work and insulate the ground with boughs. It is important to keep snow off your clothing and footwear when you are near to the fire or you will quickly become soaked.

If you can't clear the snow, try improvising a platform from green wood. It will eventually sink into the snow, but in the meantime it may suffice until you are able to create a better site.

No smoke

For a smokeless fire you need to use small pieces of absolutely dry wood with the bark removed. There will be a little amount of smoke when you first light it, but this will quickly clear to a bright smoke-free fire. Keep it well constructed in a loose, upright tower. If the fire collapses, it will smoulder

No smoke, no flame

The best method of producing a fire without smoke or flame is to burn charcoal. This can be found on fire sites left by careless campers or on the stumps of old forest fires. The most efficient way to burn charcoal is in a brazier, which can be improvised from an empty catering tin can. This is an ideal fire for cooking. For a basic brazier, simply punch some holes in the sides of the can; for a more sophisticated version, ventilate the base and adapt the rim to support your cooking pot. Silent and smoke-and-flame free, these stoves are a delight to use and excellent for deep-frying or stir-frying with a wok. You can even press them into service as a makeshift barbecue. They are so efficient and environmentally friendly that many of my students now carry these braziers instead of hiking stoves, along with a small stuff sack of locally produced lumpwood charcoal. They will also burn twigs and dung, although not without producing smoke.

Stir-frying in a wok over a basic brazier.

Portable fires

In an emergency it may be difficult to light a fire, and you will be reluctant to allow it to go out. You can keep a fire going overnight by adding firewood and then when it is burning away excluding the air supply by covering with ash or mineral soil. In the morning expose the few remaining embers, add tinder and kindling and restart the fire, blowing if necessary.

If you are forced to move on and need to carry fire with you, follow the example of the Mbayaka Pygmy – and the European 'ice man' of 5,000 years ago. Take along a few good embers or a glowing bracket fungus wrapped in green leaves and other insulating material, carrying them in a bag, basket or similar container.

SHELTER

While today we may be guided in our choice of clothing and equipment by outdoors adventurers who conquer mountains, walk over frozen wastes, ski impossible slopes or paddle turbulent rapids, it is humbling to remind ourselves that the greatest age of human adventure was many thousands of years ago, when our ancestors were reliant on tools made from bone, stone, wood and antler. We will never know the names of the early adventurers who pioneered our first trails, but it is their skills and knowledge that established the techniques and principles of shelter construction we will be studying.

From 1755 to 1759, James Smith, a colonel in the British army, was held captive by the Caughnawagas, a branch of the Mohawks allied to the French in the war for the control of Canada. He was nevertheless given a degree of freedom, even being allowed to accompany hunting parties. In December 1756, at the age of nineteen, he was out hunting racoons when he became separated from the other members of the hunting party. Lost in the deep woods of Ohio, confronted with spending a night alone outside with a snowstorm about to break, he faced an age-old problem.

'As I had only a bow, arrows and tomahawk with me, and no way to strike fire, I was in a dismal situation. The air was dark with snow, and I had little more prospect of steering my course than I would in the night.

At length I came to a hollow tree with a hole at one side that I could go in at. I went in and found that it was a dry place. The hollow was about three feet in diameter and high enough to stand in. There was also a considerable quantity of soft, dry rotten wood around this hollow. I concluded that I would lodge here, and would go to work and stop up the doorway of my house.

I stripped off my blanket (which was all the clothes I had, excepting a breechclout, leggings and moccasins). Then I went out with my tomahawk and fell to chopping at the top of a fallen tree that lay nearby. Carrying the wood back, I set it on end and against the opening, until I had it three feet thick all around, excepting a hole I had left to creep in at. I had a block

prepared that I could haul after me, to stop this hole. I also put in a number of small sticks, that I might more effectually stop it in on the inside.

When I went in, I took my tomahawk, and cut down all the dry, rotten wood I could get, and beat it small. With it I made a bed like a goose nest or hog bed, and with the small sticks stopped every hole until my house was almost dark. I stripped off my moccasins and danced in the centre of my bed for about half an hour, in order to warm myself.

The snow, meanwhile, had stopped all the holes, so that my house was as dark as a dungeon, though I knew it could not yet be dark out of doors. I coiled myself up in my blanket, lay down in my little round bed, and had a tolerable night's lodging.'

'A tolerable night's lodging'. What a simple phrase to describe something that can be so difficult to achieve – and all the more so living in the eighteenth century without the advantages of modern equipment and outdoor clothing. But necessity is the mother of invention and James Smith survived by evaluating his situation and responding positively to the challenge. With no thought of failure, he harnessed his resourcefulness and his knowledge of the forest to provide himself with a makeshift home.

Any experienced woodsman or woman will recognise in his account the physical needs that he would have to meet to be safe and comfortable. Those needs still have to be fulfilled today in similar circumstances, but because our excellent outfit deals with many of them for us, they are often less well understood. It is only when our equipment is no longer available to us that our knowledge is put to the test and our weaknesses are revealed. One observation I have made among my students is that many experienced hikers and campers have only a rudimentary appreciation of how to make a shelter comfortable. So a basic understanding of shelter techniques becomes even more important as the continuing advances in outdoor clothing, tents and bivouac equipment cushion us further from the need to use such skills in the normal course of events. Moreover, it will encourage us to be adaptable and resourceful and to respond to life's challenges with a lively and positive spirit.

Good bushcraft is largely a product of sound reasoning, and it is in shelter-building that this is most obvious. While experienced campers will swiftly provide themselves with a cosy nest, others will take short cuts that result in draughty shacks that sap energy, sleep and peace of mind. To make sound judgements we need to have an appreciation of the physical forces we are contending with and a knowledge of the kinds of shelters our Aboriginal cousins have found to be most effective and the natural materials that can be used to construct them. It is also as well to consider what types of portable shelter we might carry with us into the wilderness.

Wild country nourishes the soul, drawing us like a magnet to walk, climb, ski or canoe in tranquil surroundings. With the ever increasing availability of commercial flights to remote destinations, nowhere on the planet, with the possible exception of Antarctica, is more than a few days' travel away from our front doorsteps. So today's wilderness adventurer must have a truly global perspective on the skills of bushcraft. No matter what language we speak, or our culture, or the colour of our skin, our behaviour is locked in a daily synchronicity with every other organism on Earth as we meet the challenges our planet poses. Locked as we are into a dependency on sunlight, we constantly adjust our behaviour according to its influence.

Wherever we are standing on the Earth we each spend part of every twenty-four-hour period being warmed by the sun, and part of it losing our heat to the coldness of space. The point on the globe at which we find ourselves and in what season greatly influence the extremes of these effects. At the equator we encounter generally hot, moist conditions, with more or less equal periods of day and night; as we move north or south towards the tropics of Cancer and Capricorn respectively, we meet drier desert conditions where we can experience both intense heat and freezing cold. Beyond these climatic belts lie the temperate latitudes, where seasonal cycles demand of us the greatest adaptability. North of the temperate zones, we reach the boreal and Arctic regions, which, though dominated by cold in the winter and biting insects in the summer, have been inhabited for thousands of years. In the extreme south, meanwhile, is the Antarctic, the least inhabited area of the globe. Here human life is sustainable only with the help of the resources we carry with us.

Every organism on our planet must have a strategy to cope with the extremes of the Earth's environmental conditions. Some creatures are equipped with fur or feathers that enable them to sleep outside whatever the weather, others store food and fat and sleep through the winter in full or partial hibernation, while our cold-blooded cousins draw their body warmth directly from the environment. Most animals must therefore limit their range to the latitudes that suit their particular physiology.

The human body, meanwhile, must maintain a constant body temperature of 37 degrees Celsius. If that temperature drops or rises by only a few degrees, we will die. Our evolutionary strategy for maintaining this narrow temperature band in the face of environmental extremes is to improvise cocoons of life support, in other words, clothing and shelter. Thus equipped we are able to venture wherever we dare. So successful is this survival strategy that our species has walked, for better or worse, over almost every land surface on the planet, and even on the Moon.

Honduran rainforest, the morning after the night of a monsoon rainstorm. This impromptu shelter of palm fronds and polythene was hastily erected to protect the campfire. Without warm drinks hypothermia might have struck the group.

Shelter principles

The primary aim of any shelter is to protect us from environmental conditions that threaten our well being. From the moment we perceive a need for shelter, we must ensure that the shelter we construct is appropriate to our specific needs. No one design will suit every circumstance. Ideally the shelter should not only shield you from environmental hazards, but also provide a refuge where you can comfortably rest and recharge your batteries.

Probably the single most common mistake made with shelter-building is to leave it too late. Shelters are most easily and effectively erected while you still have an ample reserve of food energy within your body. So if you find you are going to have to build one unexpectedly, don't go into denial about the necessity to do so. The more exhausted you become the more prone to cold injury you will be, and the more difficult it will prove to do the job properly. You will be more inclined to rush in and throw up what seems to be the easiest shelter, an expenditure of energy that will be poorly rewarded by the result.

In building your shelter, remember one of the golden rules of bushcraft: seek to maximise your efficiency for the minimum of effort. Accordingly, your first consideration should be to position it close to necessary resources and away from hazards, and the second to construct it to a quality appropriate to its intended lifespan or to your own energy level. Successful shelter-builders think like engineers. At the design stage, the most important phase, they establish exactly what the shelter is intended to provide protection from, which determines their choice of site, guides their search for materials and ultimately dictates the shelter design itself. To put this approach into practice you need to be aware of the physical threats that our environment can present and of the range of possible responses to them.

In the cold and wet it is tempting to just sit and shiver. Instead act to improve your circumstances by reducing heat loss.

Heat loss

In cold conditions we lose heat through a number of different processes which, left unchecked, will eventually reach the point where the body loses heat faster than it can generate it. Unless protected by clothing and/or shelter, the body will lose heat to the surrounding environment at temperatures lower than 25 degrees Celsius. This will lead to a lowering of our internal, core temperature and, if ignored, result in hypothermia and, finally, death.

Radiation

Radiated heat is transferred by electromagnetic waves from warm to cool objects. We lose up to 65 per cent of our total heat through this process alone. Radiated body heat warms the cool air or moisture around our bodies, which is then stripped away by conduction or evaporation. Radiated heat loss is greatest from exposed skin, particularly on areas of the body that have a large blood supply and from the head and neck, where blood vessels are not as well insulated and our ability to reduce heat loss by vasoconstriction – a narrowing of the arteries in response to cold stress to reduce the blood flow – is less effective. It is vasoconstriction that is responsible for the pale, cold skin and our loss of dexterity when our hands get cold.

Radiated heat loss is best reduced by covering up, especially with hats, balaclavas and hoods. Reflective foil blankets have been suggested as a way of reducing it further, but so far tests have failed to demonstrate that they provide any significant advantage over the cheaper and more readily available polythene survival bag.

We can also receive radiated heat to warm ourselves, either directly or by reflection. Typical sources are the rays from the sun or the heat from a campfire. Your shelter can be designed to maximise your exposure to such warmth and you can adapt your fire to emit radiated heat into the shelter by placing a reflector on the opposite side of the fire to bounce the heat in your direction.

Convection

The body constantly heats the layer of air or moisture next to its surface. When this layer is disturbed by cold air passing across our bodies – the wind, for example, or as a result of the pumping movement of clothing caused by our own movement – the heat is lost by convection. This effect is substantially reduced by windproof clothes and bivouac bags.

In shelter construction you can minimise convection heat loss first by choosing a site that affords as much natural wind protection as possible. A second defence is to make the shelter as draught-free as possible. In barren wilderness devoid of trees, you will have to carry some form of windproof shelter with you.

The classic sources of convected heat we can use to raise our temperature are the warm air produced by a campfire or, best of all, a tent equipped with a wood-burning stove, space-heater or firebox.

Conduction

Conducted heat is that transferred by contact direct between one object and another. The rate at which our body heat is lost by this process is determined by the conductivity of the material with which we are in contact.

Rates of conducted heat loss

Air	0
Wool	1.4
Wood	4
Nylon	8 – 10
Water	23 – 25
Ice	86
Steel	1,700
Aluminium	9,300
Copper	15,000

Therefore, aluminium is one hundred times more conductive than ice, steel twenty times and copper one hundred and seventy five times.

For example, if two climbers, each dressed identically wearing thin gloves, are digging a snow cave, one with an aluminium shovel and the other with a wooden-handled shovel, the climber using the aluminium shovel will be losing heat from his hands over 2,000 times faster than his colleague. This means he will become exhausted more quickly and be more prone to cold injuries such as hypothermia and frostbite. Small wonder, then, that 90 per cent of the circulation to our hands is used to keep them warm.

A good illustration of the great significance of conducted heat loss in extreme cold is the winter war of 1939, during which the Finnish army had fewer casualties with frostbitten feet than the Swedish army, purely because they were using a more old-fashioned ski binding which allowed less conduction.

To reduce conducted heat loss, insulate your body from a cold surface by placing a poor conductor of heat between you and the ground. In a shelter this means erecting a bed of some description, preferably one which raises you clear of the ground. Alternatively, you might arrange some sort of underfloor heating, with warmed rocks, for example. Remember that all heat loss needs to be replaced with calories from your food supply. Canny cold-weather adventurers pay constant attention to the surfaces with which they are in contact. For example, if they are taking a rest, they might place a few spruce boughs on top of a cold rock before sitting down on it.

Left open at the sides for ventilation, this shelter made from whale bones on Namibia's skeleton coast provides shade and some insulation.

Evaporation

To change from liquid to a gas, water requires energy. So when we sweat, or when moisture in our clothes evaporates, the fluid draws energy from our body warmth to make the transformation. In hot weather this type of heat loss can be used to keep you cool – by wearing a jungle hat dipped in water, for example – but in cold climates it will work against you.

Because water conducts heat twenty-three to twenty-five times faster than air, the first consequence of sweating in cold weather is an associated loss of insulation and an increase in conducted heat loss as the warm air trapped between the layers of your clothing is replaced by sweat. Then, as the wet kit dries on your body, heat is lost directly by evaporation.

To reduce the effect of evaporative heat loss you must strive to remain dry. Wear effective waterproof clothing and maintain even body temperature by adjusting the layers of your clothing according to the ambient temperature and your level of physical activity. For instance, remove some layers of clothing before the physical exertion of building your shelter so that you have warm, dry things to wear when at rest. As for the shelter itself, you may design it to trap warm, dry air inside. If not, at the very least you should be able to dry clothes beside a campfire.

Respiration

As we breathe in cold air we warm it and humidify it. When we exhale, our breath expels heat. This loss of warmth increases in the dry atmosphere of extreme cold environments, where more heat is lost as energy during the humidification process. You must stay alert to this depletion of warmth. Aim to create a warm-air environment inside your shelter whenever possible. Here once again, a heated tent is advantageous.

Metabolism

As we metabolise our food to create warmth, we are consuming our supply of food energy. Although this process does not in itself cause heat loss, if expended energy is not replaced we become exhausted and cannot generate the necessary internal heat to maintain life. Exhaustion is a major contributor to hypothermia in outdoor activities during which high energy output in cold or wet weather can require greater food supplies than anticipated. Time after time this is a key factor in cases where mountain walkers have become lost in bad weather. Even if they have been clad in the best and most efficient outdoor clothing they are often too exhausted to stave off the effects of the cold.

It is vital, then, to remember to keep eating. The harder we work the more food we need, so when food is scarce we must try to work less hard.

Hypothermia

Hypothermia is the greatest hazard of the bush. It can occur in virtually any latitude on land or at sea. It is avoided by wearing appropriate clothing and staying dry, well fed and well watered. Hypothermia occurs when the body loses heat faster than it can generate it, leading to a situation where the body core is unable to maintain sufficient warmth to allow the proper function of vital organs. Ultimately, if unremedied, hypothermia will lead to death. Essentially, there are two types of hypothermia:

- exposure hypothermia, which is caused by prolonged exposure to cool or cold weather, usually associated with exertion and exhaustion

- immersion hypothermia, which is caused by the rapid cooling usually associated with immersion in cold water. While the symptoms of these two forms of hypothermia are similar, the treatment for them can vary greatly.

Exposure Hypothermia

We must never underestimate the risk from hypothermia. Perhaps the most dangerous situation of all is when an inexperienced party of hikers in mountainous country ignore the signs of worsening weather, and the effect that bad weather will have on the likelihood of them completing their intended route.

Experienced travellers in back country areas know that when weather closes in, adjustments must be made to the programme, escape routes may need to be sought or shelter erected to wait out bad weather conditions. Wind, wet and cold are the key environmental factors that cause hypothermia. Cold alone or a combination of any two of these factors is enough to set the cooling process in motion - wet and wind, wind and cold or wet and cold. How these environmental factors affect an individual is to a large extent influenced by that individual's experience. An experienced back country traveller will in the first instance be correctly clothed for the weather conditions. That is not to say they will just have good waterproof clothing, but also that they will know how to wear that clothing so that they vent out moisture as they are exerting themselves, and add layers as they become chilled. Staying dry is vitally important. If your clothing becomes damp you will lose moisture up to twenty-five times faster than if it is dry. Experienced hikers are able to manage themselves and their clothing.

Fitness is also important. Obviously it is a good idea to be fit when travelling in the outdoors, but even more important than this is choosing your route plan to suit your level of fitness. One of the greatest dangers is when an inexperienced party takes to the hills and attempts a journey that is beyond their level of fitness and conditioning (particularly when they have travelled a long way from home to be in the mountains, increasing the pressure to complete a journey that is perhaps beyond them given poor weather forecasts).

Food is also of great importance. The experienced traveller knows that when hiking, days are long, journeys are more exhausting and temperatures can be energy-sapping; as a consequence much more food than normal will be needed.

Experienced travellers also know the value of carrying shelter of some form, a tent, a wind bivvy sack (often carried today by parties of hikers in moorland or mountain areas) and a sleeping bag. These simple items are often forgotten by day hikers, who wish they had remembered them when they find themselves stranded for the night in the hills.

Leadership plays a very important role in dealing with high-risk hypothermia conditions. A well-led party maintains good morale, each individual staying in touch with the progress of the whole group over their intended route. A good leader makes certain that everybody is looking out for everybody else and maintains a weather eye for early signs or symptoms of hypothermia, so it can be nipped in the bud should it occur. A good leader will make bold, un-muddled decisions in regard to the route to reduce the party's exposure to the bad weather. It is very important that all outdoor leaders consider it their highest duty to prevent members of their party developing hypothermia as, once you have had hypothermia, you become more susceptible to suffer from it on a future occasion. Perhaps the worst-case scenario is that of an inexperienced group with an injured member in their party becoming lost on moorland in worsening weather conditions. Hypothermia in these circumstances can set in extremely fast, far more quickly than might be realised by the inexperienced leader. Anyone suffering from an injury is far more prone to develop hypothermia, as are people who are anxious or who have low morale. If, as is so often the case, the inexperienced leader has been striding ahead of the group with a map and compass and not involving the team in the decision making process, many of the team members may have become uninterested in the overall activity. Doubtful or even resentful of the leader, their morale will be slipping. In these circumstances the risk of hypothermia is far greater.

It has been said so many times but it needs to be said again: prevention is better than cure. This is particularly true with hypothermia, which can be extremely difficult to rectify in the field. In your planning and preparations make sure every member has sufficient clothing, food and water to take with them. If you are travelling in areas that don't offer natural protection from the elements, make certain that you carry with you some adequate form of shelter. As the journey develops maintain a keen eye on every member of the party, searching out the slightest sign or symptom of hypothermia and acting promptly to avert any worsening of the circumstances. Always march to the pace of the slowest member of your group, and if someone should become injured or start to develop obvious signs of hypothermia, act immediately to deal with the situation. It is no good thinking, 'we will just press on and everything will be all right' - this can be a fatal decision. Bear in mind also that children and teenagers lose heat faster than adults because their body surface area is larger in proportion to their body mass. Also, they generally have less insulating fat than older members of the group. Ensure, too, that people are not carrying loads that they need not carry. Every ounce of luxury must be weighed against its potential danger. Remember the old maxim - 'LIGHT IS RIGHT'.

If a member of your party becomes hypothermic, or you decide that you have to wait out bad weather to be able to complete your task, you must break the processes by which your body is losing warmth to the environment.

Effects of cold on our body

When our body begins to feel a drop in temperature it takes automatic steps to prevent further unnecessary heat loss, the most obvious sign of which is the pale colour of our skin. Our body restricts the excess flow of blood to the surface of the skin by contracting and narrowing the vessels that carry blood to our extremities - a process called vasoconstriction. In so doing the blood supply that would otherwise be going to extremities moves to our body core, helping to maintain core temperature. Associated with vasoconstriction, our manual dexterity decreases to a point where it can become difficult to touch the tip of the thumb to the tip of the little finger on the same hand. This is a result of the reduced blood supply to our extremities and is a very important sign that steps must be taken to effect rewarming. Ideally before you reach this point you should have sought shelter, replaced wet clothing with dry clothing and added insulative layers to your extremities – gloves for the hands, a hat for the top of the head, and some form of neck cover. Because our body must maintain a supply of blood from the heart to the brain for body function, the head and neck areas are particularly vulnerable to heat loss; vasoconstriction is negligible in these areas. Hence it is vital in cold weather to always have with you some form of head and neck cover.

Vasoconstriction also leads to our becoming more prone to other forms of cold injury, such as non-freezing cold injury and frostbite. We will also notice that, as the blood that once circulated at our extremities moves to our body core, we feel an increased need for urination. Consequently it is very easy for us to become dehydrated, a situation which impedes efficient blood flow through our narrowed blood vessels, and thereby intensifies the risk of cold injury to the tissues of our extremities. As a result we should train ourselves to respond to this increased urination by drinking more liquid. Ideal for this are warm, sweet liquids – particularly drinks such as hot chocolate which will warm us, give us calories and, particularly in the case of caffeine-enriched drinks, help to spark up a lively mental response to circumstances.

Mild hypothermia

If we do not take steps to prevent further cooling of our body we will become hypothermic. It is very difficult in the field to accurately monitor an individual's internal body temperature so we must look for obvious signs and pay great attention to them. The most obvious sign of someone having become mildly hypothermic is when they begin to shiver, which occurs with a body temperature at or around 35°C. In the short term shivering is beneficial in that it is an involuntary means of producing body warmth by muscular activity. However, if we don't pay attention to shivering and provide further insulation and warmth, the shivering itself will more rapidly exhaust our body's energy supply and, in the long term, lead to a rapid deterioration of the casualty. So in short, shivering is the first and most obvious sign of mild hypothermia and is a symptom which must not be ignored. **If someone is shivering we must do something about it.**

Also associated with mild hypothermia are mood changes which can sometimes be difficult to spot within an individual, particularly for leaders working with large groups of young people whom they may not be familiar with. Classic mood changes associated with mild hypothermia are irritability and perhaps most of all withdrawal. Very often mildly hypothermic casualties become very insular and withdrawn within themselves and can very easily be overlooked if they are members of a large party. If the casualty is allowed to cool further the shivering will increase and eventually become completely uncontrollable and extremely convulsive. People who have recovered from such bouts of shivering are extremely exhausted.

If the body temperature drops below 35°C we will begin to see increased clumsiness, irrational behaviour and a generally confused state. In fact, the casualty may have the appearance of someone who is inebriated. It is vitally important with hypothermia cases that they are handled extremely gently, given the best possible opportunity to rest, protected from cold or further heat loss. They must not exercise as they are now exhausted and have insufficient energy to generate heat, let alone exercise. Exercising to rewarm someone of this profound cooling will only hasten the deepening of their hypothermia. It is also vitally important that no external warmth is applied to their extremities. If you take someone in a hypothermic state into a warm room their body automatically responds to the warm environment, causing an opening of blood vessels called vasodilation, and subsequent redistribution of warm blood from the body core to the extremities. This can cause a general cooling of the body core temperature

sufficient to push the person into a coma. It used to be suggested that the best policy was to place the casualty into a sleeping bag with a fully fit member of the party to act as a warming element. However this is now not considered to be the best policy. It is thought that placing the casualty alongside a warm member of the party only ceases to reduce the rewarming effect of shivering; it may be more effective to place the casualty into one or two sleeping bags to gain maximum insulation from the cold, where their shivering can help to generate a gradual rewarming of the body at a more natural and controlled rate. If the casualty is able to take liquids they should be encouraged to drink warm sweet drinks, warm chocolate being particularly good, with honey in it to give maximum calories to help stave off the effects of exhaustion. Also associated with mild hypothermia – at the more extreme end of the condition, at about 33°C internal temperature – is the beginning of muscle stiffness. When the casualty starts to complain of muscle stiffening we must monitor their pulse rate and their breathing, restrict all their activity, encourage them to lie down with their feet slightly raised and seek the most urgent medical assistance.

Recent research has shown that prolonged exposure to cold, wet conditions in conjunction with a reduced calorific intake can lead to a reduction or even loss of an individual's shivering response. This means that other symptoms may become more important in the early diagnosis of mild hypothermia, particularly changes in mood and signs of loss of manual dexterity.

Severe hypothermia

The most obvious sign of serious deterioration of a casualty's hypothermia is when the shivering ceases. At this point we consider the casualty to be severely hypothermic, and their life is seriously imperilled. It is vitally important to arrange the most urgent transfer of the patient to hospital. From this point forward the casualty must not be given anything by mouth and we should pay careful attention to check that their airway remains open. If their temperature continues to drop further it is likely that the semi-conscious patient will slip into unconsciousness, and may even lose response to painful stimulus. At this point we must particularly make sure that the airway is kept open, and monitor their pulse rate and breathing rate extremely carefully. Under no circumstances should a hypothermic patient be left alone. A competent first aider should remain with the severely hypothermic casualty, while the most able member of the party seeks professional assistance.

It is important to understand that there is no effective means of rewarming a severely hypothermic casualty in the field. All the first aider can do is prevent further heat loss by protecting the casualty from the environment, providing them with the maximum amount of insulation, monitoring their vital signs and providing first aid in terms of emergency breathing - if necessary, cardio-pulmonary resuscitation. At all costs the casualty must be treated with the greatest amount of gentleness, as rough handling can cause ventricular fibrillation. If you have to move the casualty do so with their head downhill to help maintain blood pressure.

Deep hypothermia

When the body's core temperature falls below 28°C they are considered to be deeply hypothermic. To all intents and purposes they may appear to be dead, with no vital signs and an extremely cold appearance. However it is important you do not give up on treatment. There are many cases of people who, having been apparently dead to observers, have recovered on rewarming; many people have actually survived with up to several hours of rescue breathing and CPR. Bear in mind that it is impossible for a doctor to certify a body dead until the body has been rewarmed to normal body temperature.

Immersion hypothermia

Perhaps the most dangerous aspect of falling into cold water is the gasp reflex, which is the first shocking result of immersion in cold water and which often leads to panic and drowning. Second to this is hypothermia, which sets in very rapidly in situations where the body is immersed in cold water. Water conducts heat from a human body twenty-five times faster than air. For a survivor of a boating accident it is worth bearing in mind that energetic swimming or treading water rapidly causes exhaustion and exposure to cold. A flotation aid can improve your survival chances by up to three times.

When rescuing a victim of cold-water immersion the handling of the patient can be critical. The Royal Navy discovered that, after winching people from the sea, many of the survivors subsequently died from the profound cooling of their body core. For many years the cause was a mystery. The answer came after a remarkable piece of research by a naval surgeon: he exposed himself to cold water immersion hypothermia, and was then winched by helicopter from the sea with monitoring devices attached to his body. It was discovered that the after-drop in temperature associated with helicopter rescue was not caused, as had been suggested, by a massive evaporation from the downdraught of the rotor blades, but was in fact caused by the loss of water pressure on the legs of the victim. When someone is lifted from the sea the removal of water pressure from the thighs and calves causes blood to flow down from the core into the lower limbs, and thereby causes a reduction in the core temperature - which was, in many cases, proving fatal.

Today when people are removed from cold water conditions after a prolonged exposure they are lifted as much as possible in a horizontal or foetal position. When we consider casualties coming out of cold water we should think of them in two categories: unconscious or conscious.

- Unconscious immersion hypothermia casualties must be given appropriate first aid following the usual ABC procedure, and evacuated to hospital for rewarming. Again, even if they exhibit all the signs of death they must be treated as a viable case for resuscitation.

- Conscious patients provide a slightly more complicated scenario. If we take the case of a warm and well-hydrated, well-fed individual - perhaps on a dog sled trip - who falls through ice into cold water, this individual must be removed from the water as quickly as possible and can then be rewarmed and dried quickly. There are many cases of people who have experienced such situations who, on climbing out of cold water, have been able to rewarm themselves very rapidly by moving around and generating muscular warmth – running up and down, waving their arms, shaking and then lighting a fire. If, on the other hand, we are talking about a conscious patient who has had a prolonged exposure in cold water, we must be much more careful and treat them as we would an exposure hypothermia casualty.

Heat gain

Contrary to what most people think, the human body is in fact better able to withstand cold stress than heat stress. In hot climates as the body temperature rises we become progressively less able to work or think rationally. An increase of just six degrees can prove fatal in some circumstances. While many outdoor enthusiasts are pretty clued up on the effects of hypothermia, fewer of them appreciate how dangerous heat injuries can be or how quickly they can develop.

The physical processes of heat exchange affect the body's performance in hot environments as well as cold ones, but they work in a subtly different way. Although our normal body temperature is 37 degrees Celsius the temperature of the skin is usually cooler by several degrees. For this reason, when the ambient air temperature rises above 32 degrees Celsius we begin to absorb heat. When it exceeds the body temperature of 37 degrees Celsius we absorb the heat much faster. In these circumstances be certain to remain well hydrated so that your body's natural cooling mechanisms are working at full capacity. This may mean siting our shelter within comfortable reach of water.

There is little that can be done to counteract the warming caused by hot air itself, but you can prevent exacerbating matters by reducing your exposure to other sources of heat. Indeed, if you take care to minimise the effects of these it is perfectly possible to operate efficiently. I have several times been forced to work in temperatures of 55 to 57 degrees Celsius. Although the days were tiring and I longed for the cool of night, I was still able to remain productive. The solution is to make sure that you have plenty of water, to dress to keep cool and to provide yourself with full shade, such as a stretched out tarp.

Radiation

A bushwoman once told me that it was important not to sing or laugh in hot weather. When I asked her why, she explained that if the sun heard you, he might think you were enjoying his attention and oblige you by intensifying it. Radiation in the form of the sun's rays is one of the most serious threats to your wellbeing. Not only are you hotter in the sun, but you are also at risk of sunburn from ultraviolet rays. In extreme desert conditions, the sun can seem to batter you into the ground. Wear a large hat and long sleeves.

Experienced backcountry travellers value trees as shady resting places, but they provide only partial protection from sunburn. When siting your shelter, choose natural shade and then try to improve on it by giving the shelter a thick roof. If you have only fabric to work with, use it in a double layer if you can, keeping the layers 30cm apart. Bear in mind that, like the canopies of trees, thin cotton fabrics and cloud cover do not offer full protection. Be aware that some trees such as the Mopane tree have leaves which fold closed at midday, reducing the shade value of the tree.

Large objects, such as rocks and vehicles, that have absorbed heat can act as sources of radiated heat. Avoid resting near any of these during the hottest part of the day. After dark, on the other hand, they may be useful in countering the chill of a desert night.

Dry season shelter made from paper bark, Arnhemland, Australia. The fire keeps insects away.

Convection

One of the most disheartening elements of extreme heat is a hot breeze. It makes you feel as though you are living inside a fan-assisted oven. In these conditions seeking shelter from the breeze is essential, as is, yet again, an ample supply of water.

If the breeze is cooling, open your shelter to allow it to circulate. Don't take such luxuries for granted. Driving through desert, people unused to the climate often become accustomed to cool air rushing through an open window or the chill of an air-conditioning unit, only to be poleaxed by the oppressive heat they encounter when they have to stop to dig themselves out of soft ground or change a burst tyre.

If you have a limited supply of water you will have to balance the effects of the cooling evaporation of your sweat in breeze with the loss of water this will involve.

Conduction

We collect warmth by conduction from any object with which we are in contact that has a temperature of 32 degrees Celsius or above. So just as you do to prevent heat loss through contact with cold surfaces you need to insulate yourself with the poorest heat conductor you can find. For example, if your 4 x 4 breaks down in the desert, you could strip out the seats to improvise an insulating bed.

Conversely, if you find a surface that is cooler than your body you can rest on it to allow heat to be conducted away from you. In deserts you can sometimes dig down to a cooler layer of ground. Or lie on a raised sheet of wrinkly tin scavenged before sunrise and placed in the shade. Always be careful when picking up such items as they often harbour snakes and scorpions.

Evaporation

When moisture evaporates from the surface of our skin it carries heat away which is the purpose of sweating – the body's natural cooling system. In hot, dry conditions you can increase evaporative heat loss by wearing soaked cotton clothing. When the risk of sunburn is not too high try to wear loose-fitting clothing with the sleeves rolled up to allow your perspiration to evaporate.

In the hot, damp conditions of a tropical rainforest, evaporative heat loss is greatly reduced by the high humidity in the atmosphere. Here, with one of the principal methods of cooling denied us, we must be very careful not to overheat. Probably the biggest threat to our wellbeing in this type of climate is overexertion, which causes our bodies to heat up faster than we can lose heat. Be alert to early sensations of dizziness, thirst or nausea, and where it is safe to do so, cool off in forest streams at every opportunity.

Respiration

Respired heat loss, through panting, is the main way dogs and other animals stay cool. Unfortunately, for humans, respired heat loss is negligible. Hot, dry air, like cold, dry air, is humidified as part of our respiratory process, which means that when we breathe out we are expelling moisture as well as heat. We will lose more moisture in arid conditions than in the humidity of the rainforest.

Metabolism

Heat is a byproduct of physical effort, so in hot climates be careful not to overheat yourself by working too hard. It is sometimes safest not to work at all during the hottest part of the day. Whenever practical it is a good idea to follow the siesta routine practised in many hot climates, resting when the sun is at its hottest and working during the early morning and evening.

Vehicles as shelter

Planes or cars are an invaluable source of useful equipment and highly visible markers of your position, but generally speaking they offer poor shelter. Effectively metal boxes, they can turn into ovens in extreme heat and refrigerators on a cold night. So unless you find yourself in an exceptional situation – perhaps, say, with your car caught in a snowdrift – it is usually best to improvise some sort of more efficient shelter alongside the vehicle, remaining close to it to improve your chance of being found by rescuers if you are in trouble.

In any event, whenever you are travelling in risky areas you should stock your vehicle with survival equipment such as plenty of water, a sleeping bag, a shovel, some food, spare parts and a means of communication with the outside world. In deserts, the golden rule of survival is *NEVER LEAVE YOUR VEHICLE*.

Choosing a shelter site

It would be wonderful if temperature and weather were all we had to cope with when shelter-building. But of course, nothing is so simple in outdoors life. The location of your shelter is a vital factor: it can make the difference between a comfortable, relaxed rest and a night of torture by insects, sleepless worry, or in extreme circumstances sudden death.

I've found, when asking a group of students to create a shelter for the night, that most people tend to launch straight into construction without spending any real time considering the site. So remember how important it is to get it right before you start.

Resources

The first thing I look for when choosing my campsite is the necessary resources: wood, the main body of the shelter; brush wood, grass or forest litter for thatching; firewood and a convenient supply of water.

The ground

If you are going to be using a tarp, search for a good piece of level, well-drained ground with trees a suitable distance apart. If you will be sleeping in a hammock, level ground is much less important than trees of the necessary strength and spacing. Wherever possible I prefer a discreet campsite which allows me privacy, and other hikers an unspoiled appreciation of the landscape. If I am setting up a camp in country where security is an issue I try not to present an opportunity for a problem, choosing a site where it is difficult for anyone to approach me undetected. Depending on the level of threat, I may wait until after nightfall before pitching camp. I certainly won't cook or light a fire.

Potential hazards

Having found what seems to be a good site, look at it from the point of view of other threats. Like so many bushcraft skills, what seems initially to be rather complicated becomes second nature with practice and experience. It is easy to be lulled into a false sense of security if you are used to camping where there are few hazards, so be alert when you are in unfamiliar territory. Remember that complacency and laziness are dangerous.

Is the ground liable to flood? Flash floods are not uncommon; a sudden thaw of snow cover or rain in the hills can cause streams many miles away to rise suddenly. Sometimes flash floods happen so quickly that they surge like a tidal wave, bringing with them dead wood, fallen trees, boulders, mud and any other debris caught in their path.

Are there any overhangs to avoid? Both branches and rock overhangs can prove fatal. In woodland, always check above you for dead branches, so aptly named the widow-makers, which may be sitting there poised to come crashing down if disturbed by a breeze. Even slender branches, if they fall from high enough, can be lethal. Dead branches are a particular hazard in rainforest – in fact I can recall only one visit to rainforest where I have not heard or seen one of them drop, to say nothing of whole trees falling after heavy rain.

Rock overhangs, too, can be dangerous. Be aware of cracks and fissures that suggest the rock might shear away. In no circumstances light a fire against the wall of a cliff as the heat can trigger a rock fall.

Are there any particular insects you should avoid? Camping close to an ants' nest or hitching your hammock to a tree can result in premature and painful awakening. Ants can be temporarily deterred by cold ash from your fire placed around the foot of your shelter supports. If mosquitoes or biting flies are a nuisance, is there another spot where the breeze will keep them off? Is there a lot of dead wood and leaf mould on the ground? If so, think about the potential threat of scorpions and centipedes. It may be that you can find a clearer site. If not, knock up a makeshift brush to clear away the debris.

Are predatory animals likely to be a danger? If so, is there the wherewithal to form a thornbush stockade around the camp and sufficient firewood to keep the fire bright through the night? If you are not alone, you may be able to organise a watch rota. Have you got food or strongly scented toiletries with you that may attract the innocent but unwanted attention of a bear? If in doubt, stow them out of reach a quarter of a mile from your camp, and set your cooking facilities well away from where you are planning to sleep.

Is this campsite at risk from avalanche? This is particularly important when constructing snow caves (see page 124). Never camp below a potential avalanche slope.

Is your tent liable to be covered by a snowdrift? In temperate lands we are used to pitching our tents in the lee of a rock or other wind barrier. In the treeless higher latitudes of the barren Arctic, however, setting up camp in the lee of a rocky outcrop or iceberg can prove fatal in a blizzard, because snowdrifts build up in the lee (wind-protected) side of such obstacles. In bad storms such drifts can bury tents and suffocate the occupants.

In the Siberian Taiga I recline in a classic northland lean-to. The long log fire burns the length of the shelter, keeping me warm in sub-zero temperatures without a sleeping bag.

Building the ideal shelter

Let's recap on our design criteria. It should now be clear that our ideal should:
- be as easy to construct as possible
- be sited close to water and building materials
- not be sited on land liable to flood
- be away from overhanging dead branches or rock
- not arouse the interest of dangerous animals
- be away from insect pests
- keep us dry
- provide us with a raised platform or insulating bed
- in cold weather provide a warm, dry atmosphere
- in hot weather, provide shade and a cooling atmosphere

It is not, of course, always easy to fulfil these requirements. For instance, you might be injured, unable to light a fire or equipped insufficiently. However, there is a wide range of techniques available to us, and these can be adapted to help us cope with new or unexpected circumstances.

MAKING A BED

In almost all the types of shelter described in the following pages, you will need to fix yourself up with a bed of some kind, so we should cover this before examining the individual shelter designs in general. The purpose of any improvised bed, besides the obvious one of providing you with a cosy nest to rest on, is to elevate the body from cold ground. The materials with which you construct it will of course vary according to the part of the world in which you find yourself, but generally speaking dead branches and springy boughs make good, insulating bedding. Use thick, heavy boughs on the ground, topping them with increasingly fine, more comfortable layers.

It makes a big difference if these boughs can be retained within a wall of one or more long logs which can be anchored in place with wooden pegs. The so-called cot-wall bed is therefore the most popular choice for sleeping in a shelter. The most important point to remember with this bed is to make sure that your body doesn't sink below the level of the retaining log. If it does, you will rest in the shadow of the log and be cut off from the light and radiant warmth of the fire.

In open-fronted lean-tos in cold weather it is usually best to create a sleeping platform at chair height.

If you are occupying your shelter on a longer term basis, it might be easier to weave yourself a blanket from natural vegetation, either by improvising a loom or by hand, which is probably the simplest and most effective way of going about it.

The simple leaf hut

This is one of the simplest of all shelters, which is not to say that it is any less functional than any other. Indeed the ease and speed with which it can be erected are advantages that put it streets ahead of many better-known shelters. It incorporates techniques that are used in a lot of designs and with which we are therefore likely to be familiar.

Measure out the size of the shelter.

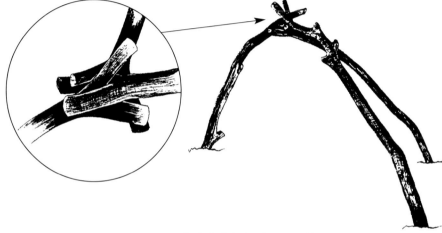

Look for forked sticks to avoid having to make cord.

Having found a suitable site, begin by measuring out the shelter size, lying on the ground and marking your body length with two sticks, one at your feet and the other at your head. Next fix three main supports. Choose naturally curved fallen branches ideally with forked ends that can be interlocked at the shelter apex. These should be stout, as they will need to bear most of the thatching; always allow for the extra weight of the roof after rain. Now lean a rough lattice of fallen branches against two sides of this basic framework with the aim of creating an overall matrix that will provide a basis for a covering of forest-floor debris. This lattice doesn't have to be regular: all too often shelters are given uniform square lattices which are unnecessarily complicated and time consuming. Concentrate instead on gearing to the kind of thatching material you are using Make sure that the gaps in the lattice are not so large that the leaf mould can fall through, and that the end of these sticks will not extend beyond the apex.

After setting up your bed, erect the shelter framework.

109

Starting at ground level, pile decaying debris from the floor on to the lattice, gradually working upwards in layers until the shelter is completed. Check that none of the supporting sticks or lattice sticks are poking through the thatch. If they are, rain will run straight down them to the inside of the shelter. The thatch should be at least 30cm deep all over. Once it is in place, anchor it against breezes by leaning a light covering of small, dead branches on top of it.

This shelter should be equipped with a cot-wall bed and a long log fire (see page 93)

Use dead branches for the rafters.

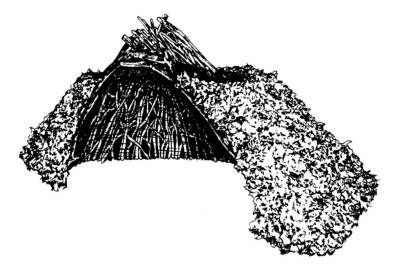

Thatch the shelter with leaf litter starting from ground level and working upwards in layers.

Note shelter sited under tree canopy for extra protection.

This shelter is intended to be used with a fire providing warmth.

The enclosed leaf hut

The enclosed leaf hut takes slightly longer to construct than the simple leaf hut and requires more accurate measurement. Its great advantage is that it does not need a fire, as the design preserves your own body heat to provide warmth.

Mark out your body length, then arrange a stout, strong ridgepole the full length of the shelter. Prop it up at one end with a small bipod or single forked stick set securely into the ground. This support arrangement must be very strong, as it will bear the full weight of the thatch. Again allow for the extra weight of the roof after rain. It is important that the ridgepole is propped up at a height that will minimise the internal space of the shelter to maximise warmth but at the same time provide enough space for comfort. Lay down your bed at this stage so that you know it will fit inside. The only way to be sure of getting the size right is to continuously check the dimensions of the structure as you build it, as the internal dimensions will shrink slightly under the compressive weight of the thatch.

Against the ridgepole, lean a lattice of small fallen branches as you would for the simple leaf hut, once again ensuring that none of the sticks protrudes above the shelter apex. Allow for an opening to the shelter either at the head end or, preferably, just to one side to form a funnel-like doorway.

Like the simple leaf hut the shelter can be thatched with whatever forest debris is to hand, to a depth of at least 30cm all over, and hold it in place with a light covering of small, dead branches.

Shelter above has a good covering of leaves with inner thatch absent to show sleeping space to retain warmth.

Two-person shelter

The two-person shelter is a logical extension of the enclosed leaf hut – a warm shelter to use when you cannot light a fire – and only takes slightly more work to construct. Think of it as two sleeping-bags joined at the head end. As with the enclosed leaf hut, your bed should be laid down at the point where you are testing the ridgepole height. The walls of the shelter will enclose your bedding and prevent it from spreading. Instead of one ridgepole, this shelter has two sharing the same support stick, forming a low tripod shape with one short leg and two long ones. The ridgepoles are splayed out and thatched in the same way as the enclosed leaf hut. Allow for a central entrance. In the small living space between the beds, a candle can be lit for heating – though you will need to be careful not to set the shelter alight.

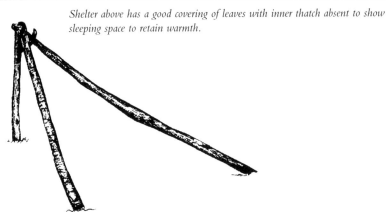

Brush tepee

This is not a design I use very often, as it requires big investment in terms of labour and materials. There is a lot of thatching involved because of the height of this shelter, and it needs to be thick enough to shed rain properly. Lower-roofed shelters are generally much easier to build and to make weatherproof, so I'd consider the group shelter ahead of this one. However, if in a country

The same brush tepee design built to a larger size in Lapland.

offering a wealth of many small branches you can use without damaging the forest, the bush tepee is a viable option.

Begin by constructing a tripod of strong, straight, mature saplings 4–5 metres in height. Lash them securely with roots or withes at the top. Whittle the ends into a point and thrust them securely into the ground to prevent the tripod from collapsing when loaded. A metre and a half from the apex lash three crossbars on to these poles. Now shorter upright poles can be leaned against this framework and the crossbars lashed into place to accept the thatching materials. Rather than attaching all the crossbars first and then thatching it is best to tie the crossbars on as you thatch. This way you use only as many crossbars as you need, and they will be correctly placed. Start thatching at ground level, ensuring that you cover the ground well here to prevent draughts, and work upwards. Leave a space 80cm wide for an entrance and improvise a thatched frame for the door.

Inside you can light a small fire in a wok–shaped fire pit no more than 15cm deep. The pit will help to keep the embers alight even if the fire dies low. In extremely cold, snowy conditions, the bush tepee can be overthatched with snow for insulation. Remember to make a ventilation hole near ground level with a stick or ski pole to keep it open in snowstorms (see page 124).

Internal view showing beds and fire pit - only a small fire is necessary to heat this shelter.

Wiltja

The shelter traditionally used by Aboriginal peoples of the Australian desert is called a wiltja. Since few flexible saplings are available here it is usually made from mulga branches and thatched with spinifex. The basic construction is very similar to the simple leaf hut, except that the shelter is much deeper, enabling several people to sleep in it side by side. The upright poles chosen for their curved shape are set securely into holes excavated with a digging stick and covered with a loose lattice of small, dead branches, which is thatched with clumps of spinifex bush. The sandy ground is carefully cleaned of any dead sticks or thorns, and if necessary a dry-grass bed is laid. At the entrance a small mulga-wood fire is lit and a windbreak is quickly put together from some dead mulga branches and more clumps of spinifex as necessary. This can be moved as the wind changes.

I have particularly fond memories of living in a wiltja. At night its upside-down-cradle shape is accentuated by the scarlet firelight reflected in the red desert sand, and the scent of the spinifex thatching mixes with the dry smoke of the mulga-wood fire to create an atmosphere of calm and wellbeing. One night, as I lay motionless, looking out of this miniature Sydney Opera House, the shooting stars crossing the perfect desert sky, I was rewarded by the sight of a pack of dingos, just visible as faint silhouettes in the glow of the fire, howling to announce their presence. As I watched, a young dingo stepped closer into the firelight, desperately trying to emulate the howl of the adults. And then the flames died to embers and the light went out. By the time I quietly pushed in the brands to bring it to life again, they were gone, leaving only their paw prints behind them.

Simple but effective desert shelter breaks a cold breeze or rainfall.

Tightly woven shelter protects against rainy season storms. Note the door.

Wickiup

Another desert, another shelter. The wickiup was the shelter traditionally used by peoples such as the Chiricahua Apache, in south-west America. Interestingly, the basic design is remarkably similar to that of the shelters of the bushmen groups of the Kalahari and the Hadze of Tanzania. In Africa it is customary to keep a fire burning in the entrance to such a shelter, usually a three-stone cooking fire. This not only shields the occupants from the chill of the night but also wards off leopards. The ground is cleaned of thorns and sticks and an animal skin laid down as a bed

The wickiup is made up from long, flexible saplings set into the ground in a circle of holes excavated with a digging stick. The saplings are bent over and interlaced to form a very upright, dome-shaped structure. This is thatched with bunches of grass kicked out from the ground and held in place with encircling bands of natural cordage or other saplings. As always, the shelter is thatched from ground level upwards. The top is finished with a good depth of thatch.

It was difficult to find, but when I was filming a programme for the BBC on the survival skills practised by Geronimo, the famous Chiricahua Apache warrior

A timeless scene: San bushmen at home. Children play the melon game, others prepare food and crafts.

of the late nineteenth century, I was able to reconstruct an Apache wickiup on an old village site at the foot of the Chiricahua mountains in Arizona. In this dry region with few resources the small canyon that had once been an Apache camp was a revelation. Here, hidden in the midst of this seemingly barren land, was an oasis: where fires could burn away undetected and where soap-tree yucca, bear grass, agave, squaw bush and greasewood – all mainstays of Apache survival – proliferated. The only difference from those days was that with the Apache people gone, the old brook which had once flowed here had dried up. The lowering of the water table was probably caused by the change in land usage.

In Tanzania the Hadza build a virtually identical desert hut.

First a triangular frame is made.

Next this is given long cross pieces.

Wild banana leaves act as massive roofing tiles.

In the head-waters of the Orinoco River in Venezuela I used one of the most remarkable jungle shelters I have ever encountered. Its architects are the Sanema, and their design and technique are so efficient that, as I watched them, working in groups of six, they created overnight accommodation for fifty people in the space of thirty minutes.

To build the shelter they need to find three trees, which must be strong enough to support hammocks, growing in a triangular configuration and close enough to one another to be joined by a shelter frame. If the hunters can't locate three suitable trees they can manage with two and a pole fixed firmly into the ground.

Three cross poles are then lashed with lianas to the uprights to connect them, one positioned horizontally 2.5 metres above the ground and the other two at an angle to meet at a higher point. Across this triangular frame a roof of straight sticks, about 3 metres long, is laid. A layer of overlapping wild banana leaves, anchored with a few extra sticks, is placed on top of this to make the roof waterproof. The occupants tie their hammocks in pairs, one above the other, between the three posts, so that each shelter holds up to six hammocks. Anyone who hasn't brought his hammock with him will quickly improvise one from the split lianas.

In the middle of the shelter, dead wood is feathered with a machete and a fire lit. The cooking pot is suspended over the fire with a simple pot crane. Smoke from the fire lingers in the shelter, deterring insects.

Hammocks are stretched between the three corners.

Jungle lean-to

Any jungle shelter needs to have a rainproof roof, a raised sleeping platform and, if possible, some protection from mosquitoes. Of these three requirements mosquito protection is the trickiest to achieve.

In Zaire I have seen makeshift box-shaped mosquito nets, traditionally fashioned from small rectangles of fine bark cloth sewn together with bark thread. A more modern solution is to use flour sacks, opened out, stitched together and hemmed. These box nets are suspended from the four upper corners of the shelter with the hem resting on a tightly woven and therefore mosquito-proof mat. But mosquito mats are difficult to improvise, so it is essential to carry with you anti-malarial drugs and a mosquito net or clothing that mosquitoes have trouble biting through. The raised sleeping platform and roof are relatively easy, on the other hand, thanks to the abundance of raw materials in the rainforest.

In an emergency, fall back on the open-fronted lean-to, which is a straightforward shelter design to remember. Build a raised sleeping and sitting platform at chair height, so that you will be able to sit comfortably inside the shelter. Set up a ridgepole and lean several long poles up against this, lashing them all together securely with lianas. Depending on the type of palm fronds available, create cross members either from midribs of long palm fronds, such as the coconut palm, or long pieces of liana tied in place. Starting at ground level, thatch the shelter to give a good overhang projecting beyond your sleeping platform.

If possible, light a fire to ward off insects and to warm your body and spirit.

Open lean-to of paper bark in Arnhemland, Australia.

Open lean-to with raised bed in Costa Rican rainforest.

A strong roof design lashed together with sago palm midribs.

Built in one hour, this shelter will survive at least six months.

Palm-frond hut

Perhaps the most commonly encountered shelter design in the tropics is a hut with a pitched roof and a raised sleeping platform. These can be made from a wide range of materials. The framework can be of bamboo, wood, or even the midrib of palms such as the coconut palm. For the roof thatching you can use split and thatched palm fronds, sago palm leaves folded over a split midrib and stitched in place with a thin, flexible splint from the midrib, grasses or large, flat leaves.

Set the major uprights firmly into the ground and add a ridgepole. Next the corner posts are erected. The ends of the poles should be as level as possible. Set secondary eave ridgepoles on their tops and tie them securely into place. Lash the diagonal supports securely from the ridgepole to the eave pole. If fresh bamboo is available this is easily done: just cut a pole long enough to be bent over the ridgepole and tied down on to both eave poles. Cut out a section of the bamboo where you want to bend the pole.

Pygmy hut

The Mbayaka Pygmy of Central Africa hold a special place in my heart. I have yet to travel with any rainforest people who are more in harmony with their environment. Indivisible from the forest is how I think of them, and they are a great example to us all in how we should accept and enjoy our dependence on nature rather than try to conquer her. In the vast rainforests of equatorial Africa they make small dome-shaped shelters from flexible saplings. The roof is thatched with large mongogo leaves by shaving up a sliver of the midrib into a hook, to which the leaves can be attached like roofing tiles. Inside they sometimes build a raised sleeping platform, running up a blanket from a sheet of suitable bark. It is sad that they are so often considered oddities because of their diminutive size. It actually is a real advantage when it comes to shelter-building, and walking through undergrowth – when you travel with the Mbayaka you soon begin to envy them their stature. And in their own forest they are true giants.

Arctic open lean-to

Within the Arctic Circle there are still people travelling in the forests who do not possess a sleeping-bag. Every night they sleep out they must construct a bed and a good, long log fire to keep them warm throughout the night. If the weather is threatening they also need a bivouac that will keep the weather at bay, while at the same time allowing the heat of the fire in. Although these travellers usually carry with them a tarp or other portable roof the most frequently used method of pitching is a direct descendant of the Arctic open lean-to.

At first glance the concept of this ancient design is simple. Consequently, it is the first shelter that most people learn to build. But, as with so many other aspects of bushcraft, there is a right way and a wrong way to construct it. If you get it right you will sleep comfortably and keep reasonably warm; if you don't you will hardly sleep a wink and will spend the night either shivering with cold or choking on smoke.

This shelter is geared to the great boreal forests where mainly tall, straight timber is thick on the ground, and the axe is carried as the primary survival tool. You should not build it using green wood where the cutting of such wood will cause lasting damage to the forest, as would be the case, for instance, in broad-leaved deciduous woodland. Here, choose the simple open lean-to instead. The effect is the same and it can be achieved with dead branches and leaves from broad-leaved trees.

Find two trees 2.5 metres apart aligned at 90 degrees to the prevailing wind. This angle will minimise the amount of smoke from your fire entering your shelter. In breeze-free conditions, build at 90 degrees to the slope of the ground: cooling air running downhill at night can drive in the smoke. Fix a strong ridgepole to the trees, lashing with roots or withes, or by propping it up with fork-ended branches. Next construct your bed at chair height. It must be positioned so that you sleep side on to the fire, and it needs to be level. Take time to get this right.

Now add the roof, by leaning straight poles against the ridgepole and tight up against the bed. In wet weather give the roof a very steep angle; in drier conditions the slope can be gentler. In spruce forests you can use small trees for this,

Classic northern lean-to in Rocky Mountains. Steep roof gives best rain proofing.

cleaning them of their boughs, which you can save for thatching. Finish the roof from ground level – as always – with a thatch of thick layers of boughs.

Lay some fine branches on the sleeping platform in an overlapping herringbone pattern with the soft tips at the head end to give extra depth by way of a pillow.

Finally light a long-log fire in front of the shelter, at least one full pace from the bed, and stock up on enough fuel for the night. As long as you build the fire properly its warmth will convect and radiate heat towards your body, from the side and from above, too, as it will bounce back from the roof. It will also warm you a little from underneath the sleeping platform. It is rarely necessary to use a reflector, or backlog fire, with a long-log fire. If you need extra warmth you can heat dry rocks, not rocks from rivers or damp ground which are likely to explode, as are lumps of concrete or glassy stone such as flint, in the fire, and position them with forked sticks under the sleeping platform as underfloor heating. Obviously you will have to take care not to heat them to the point where they will cause a fire.

At −48 °C a quinze is a welcome shelter.

The quinze

The quinze is a first-rate snow shelter ideally suited to northern forests when the temperature is below −10 degrees Celsius. In such conditions snow remains fine, dry and powdery, and even making a snowball let alone cutting snow blocks is impossible. Instead, using shovels or snowshoes form a large mound of snow around 3 metres in diameter and 2 metres high. If there are enough of you the easiest way to do this job is in a team of three. Put one person in the centre on skis or snowshoes to trample down the snow while the other two pile it inwards. The stamping action breaks the snow crystals, encouraging them to stick together in a solid mass. Once the mound has been completed, take pencil-thick sticks of equal length, about 30 centimetres, and push them into the snow at 90 degrees to the surface. In very cold temperatures you can begin to hollow out a shelter at once, although it is usually best to leave it for a while to give the snow a chance to refreeze. In the meantime you can have a warming drink and collect firewood and spruce boughs for bedding insulation.

Returning to the mound, excavate the snow from ground level, carefully hollowing it out until you expose the ends of the sticks you have placed in the quinze. This will ensure that the thickness of the walls remains constant to prevent you from inadvertently digging too far and weakening the structure.

Inside you must add a ventilation hole and form a raised sleeping area so that cold air sinks to below the level at which you are sleeping. Insulate the sleeping platform with plenty of spruce boughs. A candle inside the quinze will provide some warmth and a cheery light, and can prove a useful warning of an excess of carbon monoxide build-up which will make the flame sputter or even go out altogether. Check that your ventilation hole is clear and that you have a means of keeping it that way from inside the quinze. Store your shovels inside the quinze and leave your skis outside in a place where they can easily be located if there is a heavy snowfall. Snowshoes should be hung on a nearby branch.

Spruce-tree bivouac

In deep snow in the northern forests, you can build a quick shelter by excavating a space under a spruce tree. In colder temperatures, −10 degrees Celsius and above, when the snow is damp and heavy, this design is less efficient than the quinze and more labour intensive because very powdery, dry snow is more difficult to move.

Search for a spruce with a wide spread of branches at its base and a good depth of snow all around it. If you can find the right tree to start with you are halfway there. Choose one growing on high; if you site your shelter in a gully it will fill with cold air during the night.

Dig a space between the canopy of the branches, breaking off the lower ones as necessary, to create a living area. Reinforce the lower branches of the tree with extra sticks and boughs, piling additional snow on top to create a volcano-like wall round the shelter. Choose a side for an opening. If you are on a slope, try to ensure that the opening is facing away from the wind, looking along the slope rather than up or down it, as this will reduce the likelihood of smoke filling your shelter. In the opening lay a long-log fire with a reflector behind it. Inside the shelter, clear the snow back to the ground, or as far as you can, and if possible make a sleeping platform with a spruce-bough covering. If it isn't possible fill the sleeping area of the shelter with spruce boughs taken from another tree.

Quick to construct, the spruce tree bivouac is cosy for one but cramped for more.

Snow cave

Snow caves have saved the lives of hundreds of mountaineers caught in blizzards. The principle of digging into a snow bank to get out of the weather is so simple that these shelters have been successfully created by mountaineers with no formal instruction in how to make them. For a basic snow cave all you need to do is dig straight into the snow slope and hollow out a sleeping space to the left and right in a 'T' shape – that's it.

A more elaborate shelter for two people can be even easier to produce. Look for a snow bank with a short slope about 3 metres deep at its top. Not only does digging your cave at the top of a slope put you in less danger of starting an avalanche, but removing the snow is easier as you can just throw it down the bank behind you.

Although snow is soft, digging out a snow cave is hard work, so having the right tools for the job makes a great difference to the energy you expend and thus to your chances of survival. Most people recognise that a snow shovel is an essential piece of equipment for winter mountaineering, but you should also have a snow saw that will enable you to cut out the snow in blocks with the maximum of speed and the minimum of effort. I would estimate that using a snow saw takes only a third of the energy your body would have to devote to digging with a shovel alone. As a result you will be less tired, drier and in a happier frame of mind as you work and afterwards.

Flatten the snow in a vertical face 2 metres wide by 2.5 metres high, and with your saw make two vertical incisions 60cm apart and 1.5 metres long. Connect them with horizontal cuts top and bottom to form a rectangle. Next make two vertical cuts 20cm inside your original cuts so that they meet the first vertical incisions in a wedge. (1.) Start to remove the snow with an upward movement of the saw, beginning 50cm below the highest horizontal incision at about 30 degrees to your last vertical cut. (2.) The snow should break away in wedges and slide into your gloved hands. Toss it over your shoulder so that it falls down the slope behind you and out of your way.

(3.) Continue cutting in this way until you have taken away the snow within the rectangle to the depth of the saw blade. Then create a 'T' shape by slicing the snow on both sides of the upright cuts, and excavate the snow until you have carved out enough space for sleeping platforms. Already you will be shielded from the weather and feeling the benefit of the shelter. Add the ventilation hole and plug the top bar of the 'T' shaped entrance with one long block of snow and two smaller ones.

As always, store your shovel inside the cave and keep a means of clearing the ventilation to hand. Place insulation beneath you and smooth the inside of the roof to prevent crests, which drip melting snow on to you. The original entrance

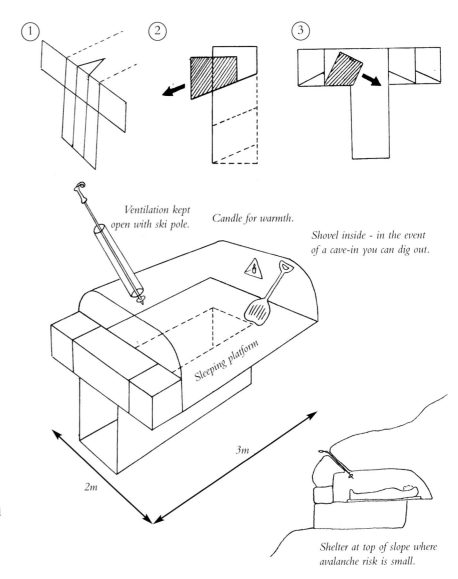

Ventilation kept open with ski pole.

Candle for warmth.

Shovel inside - in the event of a cave-in you can dig out.

Sleeping platform

3m

2m

Shelter at top of slope where avalanche risk is small.

to the cave doubles as a cold well, ensuring that the warmer air rises to the top of the shelter where you will be sleeping. Check that the roof is not too low to allow free movement because it will gradually sink under the weight of the snow. Novice snow-holers are often alarmed by this movement, which is quite normal and not a worry in itself. However, it does mean that you will be lucky to get three days out of a cave without having to increase the roof space, or make a new cave.

Snow trench

The snow trench is a quick overnight shelter suited to dry, cold conditions when you do not anticipate a heavy snowfall. It is an excellent bivouac on a cross-country journey in the boreal forest, for example. Dig a trench in the snow deep enough for you to lie in, well down out of the wind. Make it wide enough to stop you coming into contact with the walls when you turn over in your sleep. Insulate the trench with a good depth of spruce boughs, and try to arrange some simple cover at the head end to keep the snow from falling on your face – perhaps your jacket laid over crossed skis.

Fighter trench

In the mountains, where you are likely to find snow firm enough to be quarried, the snow trench can be modified and improved. Search for deep, hard packed snow on a flat, avalanche-free surface. Test for 1 metre depth of snow. Dig out the snow with your saw in blocks measuring 90 by 45 by 16cm. Next dig your trench, and around the inside edge of it carve out a recess to accept the base of the blocks. Cut one of the blocks into a triangular shape and stand it at the end of the trench. Cut another in half and set it on to the recess, leaning against the triangular end block. Repeat this process with the full-sized blocks, staggering the positions of the blocks as you would in brickwork, until the trench is roofed. At the point where the blocks meet, cut vertically through them and they will become perfectly bevelled and sit solidly against each other, forming an angled roof over the trench. Continue until the whole trench has been roofed, block in the ends and make an entrance. If the snow is deep enough, dig a cold well in front of the entrance to collect cold air. As always, attend to the insulation beneath you and ventilation, and keep your shovel inside the trench.

Igloo

In the high Arctic the igloo was the traditional winter shelter. Inside it was heated by a koodlik seal-blubber lantern with a wick made from cotton grass and dried moss. Today the indigenous Inuit tend to use heated frame tents, which are quick and easy to erect, along with modern sleeping-bags, stoves and space-heaters, but the art of igloo-building has not been forgotten. I count myself as very fortunate to have had the opportunity to learn how to build igloos from men who really lived in them as children. I could include here details of how the blocks are cut and fitted but, while experienced practitioners can assemble an igloo in thirty to forty-five minutes, the truth is that it really does take more skill and expertise than can be picked up from a book. So, if you are setting out into these barren northlands, go well equipped and devote the time to learning igloo-building from the masters.

Group shelter

The group shelter is a more sophisticated amalgam of many of the construction techniques we have so far covered. In essence it consists of a circle of joined open-fronted lean-tos facing inwards. It is one of the best designs of all, in terms of both the effort it takes to build and its effectiveness as a temporary home, offering a warmer and more comfortable living space than any other shelter.

The ideal group shelter accommodates four people although the design can easily be adapted to suit three or a more sizeable team. I have several times built one for a group of twenty, although for this many occupants it needs to be oval rather than round and you have to factor in more space for the fire.

Begin by getting each person to lie down, end to end in a circle, and marking out his or her body length to gauge the shelter dimensions. When calculating these, allow extra space for a doorway and storage areas. The middle of each bed should be one pace from the rim of the central fire pit. Then plant your upright forked sticks into the ground. These will support the weight of the roof, so they must be strong, well dug in and all installed at the same height. Connect these sticks with short ridgepoles resting securely in the forks. If you can't wedge them in tightly, bind them in with withes. You will now be looking at a henge-like ring.

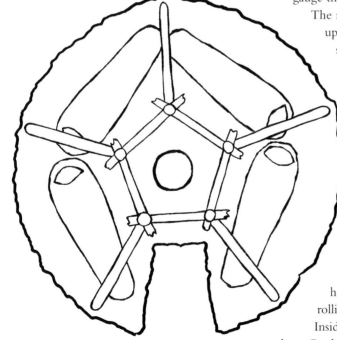

Next lean strong diagonal supports against the forked sticks, digging them into the ground at the outer edge of the sleeping space. By this stage the shelter should be pretty solid. It is important to keep it symmetrical so that it is self-supporting and won't collapse. For the roof, lay sticks diagonally against the ridgepoles and thatch the hut with forest debris, starting as always at ground level and working upwards. For the fire the opening at the apex should be 1 metre in diameter, which will allow smoke to escape even in cold weather and at the same time help to trap warm air inside.

Make a lintel for the doorway from a faggot of small sticks. This should be about 30cm in diameter and slightly longer than the length of the doorway. Restricting the height of the entrance in this way will reduce heat loss from under the shelter and help the fire to draw properly so that the interior doesn't become too smoky. Using withes, secure the lintel horizontally across the doorway at about sternum height, and thatch the roof above it. Hang a rolling blind mat over the entrance to keep the warmth in and the wind out.

Inside, the sleeping area will consist of one continuous cot-wall-type bed running in a circle round the hut. Cooking pots can be positioned over the fire in pot-hangers suspended in the centre on a single wooden stick across the opening in the apex.

Complete the shelter by removing any protruding branches or sticks that may cause you injury or discomfort. If you don't do this, you are certain to regret it after dark.

Seen up close, the group shelter resembles a small volcano. Its shape naturally encourages an updraught that draws smoke away freely. If you build the shelter properly, it will be warm and cosy and space will not be too restricted; built wrongly, it will be either cramped or cold and draughty. It does take practice and experience to gauge the dimensions to perfection. Another of its advantages is discretion. There are no obvious angles or shadows discernible from the outside and because it has been created from local debris it blends almost invisibly into the landscape, muffling the sounds made by its occupants and concealing the glow of their fire.

There are two main risks with this shelter: collapse and fire. Avoid any accidents by appointing one team member to be responsible for ensuring that it is correctly constructed at each stage. In a group of young people, the shelter captain should be an experienced adult, preferably with some training in bushcraft and first

aid. It certainly shouldn't be anyone who hasn't successfully built one of these shelters before. If you have sleeping-bags you can dispense with the fire risk altogether, by not lighting one, but if you don't you will need warmth. Stay safe and comfortable by sticking to the following guidelines.

Fires produce the most smoke and flames when they are being lit. Keep your fire small and set it into a shallow wok-like depression, which will give it a good ember base so that you won't be continuously relighting it.

Burn only dry, dead wood to minimise smoke. Use firewood that burns long and warm, such as oak or beech.

Make sure that water is always kept to hand inside the shelter in a place with which everyone is acquainted. The shelter captain should be responsible for this task.

Establish an evacuation point in case of fire or any other emergency.

If you are going to keep the fire burning through the night operate a watch system to ensure both safety and warmth.

Rock overhangs provide welcome shade in arid lands, but be sure to look for snakes.

Natural shelters

As we have seen, one of the overriding aims of bushcraft is to achieve maximum efficiency for the minimum effort. When it comes to finding shelter, this means staying alert to the possibilities that may be offered by the landscape. There are a number of natural and manmade features that might provide shelter in themselves, or could be easily adapted to do so.

Caves

Caves and rocky overhangs have given shelter for hundreds of thousands of years, and archaeological excavations have suggested that Neanderthal communities may have inhabited or at least visited some caves on a regular basis for thousands of years. However, there are a few hazards of which you need to be aware. Humans are not, of course, the only creatures to seek shelter in caves: spiders, snakes and even bears may view the one that you have happened upon as home. Be on the alert for tracks and other signs of such occupancy at the cave entrance. Caves heavily soiled by the guano of a large bat or rodent population are also best avoided. Inhaled as dust, the guano can cause several dangerous diseases – histoplasmosis, hantavirus and melioidosis, to name but a few.

If you are sheltering from a storm, another important consideration is what is described as the 'spark-plug' effect in which lightning can pass across the gap between the cave roof and your head as it searches for the shortest route of conduction. Take the precaution of allowing at least 3 metres' clearance between your head and the cave roof.

As far as comfort is concerned, caves can be very draughty. You will certainly need to provide yourself with an insulative bed and possibly some form of windbreak.

Fallen trees

Fallen trees can sometimes be turned into shelter or incorporated into a shelter design as a wall or ridgepole. Keep an eye out for signs of harmful creatures that may inhabit fissures in or beneath the bark. Fallen-tree shelters are difficult to make draught-proof and they can also cause complications in construction methods.

Stone walls

On moorland where few trees are to be found, stone walls may be used as a windbreak. Or, for an emergency shelter, a polythene survival bag may be pitched against a wall.

Hollows

Hollows and ground depressions have the allure of a nest, a quality that attracts many novices to build their shelters in them. But for the most part, ground depressions are damp places in which to pitch camp. If you must sleep in such a place, perhaps because you need to stay hidden, search for the driest hollow you can find in well-drained ground. Lay down extra bedding or, better still, construct a raised bed and put a roof over the depression to channel rain away from its rim.

Hollow trees

Both standing and fallen hollow logs have been used as shelter. If you can find a tree with enough space in it to accommodate your body, clean it out as best you can, staying on the lookout for venomous creatures. When you are satisfied that all is safe, just crawl inside.

Sangars

In many desert areas nomadic herdsmen create sangars, small corrals with low stone walls for their sheep. These can be pressed into service as shelters with a tarp or other improvised roof spread across the top. Before moving in, clear out any rocks or dung. Watch out for scorpions which like to live underneath both dung and rocks.

Useful equipment for natural shelters

Polythene survival bag

On a mountain expedition it is best to take with you emergency survival gear such as a sleeping mat, Gore-tex bivvy bag and warm clothing or a lightweight sleeping-bag. However, many mountaineers rely on the lightweight polythene survival bag. If you need to use one of these as an emergency bivouac, put on whatever spare clothes you have with your waterproof clothing on top and search for a large rock, rocky outcrop or stone wall to shelter behind. Improvise some ground insulation: for example sit on your climbing rope. At the closed end of the poly bag, cut a small face hole to breathe through. Pull the bag over your body, put your feet inside your rucksack for further insulation and eat some of your emergency food. Keep your whistle and torch to hand for signalling.

Portable bothy

An improvement on the polythene bag that is becoming popular is the portable bothy, which is available in a range of sizes to accommodate anything from two to six people. This lightweight, portable shelter made of waterproof dayglo-orange nylon and fitted with ventilation holes provides instant protection from wind and rain. Warmed by the body heat of the occupants, it is surprisingly comfortable. To gain maximum benefit from the bothy use it in the lee of a wall or large boulder and, as with the poly bag, insulate yourself from the ground with rucksacks or climbing ropes.

Polythene sheeting

If you have some polythene sheeting available you can improvise all manner of shelters. The only major drawback to using polythene is that because it is totally impermeable, condensation will build up inside and can soak your dry, insulative layers. So try to keep your bedding away from the shelter walls and make sure you have enough ventilation for the condensation to evaporate.

Parachutes

Ex-military parachutes can often be bought in army surplus stores. They may no longer be serviceable as parachutes, but have many good years ahead of them as lightweight shelter. There are ways without end to pitch parachutes as shelters, and the fabric can be adapted to produce a variation on many of the shelters we have already looked at. The key point to remember is that parachute nylon itself is not actually waterproof so it won't offer protection from the rain used any old how. But stretching taut improves its capacity to shed rain, and arranging it in two layers 30cm apart virtually guarantees a dry shelter. Parachutes can also be cannibalised for their nylon cord and the nylon cord can be used in turn for its fibres, which can be used for fishing-line or sewing thread.

The suspended parachute tepee is the option I usually go for. Stretch the parachute fairly taut, high off the ground in a single layer. This gives you an excellent shelter to work under, and although it isn't fully rainproof it breaks the force of the rain.

Lightweight trail shelters

One of the greatest joys of travelling in remote regions is the sense of independence and freedom it gives you. To enjoy such nomadic wandering you need an easily transported shelter. My preference, for many reasons, is a lightweight tarp or shelter sheet.

First of all, it is light, weighing perhaps as little as 1 kilogram, which increases your capacity for extras such as a warmer sleeping-bag or more food. Secondly it is versatile, providing all kinds of protection, from shade in arid zones to shelter from the rain in the tropics. Under a tarp you sleep close to nature, not zipped away in an unhealthy nylon cocoon, and wake up to limitless fresh air. And a tarp shelter can be pitched in only a few moments and taken down and packed away just as quickly.

The following are varieties of shelter I use with the tarp. Stick to the same guidelines as for others when siting them.

Fixed-tarp shelter

I opt for the fixed-tarp shelter, the most permanent of these techniques, only when I plan to be pitched for more than a few days. I usually fasten two tarps to give myself more room for manoeuvre for the duration. You could do the same if you are travelling with others, as this combined shelter will comfortably sleep two to three people.

Cut forked uprights and one strong ridgepole to fit the dimensions of your tarp and set the upright supports in the ground a tarp length apart with the ridgepole between them.

Pop together your tarps, pitch them over the ridgepole and peg them taut to the ground. If your tarps don't fasten to each other, pitch one of them on one side allowing 15cm to overhang the ridgepole and peg it out with guy lines on both sides. Do the same with the tarp on the other side so that both tarps are stretched taut, overlapping at the ridgepole.

You can make the shelter more snug by enclosing the ends with simple thatching. Fully thatch one end, doing only half the other to leave a space for the doorway. Set short, upright wands into the ground, green-stick-fracture them at the tarp edge, and bend the tops down to rest just under the tarp. The ends can be interwoven to provide structural support. Interweave horizontal withes, bending down their ends, and dry grasses or plants, or other thatching materials.

Simple tarp bivouac

This commonly used shelter is particularly suited to forest camping, and gives you an enriching sense of closeness to your environment. The secret is to have your tarp already set up with appropriate guy lines so that you can pitch it easily after dark.

Among the usual criteria we apply to finding the right site, protection from the prevailing wind is a particular priority for using the tarp bivouac. Look also for an area where the trees are wide enough for you to set up your tarp between them. Pitch the tarp at about the height of your sternum (lower in very bad weather, or if you wish to keep a low profile) and peg it out with simple improvised pegs. In country which is home to insects and venomous snakes it is a good idea to pitch a mosquito net beneath your tarp. Choose one with a sewn-in groundsheet that can be zipped up.

Tarp-and-hammock bivouac

The tarp-and-hammock is my favourite way bar none of sleeping outdoors. I use this bivouac in the warm months of the year in temperate climates and most of the time in the tropics. Search for two trees at a suitable distance away from each other to take your hammock and tarp, and pitch the tarp at a height of about 2 metres, guying it out firmly. Tie up your hammock beneath it, with or without a mosquito net, depending on the conditions. I string a cord between the tarp and the hammock where I can hang my clothes and boots overnight. The whole operation takes only five minutes, and when you break camp in the morning there is hardly a trace that you were ever there, which is the perfect way of camping in forests.

Evenk slippery figure-of-eight hitch.

This is the method used by Evenk reindeer-herders of Siberia to tie a strong quick release hitch. It is one of the most useful knots – excellent for tying up taut lines.

Tarp taut hitch

Used to tie and tighten the ridge cord of a tarp shelter tightly and securely, it releases with a pull on the working end.

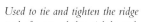

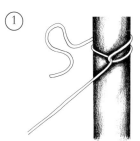

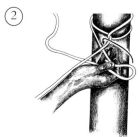

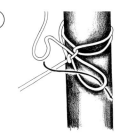

The slippery adjustable loop.

My favourite method for setting up guy lines on a tarp or shelter, it facilitates quick removal by pulling on the working end. Tie to an improvised peg or convenient sapling.

Tents

In mountains, tundra or moorland regions where trees are scarce it is best to carry a hike tent. There are many excellent designs on the market; for comfort and longevity, look for one that has:

- ☛ plenty of room to live in – there's nothing worse than having to spend several days cramped in a tent in which you cannot sit up

- ☛ zips that are not heavily strained – if they are they will certainly fail when you need them the most

- ☛ no-see-um netting – to prevent insects getting in

- ☛ good ventilation – my greatest criticism of some modern tent designs is that they often don't make enough allowance for the evaporation of condensation

- ☛ sound flooring material or an interchangeable underfloor for added protection

- ☛ large vestibule for stowage and cooking in inclement weather

- ☛ a design geared specifically to the conditions in which you'll be using it

Evenk tent, central Siberia.

Woodlore students learn how to live in a traditional Sami lavuu.

Heated tents

In forests, on canoe trips or used as a base camp transported by pack animal, dog sled, four-by-four or snow mobile, no tent provides greater cheer than a heated one.

Early heated tents were made from sheets of elm or birch bark tied on to wooden frames. More portable versions, such as the North American tepee, were crafted from animal skins. Fabric tents include the *lavuu* or *kota*, the traditional home of the Sami in Lapland, a large tepee-shaped affair housing a hearty open fire, and the *dyu* (or *chum* as it is known in Russian) of the nomadic Evenk reindeer-herders of Siberia, usually heated by a sheet-metal wood-burning stove. In Mongolia the *ger* or *yurt* – a unique shelter made from collapsible lattices of willow, covered with thick felts and canvas – remains a common sight. Inside these are very homely, with beautiful decorations and a warm stove fuelled largely by dung. In Canada heated wall tents are still popular, although they are less cosy than those with a circular floor.

My personal favourite is the tepee-style tent of northern Europe, now available in portable models with one central collapsible pole. These tents are a popular choice in the sub-Arctic and keep you wonderfully warm and dry in the worst weather, so they are ideal for the British climate – a perfect headquarters for a youth-group expedition, for example. From the late autumn through to spring, I camp almost exclusively in a very lightweight tepee that can sleep four comfortably or two in extreme luxury, yet is no heavier to carry than the average solo mountain tent. Depending on the size and specifications, these tents can be heated either by a portable wood-burning stove, with a chimney to carry away the smoke, or a small fire. For use with a fire, there are collapsible, environmentally friendly fire boxes on the market that prevent any scorching of the ground inside the tent.

135

CORDAGE

String or cordage is one of the most important resources we can carry with us into the wilderness. With it we can improvise items for use in the camp, negotiate obstacles, such as rivers or cliffs, make temporary repairs to equipment and, should the need arise, catch food.

As with so many items of our modern equipment we take for granted the presence of strong nylon cord. But in the study of bushcraft we must learn how to provide cordage for ourselves from nature. Fortunately there are many fibres to be found in the natural environment which we can utilise to make all sorts of cordage from small lines to strong ropes. An incredible story of the use of natural fibres for cordage was recounted by Hearne in his copper mine journey in 1771.

She still had a small store of provisions by her when she was discovered. She was in good health and condition, and I think was one of the finest Indian women that I have seen in any part of North America . . . The sinews of rabbit's legs and feet . . . she twisted together for snares . . . also enough skins to make a warm and neat suit of winter clothing . . . Showed greater taste and no little variety of ornament. . . Her leisure hours from hunting had been employed in twisting the inner rind or bark of willow into small lines like net twine, of which she had some hundred fathoms. With this she intended to weave a fishing net as soon as the spring advanced . . . it is the custom of the Dog Rib Indians to make their nets in this manner, and they are much preferable to the deer thong nets of the northern Indians which, although they appear very good when dry, grow so soft and slippery in the water that the hitches are apt to slip and let the fish escape. They are also liable to rot, unless frequently taken out of the water . . .

Of course, only half the story is about making cordage: it is just as important to know what to do with it once you have it. That means learning to tie knots. Although many believe that knots are difficult to learn, for the most part the opposite is true – particularly the ones we use in bushcraft.

(left) A warrior's hammock: the braver the warrior, the fewer the cords.

Improvised cordage

One of the great joys of making cordage from natural materials is that you are literally bending the fibres of nature to our aid. An added benefit is that while learning the skills you come to know the forest and other country in a more intimate way, discovering parts of trees and plants that you may not have looked at closely before.

Birch bark canoe.

Roots

The roots of many trees can be used to make cordage – the roots of spruce trees, among others, were used to lace together the birch bark canoe. The roots of coniferous trees, such as cedar, spruce, hemlock, yew, larch, and pine, are particularly adaptable, but some deciduous trees, such as birch, can also be used.

The roots that you need are the long, surface ones which are thin and flexible, found just a few centimetres beneath the ground. Generally, the best are to be found in mossy conditions where the soil is easily removed from a large area to expose them. Then they can be separated from each other and harvested. Failing this, take a short, finger-thick stick about 20cm long, and gently scrape at the ground at 90 degrees to the direction from which you think a root might radiate out from the tree. Eventually the tip will trip over a root. Once you have found your root, excavate along its whole length – never try to pull the root from the ground as it is much more firmly attached than you may imagine and will snap; instead, be patient and take your time to unearth it. Choose a root slightly thicker than its intended purpose to allow for the relatively thick bark on the root. Take only one or two roots from each tree and carefully replace the soil. That way you will harvest a resource that nature is willing to supply, and do no lasting damage within the forest.

Now prepare the root for use. First remove the bark: this is best done with a tool called a brake. To make one take a dead piece of wood that can still be split. Carve the stick like a screwdriver, cutting a V in the flat blade end about 4cm deep. Insert the root into the split and support the stick in your closed hand. Pull the root through the split and the bark will split and peel off. The root can now be dried and stored for use later in the year or be pressed into service straight away.

If you're lashing together a shelter ridgepole you need not remove the bark: choose a root strong and long enough and use it as it is. If, however, you are lacing or lashing together something that must stay tightly bound, allow the root to dry first: when it is green it will shrink considerably as it dries; if you make a lashing with it green, when the root shrinks the binding will come loose. When you use a dry root moisten it before use to make it more flexible. Traditionally, some roots, particularly those of the spruce, are improved by boiling: this increases the root's flexibility and makes it less prone to becoming brittle when dry.

You can split roots many times to make finer binding materials, and semicircular or flat binding strips that become attractive, strong and functional lashings. In northern Europe fine roots have been used to weave intricate baskets.

Roots can be a strong and easily available material, particularly in coniferous forests.

In deciduous forests withies have boundless uses.

Withies

Withies are the wire of the woods, made from thin, flexible birch, hazel, ash, and willow wands. In our rural past, withies were used to bind together faggots of firewood for transportation to bakeries in cities, to hold in place the staves of barrels and lash together frameworks of rustic poles. You will find them most useful in the construction of shelters, campsites and all manner of backwoods projects. They have even been used to make ropes for crossing rivers. In the archaeological record, withies have been found attached to heavy objects for hauling, and lashing together the planks of early rafts.

Withies can be made in winter, but you will find it easier in the summer when the sap is well up in the tree and the fibres are most flexible. First, search for a suitable wand – it should be a young shooting sapling or branch. Choose one that is flexible, long enough for its intended purpose, and which is free of strong branching stems. Begin by stretching the wand and trimming off any side branches about 4mm from the main shoot. Next, grasping the wand close to where it is attached to the parent tree, twist it until you hear the fibres pop. Now continue to twist gently, moving your hands towards the tip of the shoot. Hold the tip and bend the wand into an S shape rather like pedals and cranks on a bicycle. Turn the pedals carefully, which loosens the fibres, gradually working your way towards the base. Don't over-twist it or the fibres will fray and break. Almost inevitably in some places they will be less willing to loosen; at these spots you can encourage the twisting by stretching the withy and working it gently between your hands. Once you have softened the withy to its full length, you can cut it cleanly from the tree.

You can use it as it is, or split it in half to lash together poles or bundles of materials. Withies are remarkably strong and enduring, and can even be tied together with conventional knots, particularly the fisherman's knot (see page 152). I have used withies regularly to establish a rustic camp, lashing together ridgepoles, or support poles for kitchen utensils and implements. The lashings last a year easily and sometimes two before they have to be replaced.

Withies can also be re-used: in the eighteenth century bakers who received faggots of hornbeam bound with withies from woodland outside London sent the withies back to the woods for recycling. If they dry out, soaking will restore their flexibility.

Scrape away green outer bark.

Slice open length of inner bark.

Bark

The cambium or inner bark of some trees can be removed and processed into wide sheets or thin strips of fibre. In Zaire I learned how to process inner bark into cloth for clothing or into strips of netting which could be sewn into a mosquito net. Similar barks have been used to produce loincloths, skirts, sailcloth and even bed sheets. Perhaps some of the finest bark cloth is the *tappa* of Polynesia, made from strips of mulberry bark skilfully pounded out and glued together with Polynesian arrowroot juice.

There are several basic techniques for the removal and processing of inner bark. Although I shall describe here the trees to be found in the northern temperate zone, the same techniques can be applied to a wide range of trees found in other parts of the world.

Peel bark halfway off.

Lift out wood from bark.

Willow bark

The willow is widespread in the northern temperate zone, favouring wetland habitats. Its bark is easily removed between March and July. If you are going to use it for binding or lashing, you need only remove suitable strips and leave on the outer bark. I tend to take it from saplings 4–6cm in diameter: they provide a strong, thick bark which when cut into 5 mm–1cm wide strips, produces an excellent binding material. For finer work remove the outer bark from the willow, or the inner bark will dry and become brittle. For weaving or making of string, you will need a thinner, more flexible inner bark, found on saplings of an even smaller diameter.

The best place to look for suitable saplings or thick wands is in wet areas at woodland edges or along the banks of streams and small rivers. I try to find a willow tree that has fallen over with side shoots rising vertically from the trunk. Choose a straight sapling 3cm in diameter, with as few side branches as possible.

With care you will have a sheet of bark that can be split down to desired widths.

Save the outer bark: boil it in water with ash and bark fibres to increase the fibre's durability.

Prune it carefully, using a folding saw; in this way the tree is not damaged and you may return to it season after season to collect more saplings. Next, trim off the top of the sapling and plant it in the ground, where, because of the willow's tenacious nature, it may take root and grow into a new tree.

Scrape off the dark green outer bark with the back of your knife blade. Keep the bark scrapings. Now slit the bark all the way along the sapling, then peel it half-way off the stick on either side of the split, then lift it free. It can be used straight away to tie undemanding lashings, but for more prolonged use, or for the manufacture of fine cordage, you will need to process it. Cut the inner bark into useful-sized strips, then put it into a pot with some wood ash and the saved outer bark scrapings. Simmer it for at least 40 minutes; by this time the bark will have changed colour to a deep ruddy brown. It is now more durable and flexible. Willow-bark strips can be woven into multi-coloured straps by mixing unprocessed with processed strips twisted into two or more ply cordage.

Although in theory it is impossible to remove the inner bark from the willow during winter, I have found that by using a knife to strip off the fibres it is possible to collect thin strips 20–30cm long by 4mm wide. The fibres from winter-stripped bark are stronger, making them the best choice for thin strong cord.

Lime bark

The inner bark from the lime tree was once one of the most important sources of natural cordage. Throughout the summer months it is easily peeled away in long sheets, or even intact. Although no record survives today of how our Mesolithic ancestors built their homes, I suspect that they might have fashioned them from saplings bent over and tied together with lime bark, thatching them with large sheets of bark. In Britain today lime trees are most often seen in municipal parks and are no longer the prolific woodland tree they once were. Certainly we would never use the lime bark as a shelter thatching material today.

Place long sheet of bark in slow stream.

After a month the bark smells terrible but has softened.

Now fibres can be easily split down as necessary, rinsed and dried.

In the past the bark was probably cut low, then pulled out and down at the same time to produce long strips for use in cordage. However, a more sympathetic way of using the tree is to fell a sucker shoot and strip its bark. Lime trees reproduce well by suckering – that is producing new saplings from the base of the mature tree – and a suckers 5–15cm in diameter can be felled with no fear of damaging the mature tree. In fact, several new saplings will spring from the stump. To remove the bark from a sucker, split it the full length and pull it off like a jacket. Save the wood to season and carve; soft and light-coloured, it is a delightful wood to work with. Straight from the tree lime bark is stiff and incredibly inflexible, like plastic guttering, and seems the most unlikely material to turn into flexible cord. For quick makeshift cordage, a few fibres can be peeled away from the inside of the bark jacket. For the best cordage, though, the bark must be soaked in water for several weeks – a slow-flowing stream is ideal. After soaking it takes on a strong smell of vegetative decay and tannin which can be quite overpowering, but the layers of bark will separate freely and you can strip out large quantities of broad fibres. Wash them in fresh water to get rid of the strong smell and then hang them out to dry. In the past these were used to make strong rope, and are well suited for use in fishing lines, string, and strong cords. They can also be used for weaving – the 'Ice man' discovered in the Alps was found with several items on his person made from lime bark, including a length of cord.

Other barks

Many other trees yield fibre from their inner bark including, wych elm, oak and sweet chestnut. Once you're familiar with the processes by which lime and willow bark can be treated, you can adapt them to other trees. Sweet chestnut and oak inner barks can be stripped from the partially rotting bark found on fallen timbers. When dried, they make wonderfully soft flexible string.

Plant fibres

Many hundreds of plants around the world will provide you with fibres. Once you have become familiar with the ones available in your homeland you quickly learn to adapt the techniques for extracting them to strange plants in other countries.

Yucca *(Yucca sp.)*

Yuccas, and particularly the soap tree yucca, provide long lengths of strong cordage easily. Take fresh green leaves and begin by battering the sharp point at the leaf tip against a rock. Turn the leaf round and beat the basal end, where it attaches to the main stem, against a rock to soften it. Then take the leaf in the centre between your teeth and pull downwards with your hands until the leaf is halved. Repeat the process to quarter it. These strips of leaf fibre can be knotted together base end to base end, pointy end to pointy end, and with a simple reef or square knot (see page 113). In this way you can produce several metres of just the right sort of cordage for a wickiup (see page 116).

Agave *(Agave sp.)*

Agave has long been a favourite repair material for travellers in arid areas. The tip of the leaf has a hard sharp spike, which can be left attached to the fibres of the leaf for use as a needle. When green leaves are thick, fleshy, and cactus-like in texture soak them until the fibres pull off easily, or scrape them free, the more usual method. A word of caution here: the leaf juice may cause severe skin irritation unless it is washed off immediately after contact.

Begin by cutting a fleshy leaf with a good point low at the base of the plant – take care because the edge is covered with many tiny thorns – then slice off the edge. Next use a sharpened piece of wood or perhaps the back of your knife to scrape the flesh off the leaf – sometimes it helps to pound it a little first. Soon you see the fibres starting to free themselves. You can speed up the process by rubbing them round a nearby branch. When clean of flesh, the fibres are extremely strong and remain attached to the sharp point of the leaf. These natural 'needles and thread' were carried by Apache warriors and were strong enough to repair a damaged moccasin. Remove the sharp point to use the fibres as strong cord or string.

Pull off green yucca leaf.

Blunt the sharp point on a rock.

Bash the base of the leaf against a rock to soften it.

From the middle of the leaf, strip down the fibres four or more times.

Tie leaf strips together into long cord.

Long cord, strips and whole leaves from yucca.

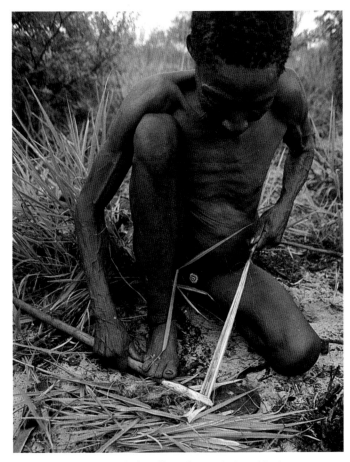

San bushman stripping pulp from fibres of Sansevieria aethiopica.

Wild sisal, Mother-in-Laws Tongue
(*Sansevieria aethiopica*)

Wild sisal is found in Africa and grows well in extremely arid conditions. It is easily recognised as it looks like pieces of green rubber hose-pipe standing upright in the ground. It is used by Bushmen in the Kalahari to produce string strong enough to snare deer or birds. A long sisal plant is cut low down, pounded with the blunt end of a digging stick, then scraped of its thick pulp with the sharp end until the strong internal fibres have been freed.

Stinging nettle *(Urtica sp.)*

The stinging nettle is a native of wetland habitats. Its fibres are so strong that they have even been used commercially to produce cloth: the nettle stems are softened in water then the fibres combed out. This is not a practical process for travellers in backcountry areas. I experimented extensively with the stinging nettle and eventually hit on a much easier way to do it. It produces cordage inferior to the commercial version, but it is more than adequate for short-term needs. First, select tall nettles: they are best collected late in their growing season just before they begin to dry and rot. When you can, avoid being stung – it is possible to remove the stinging hairs by swiftly drawing the nettle stem through your clenched hand. However, there is a knack to this and many people never acquire it. If you do not have gloves with you, use a pair of socks to protect your hands or coat your hands heavily with mud. Remove the leaves, flatten the stems gently either by squeezing them between your index finger and thumb or, if they are strong and resistant, by rolling a small stick over them on a log. Now bend the nettle in the middle to break the strong, fibrous pith inside. Remove the pith, leaving the fibres attached to the outer bark, then peel the bark into four lengths. The fibres can be used as they are for many jobs – for example, tying a fish to a stick for cooking – or can be made up into strong cord. The finest nettle cordage is produced by drying the fibres then dampening them slightly before laying into string.

Willowherb *(Epilobium sp.)*

Willowherb can be used in the winter to provide fibres when many other fibre-producing plants are no longer available. It is the outer fibres on the stem of great willowherb, *Epilobium hirsutum,* that are used for cordage. The plant can often be found in large stands beside ponds, ditches and damp ground. It is quite easy to remove the fibres as there are no stings or acrid juices to contend with. Rosebay Willowherb *Epilobium angustifolium* (right) may also be used.

Take a dry stem and pull off any leaf stalks then gently crush the stem as you would with stinging nettles. Open the stem flat and you will find that the pith is woody: to remove it snap it every 8cm along the full length of the stem, then lift out each section of woody pith from the fibrous outer bark. The fibres need no further processing as they are usually dry already. They can be laid into cordage strong enough to make a snare or fishing line. Other plants that can be used in a similar way include evening primrose, milkweed, Indian hemp and dogbane.

Lianas

One of the most wonderful cordage resources is to be found in the tropical rainforests: the liana. Hanging like pieces of telephone cable from the highest branches, lianas trail down towards the ground. Little needs to be done to make these fibres ready for use other than to tug carefully on the end so that they snap high up. Be careful not to pull too hard and bring down dead branches on top of your head. Also, don't look up: liana is elastic and can snap like a bungee cord.

Lianas (left) can be found in many diameters from 3mm to 20mm; they have been used to tie bundles of leaves, for construction purposes, and even to make improvised rope bridges across fast-flowing rivers or deep chasms. When using them, watch out for the sap: if you get it on your hands don't rub your eyes or the tender parts of your body until you have washed them thoroughly.

Hair and hide

Hair is known for its great strength and elasticity and has long been used to make cordage. In many ways a rope made from hair resembles a modern polypropylene one. Even human hair has been used to produce rope; preferred for its strength for the spring of the Roman ballista, a type of giant crossbow used in ancient warfare. Horse hair was used in the manufacture of animal snares and fishing lines, especially the hairs from the tail of a stallion because they carried less scent. Even today ropes are still made from hair: I have helped Mongolian men make beautiful three-strand hawser-laid rope from horse-tail hair.

Both rawhide and leather have been used in cordage, particularly rawhide used to make lariats. Strips of rawhide known as wangs can be used as bindings. They are usually tied in place while damp: as they dry they tighten and stiffen. You can repair tool handles with rawhide: sew a wet piece of rawhide tightly around the split and leave it to dry. It will shrink into place.

In parts of Africa animal intestines are cleaned of their contents and then stretched by spinning a heavy weight on the end. The resulting cord is very strong.

Aboriginal pulling tendons from the leg of a kangaroo.

Sinew

Animals sinews have been used for thousands of years in situations where great strength in cord is required. The most obvious use for sinew is in the manufacture of a bow string where tremendous strength is essential in a thin cord. Generally the sinews/tendons found in the legs of gazelles and antelopes are favoured although I have also encountered the long sinews from the neck of a giraffe being used because of their great length. Sinews have also been the traditional thread for leather clothing and are still in use amongst many peoples of the far north. The fibres often outlive the clothing that is sewn together with them; usually these are the back sinews as they can be easily stripped down into convenient threads. The leg sinews of an animal are thicker and shorter; at first glance they seem a very unlikely source of threads. To process them they must be dried and then pounded with a wooden mallet on a smooth stone or log to separate them into many fine strands. These strands can then be used as they are for sewing threads or can be laid into cordage. The fine strands are also frequently used to tie on fletchings to arrows – they are moistened in the mouth and then applied; the moistening seems to liberate a natural glue that holds the sinew in place.

Trusty sinews provide the San bushman's bowstring – the thread by which his life hangs.

Improvised mooring line of bull kelp.

Seaweed

Perhaps the most remarkable of nature's fibres comes in the form of algae: long strings from several species have been made into fishing lines and even improvised anchor cables. However, it was perhaps on the north-west coast of North America and Canada that seaweed was most used for cordage: there, the bull kelp *Nereocystis luetkeana* grows prolifically. In the past, its stalks were collected, cured and dried. To cure it the stalk was soaked in fresh water then dried over a smoking fire and made into fishing lines, which were kept stored in oil so as to retain their flexibility. They were often hundreds of metres long, which made it possible to catch species of fish which only inhabit deeper water.

Methods for making cordage

The 2 ply pygmy roll

1. The method is begun by tying together 2 strands of cordage fibres. These are held together with one hand (here using the left hand) while the other hand effects the twisting. Hold the strands then where they meet and using the thumb and middle finger of your free hand roll the two strands simultaneously in the same direction until they are tightly twisted, being sure to keep them apart so that they twist independently.

2. At the end of the roll, clamp the two strands between thumb and middle finger. Release the left hand and the strands will twist together as cord. Repeat the process until you have the necessary length of cordage. As the fibres in the strand start to run out simply twist in new fibres to each strand. Strive to maintain an even thickness in each strand.

The rope lay

For larger cords a similar process can be adopted. Clamp the point where the strands meet with your thumb. Clamp the lower twisted strand between the index and middle fingers of the left hand and hold the upper strand at the end of rolling. Releasing the thumb allows the cord to twist together

3-strand flat plait

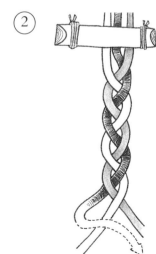

4-strand round plait

8-strand flat plait

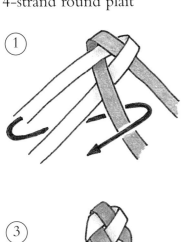

①

②

①

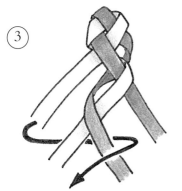

③

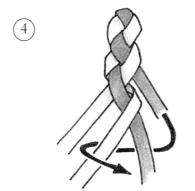

④

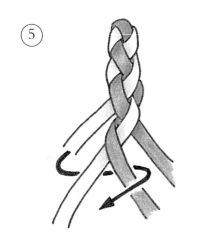

⑤

⑥

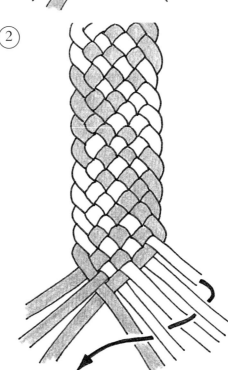

②

Handling cordage

Although today's ropes are generally lighter and stronger than the ropes of yesteryear, they may be more susceptible to some forms of damage than the natural ropes used in the past. For example, climbing ropes left in the boot of a car in hot weather may be severely weakened by exposure to high temperatures. Here are some rope rules.

☛ Know the history of your rope: *never lend any rope which you use in a life-preserving role.*

☛ Familiarise yourself with the manufacturer's recommendations: most reputable rope-manufacturing companies can supply you with all the relevant information you will need to care for and maintain your rope.

☛ Don't carry a rope when it has exceeded its recommended life.

☛ Handle your rope with care: many professional mountaineers insist on coiling their own rope, as others' poor technique can damage it.

☛ Don't tread on your rope: this forces dirt into the weave of the rope, which will abrade the fibres and weaken it.

☛ Don't let your rope come into contact with chemicals, which may affect its strength.

☛ Don't pass a rope over a sharp edge or a rough surface: pad the rope where it passes over rock with a rucksack or item of clothing. Alternatively, use a strop or sling and a karabiner to reposition the rope's passing point away from the abrasive edge.

☛ Small-diameter rope can become more tangled than larger rope: learn to hank your cord and avoid this. It will save you many hours of frustration.

Rope terminology

① Working End
② Bight
③ Loop or a single turn
④ Twist
⑤ Two round turns
⑥ Standing part
⑦ Standing end

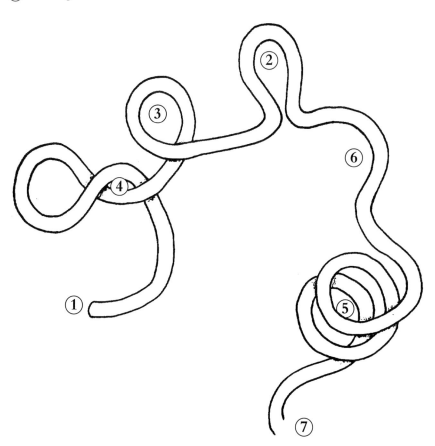

How to coil ropes

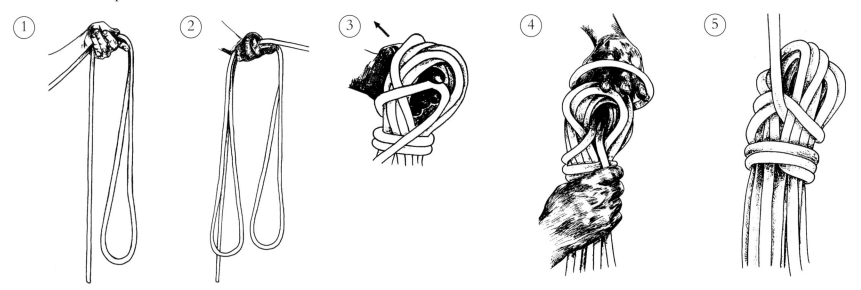

Lap coiling: a method kind to rope, popular for coiling climbing ropes as it does not kink the rope.

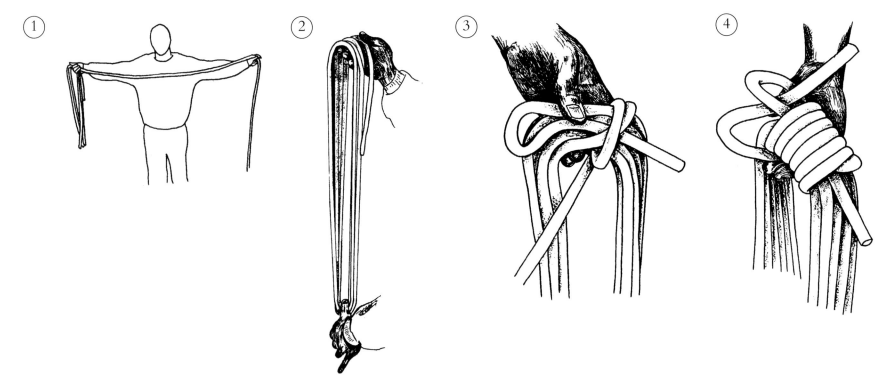

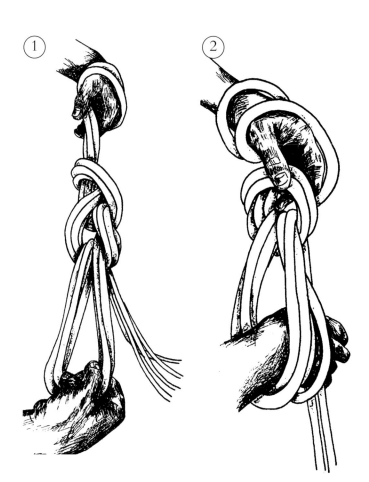

① ②

Tying off lap coil.

③

Chaining: chaining is useful for canoe lines as it prevents tangles, particularly in capsizes.

How to hank cordage

Hanking: keeping lengths of cord tidy is an everyday chore. This technique prevents tangles.

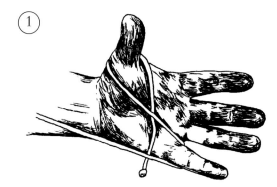

①

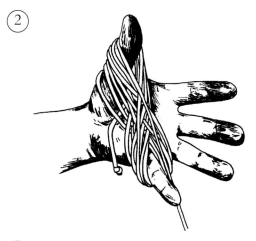

②

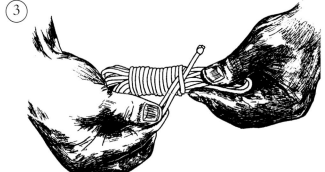

③

Knots

In an ideal world one knot would be used for every purpose, but this isn't an ideal world and we need to be able to tie for many different purposes. For instance, you may have to moor a boat, cross a river, set up a camp, and abseil down a cliff all in one journey: you'll need to know a wide variety of the knotting techniques to get past these hurdles. If you hadn't already realised it, bushcraft is an all-encompassing study! The knots we use in bushcraft are relatively simple and many incorporate similar principles. When you've grasped the principles tying the knots is child's play.

The overhand knot and its useful relatives

Probably the simplest of all knots, and fortunately it is incorporated in many others used in the bushcraft world, all of which are easily tied and relatively secure. The drawback of the overhand knot is that once tightened under load it can be hard to untie: use it with small-diameter cordage rather than ropes.

Overhand bend.
A moderately secure way to join ropes and cord.

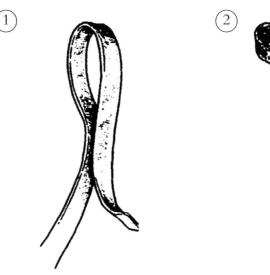

The overhand knot.
Used as a stopper to prevent a cord slipping through an eyelet or to prevent the sealed end of a cord fraying.

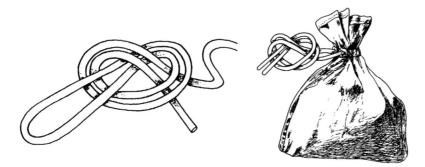

Tied in doubled cord to provide a secure loop.

Two-strand overhand knot.
A common and effective way to tie off drawcords.

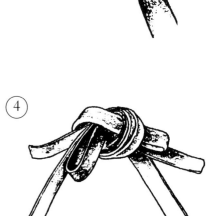

Double frost knot.
For joining climbing tapes.

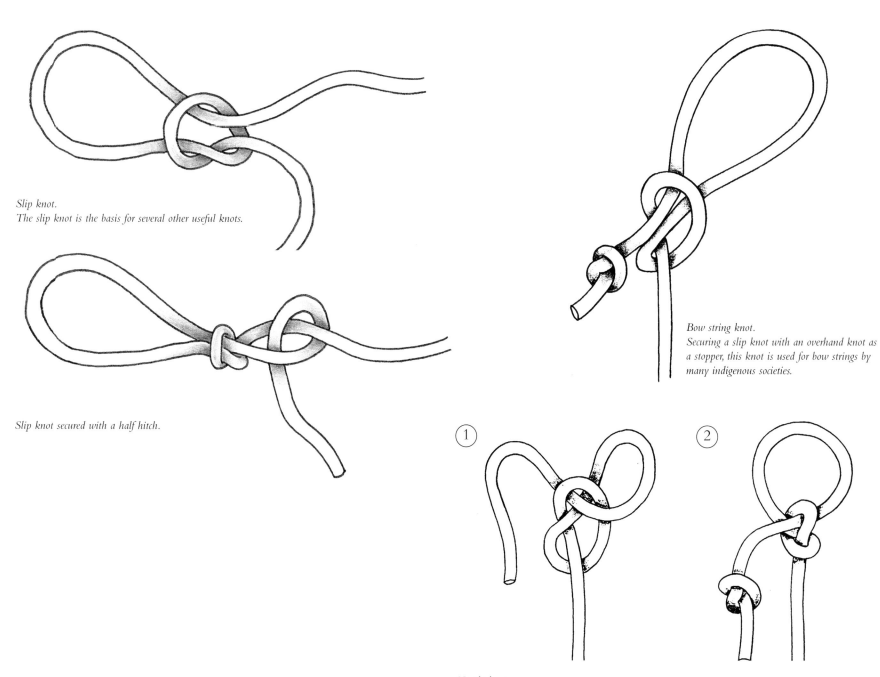

Slip knot.
The slip knot is the basis for several other useful knots.

Slip knot secured with a half hitch.

Bow string knot.
Securing a slip knot with an overhand knot as a stopper, this knot is used for bow strings by many indigenous societies.

① ②

Honda knot.
This knot was used to form the loop in a cowboy lariat as it forms a round open eye.

Fisherman's eye knot.
A slip knot secured with an overhand knot around the standing part forms a strong eye.

Overhand bend or fisherman's knot.
Two sliding overhand knots form a join between cords.

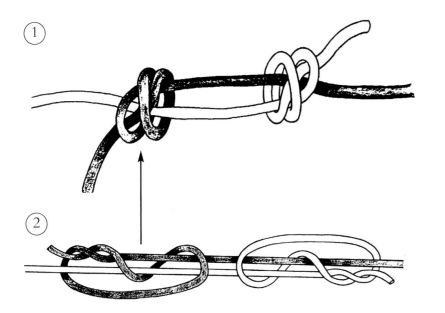

Double fisherman's knot.
More secure than the overhand bend, this knot has been used widely in mountaineering to join ropes and make strops.

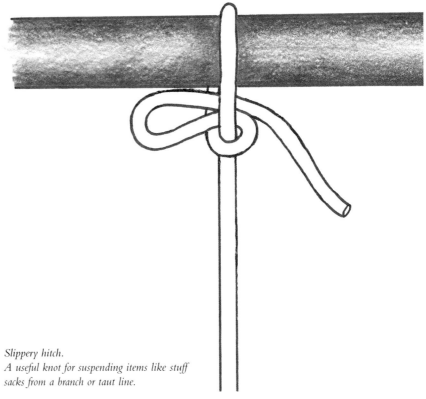

Slippery hitch.
A useful knot for suspending items like stuff sacks from a branch or taut line.

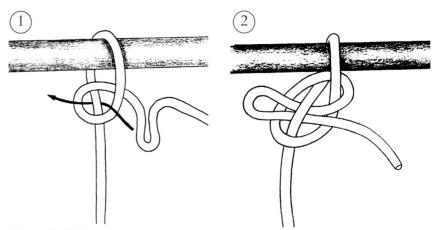

Mooring line hitch.
A knot widely used for temporarily mooring small boats, which releases when the working end is pulled.

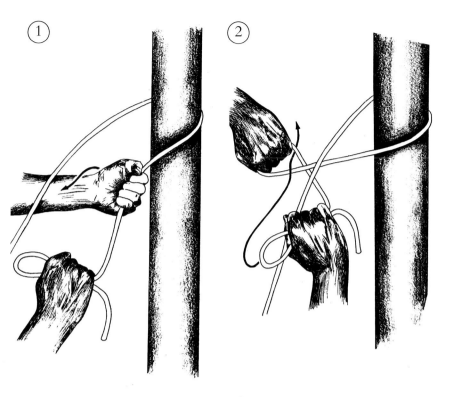

① ②

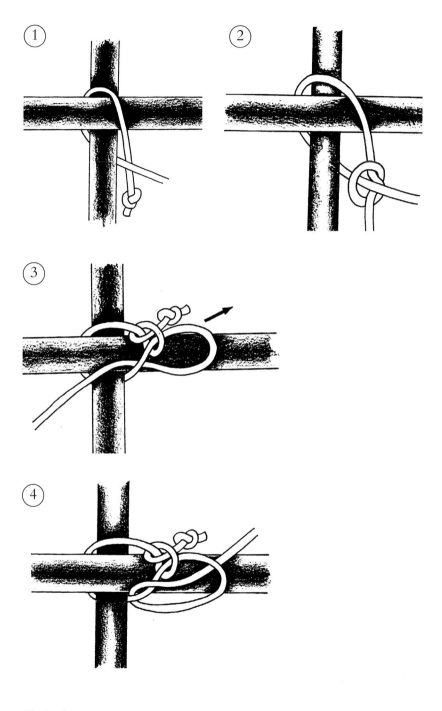

① ②

③

Evenk overhand hitch.
In Siberia, nomadic reindeer-herders employ quickly-tied release knots to minimise the time their fingers are exposed to the cold. These knots are very useful.

③

④

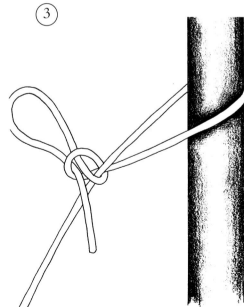

The jam knot.
The jam knot is a simple lashing, which provides strength for a minimal expenditure of cordage. It is intended for tying in nylon cord.

The figure-eight knot and its useful relatives

The figure-eight knot – or, as it is sometimes called the Flemish knot – is a more reliable knot than the overhand knot in that it is both secure and easily untied after loading. The figure-eight family of knots are among the most important used in the outdoors because of their widespread adoption by climbers and mountaineers. If the figure-eight knot is tied wrongly an overhand version is the result. This may be difficult to untie but will hold under strain. Use it in much the same circumstances as you would the overhand knot.

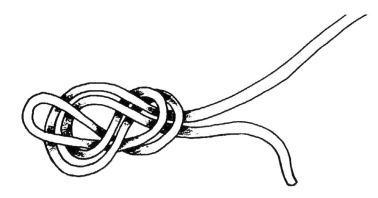

The figure-of-eight loop.
The most popular knot for tying into climbing harnesses and belays, the figure-of-eight is a very important knot.

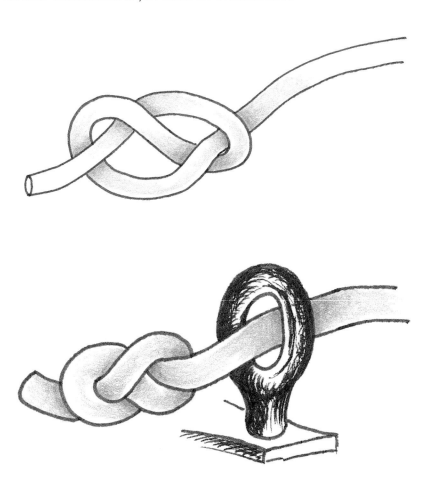

The figure-of-eight knot.
Similar to the overhand, the figure-of-eight knot is less prone to jam tight. If tied incorrectly you end up with an overhand knot which is secure, hence the figure-of-eight's popularity amongst climbers.

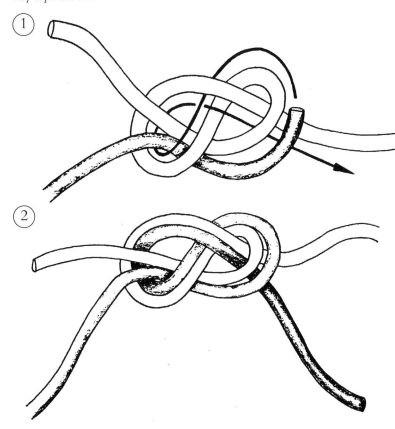

The figure-of-eight bend.
A secure method of joining ropes.

The bowline knot and its useful relatives

The bowline is one of the most widely employed of all knots, used to form a secure loop at the end of a rope. In mountaineering and climbing it has been superseded largely by the figure-eight, although it is still widely used in alpine mountaineering and at sea. Because of its great strength, reliability and speed of tying, it is a knot with which we should all be familiar.

① ② ③ ④

The double figure-of-eight knot.
This knot provides two non-slip loops and can be used to improvise emergency climbing harnesses.

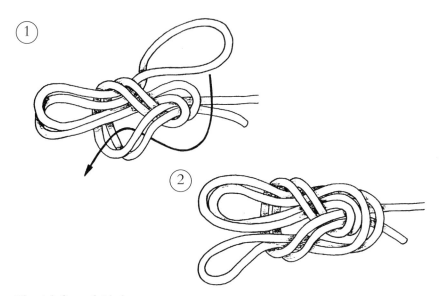

① ②

The triple figure-of-eight knot.
This knot produces three non-slip loops – excellent for an improvised harness for lowering, with one long loop around the back and shoulder and two smaller leg loops.

The bowline.
A secure, quickly-tied knot with a non-slip loop, the bowline remains popular amongst mariners and mountaineers.

The triple bowline.
Tied with doubled cordage, a triple bowline is formed with three non-slip loops. This can be used to improvise a harness for lowering.

155

The clove hitch and its useful relatives

Another widely used knot, easy to tie, untie, adjust and to learn because of its clear symmetry. It is an essential knot to be familiar with. The constrictor knot is a modification of the clove hitch: its exceptional security makes it one of the most useful of all knots.

① ②

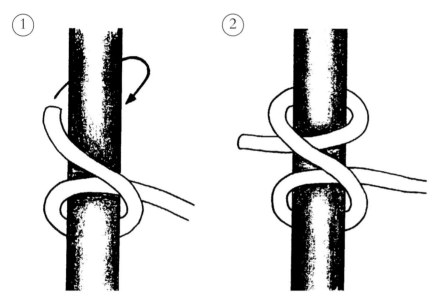

The clove hitch.
Used to attach a line to a post or rail, this is a secure fastening so long as the strain comes from 90° to the post.

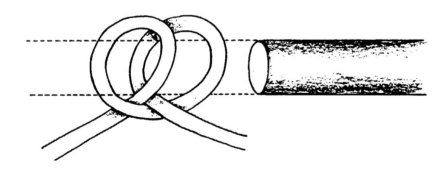

Clove hitch (tied in the bight).

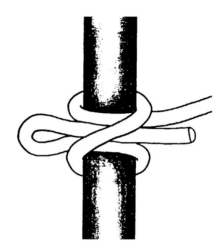

Slippery clove hitch.
A useful knot for temporary fixing, which is easily released. It can be used to guy out to saplings.

The anchor bend or fisherman's bend.
This cannot be tied under strain but with the first half hitch tucked through, the round turn forms a very secure attachment.

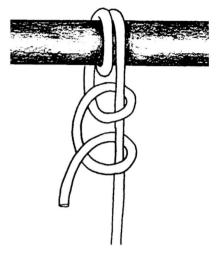

Round turn and two half hitches.
This knot can be tied under strain and forms a strong attachment. Take a round turn around post or beam and pass two half hitches around the standing part.

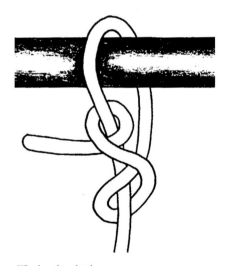

The buntline hitch.
With the end of this hitch constrained within the loop of the hitch, this knot does not work loose. Consequently it is a good knot for tarps and tents, remaining secure even when they are flapping in strong winds.

Other useful knots

①

The sheet bend.
The sheet bend is a quick way to join two cords – very effective if they are of differing thicknesses. It can also be used to attach cords to the corners of a sheet of material which has no eyelets. To do this, twist the corner until it can be doubled back, forming a bight through which to sheet-bend the guy.

①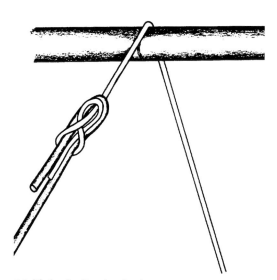

The constrictor knot (tied with an end).
A modified clove hitch, the constrictor knot binds tightly upon itself and does not work loose.

②

The double sheet bend.
A more secure form of the sheet bend.

① ②

③

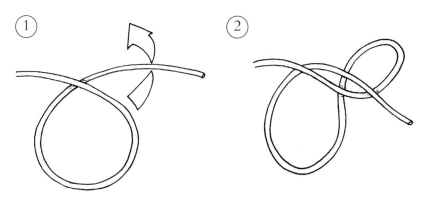

The constrictor knot (tied in the bight).

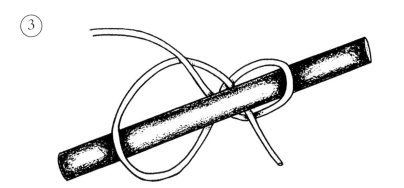

Modified or hauling sheet bend.
In this knot the working end is tucked away, streamlining the knot for hauling.

①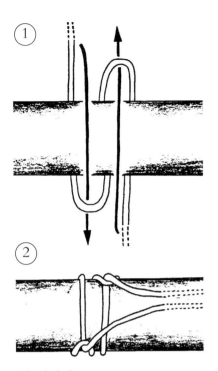

②

The plank sling.
The plank sling is more easily learned when it is tied as shown here. This knot is a first-rate binding for a bundle of tent poles or sticks. Pull the sticks tight and tie off the ends.

The timber hitch.
Elegant and simple, this hitch is a secure and economical method to begin lashings and taut lines. It is particularly useful tied in natural cordage.

① ②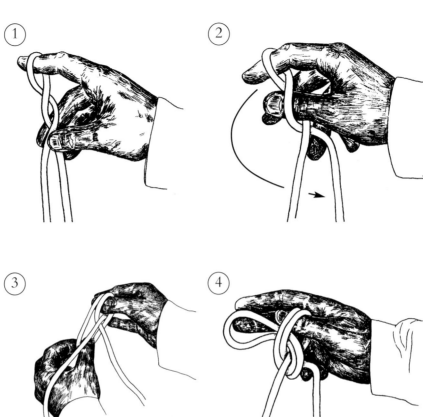

③ ④

⑤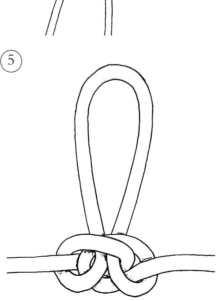

The alpine butterfly knot.
This is a non-slip knot of strength, used to tie a loop in the middle of a rope – a traditional middleman knot in mountaineering. Use it when loops are needed in a line.

The lark's foot hitch.
Simple and widely-used, it should not be relied upon in rescue situations with man-made fibres – under load they can heat up and melt through.

①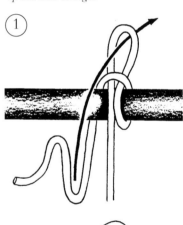

②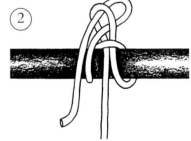

The highwayman's hitch.
A secure hitch which will release cleanly and quickly.

The waggoner's hitch.
A simple and effective means of tensioning a rope.

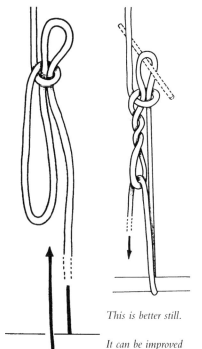

This is better still.

It can be improved by pinning here with a stout bar.

① ②

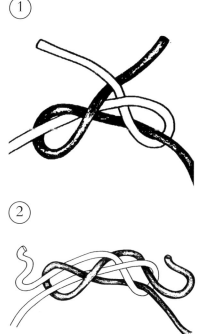

The vice-versa knot.
Will join elastic shock cord – useful for repairing the cord in tent poles.

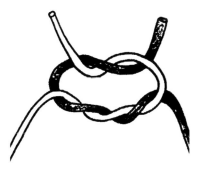

The surgeon's knot.
Used to tie off sutures, the surgeon's knot will secure the ends of nylon cord where other more conventional knots – such as the reef knot – will loosen and come apart.

The half blood knot.
A quick and easy knot for attaching a hook to fishing line. Wet the line before tightening.

① ②

③ ④

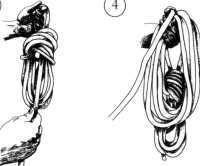

The first coil provides the weight and sufficient cord to reach from the branch down to the ground.

The second coil provides sufficient rope to reach from the ground to the branch.

⑤

The tree-surgeon's throwing coil.
This technique is used by tree surgeons to quickly cast a rope over high branches with ease, and without tangles and jams.

The adjustable loop.
Quick and easy to tie, this knot is perfect for adjustable guylines.

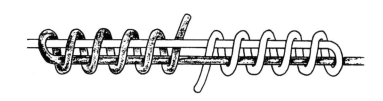

The blood knot with inward coil.
A secure and easily-tied knot for joining fishing line. When tying monofilament, wet the knot before making tight to ensure proper tightening.

159

HITTING THE TRAIL

The best thing in life is moving on.
Evenk saying, Siberia

Perhaps one of the greatest joys of bushcraft is striking out on a journey into new territory. Having spent most of my adult life engaged in this, I have come to look forward to every aspect of a journey, from planning the trip and preparing my outfit, to the challenges and rigours of life on the trail. However, in the preparation stages we can – all too easily – become too caught up in discussions of rucksacks, sleeping-bag design and the journey itself, and overlook something that may make a huge difference to our comfort and success: preparing our minds for the journey.

Mental preparation

Throughout the planning phase of your journey it may seem as though actually setting out is the smallest part of the whole endeavour and in many ways that is true. But when you do, it is important that you are working both physically and mentally at 100 per cent. Leave behind any mental baggage that may distract you from other more important considerations.

The moment the door shuts behind me I start to focus myself, switching into what I call an expedition frame of mind. From that point forward you must pay proper attention to all the details of the journey, run over all of the details so that you are completely *au fait* with the minutiae. You must become active and sharp, spotting signs in the airport ahead of others, and thereby preparing yourself for the kind of alertness that makes the difference when you are in the bush. You must become willing to adapt to new circumstances and bend with the flow of the journey, like the proverbial tree on the mountain.

- Push aside any fears you may harbour so that they don't cloud your judgement at times of crisis.
- Become considerate to others around you, suppressing your own idiosyncrasies in the interests of team morale.
- Exercise your ability to think quickly and responsively; stay alert to your location and the details of your expedition so that you remain totally involved.

- Be prepared to respond to whatever circumstances you meet.
- Take a pride in negotiating challenges and obstacles and be prepared always to respond with physical as well as mental energy. It may be that you will need to be actively aggressive to solve some problems.
- Watch out for times when your mental focus slips: be prepared to tighten the nut when you are tired.
- Taking care of expedition chores yourself should be your first priority: only when you have taken care of everything should you attend to your own kit, relax and rest.
- Expect the unexpected: things inevitably go wrong when you are on the trail, but when they do, don't complain – do something about it.
- When you are working with local guides do not assume that they will be of the highest calibre: on several occasions I have been surprised by the incompetence of guides who came bearing the highest recommendations. The important thing is to be responsible for your own safety. Do not be too willing to abdicate such responsibility to others.
- If you are acting as guide, be receptive to the history and experience of other members of your party: they may be highly competent, yet in the early stages of an expedition seem not to be so because they are adapting and acclimatising to new environmental challenges. Orientation is a key early phase of any expedition.
- Switch on your memory powers: make certain you know what items of equipment you have with you, where you put them last and what you used them for so that you don't lose anything. The simpler your outfit, the easier it is to maintain.
- Stay alert to possible threats: you may be travelling through an area where you are at risk of theft, so don't make yourself a target.
- Lastly, develop empathy with your environment: allow nature into your life while you are on the trail. Make the most of enjoying your surroundings. After all, that is why you are there.

Setting the pace

Having given consideration to the care of our mind the next most important thing on any expedition is taking care of our feet. Our feet are our means of moving and even when we are using snowmobiles or off-road vehicles in a crisis the lowest common denominator is walking. When we are walking in the back country we will most likely be carrying rucksacks loaded with a considerable amount of equipment, food and clothing; we will find that we are unable to walk as freely as though walking down a city street unburdened. It is very easy in the bush to find ourselves tiring, twisting ankles and ending up with blisters on our feet.

If you are new to walking with a rucksack and boots, bear in mind while you are planning the journey that you must condition yourself to this. Get used to wearing a rucksack with a load in it and learn to walk efficiently for long periods without injuring yourself: you will move at a very steady pace, taking care not to twist an ankle or to shift your feet unnecessarily within your boots, acquiring blisters.

One of the most important things about walking with a rucksack is to establish a comfortable pace: a good guide is your heartbeat. Try to find a speed at which you are not exerting yourself on the level. As you move uphill, shorten your stride and reduce your speed to maintain an even heart-rate. Although at first this may seem slow and uncomfortable, in the long run those who keep the steadiest pace tend to travel further for the expenditure of fewer calories. It's a good idea to stop every hour and rest for a few moments and check that everyone in your party is still in good spirits – anyone who has a sore spot in their boot can take it off and apply some moleskin to help prevent rubbing. You can also check your navigation, then update everyone on where you are going. Frequent breaks enable the party leader to maintain proper communication with the group: I always enjoy these moments when we can reflect or comment on the terrain we are passing through. Don't stop for too long, though: your body will cool and when you start again you will be stiff and more prone to muscular injuries.

Perhaps it is in the high mountains where you really see the advantage of maintaining a steady pace. Alpine mountaineers learn to move at an almost painfully slow pace: they plod along, moving only a few inches at each step, contending not only with the load on their back and the snow under their feet but also with the thin air of the Alpine environment.

With experience the pace will quicken and a party of experienced hikers will be able to move swiftly all day. But in a group of mixed ability the pace must be set to suit the slowest person. Otherwise they will not only struggle to keep up but will be more prone to injury, exhaustion and, in cold conditions,

hypothermia. An old piece of wisdom from the trail is that as you walk through rocky, steep terrain or you travel on cross-country skis you should take a little rest at every step.

In cold conditions when you stop on the trail you will probably need to put on a garment to keep you warm. It is a good idea to keep this to hand at the top of your rucksack. When you first stop you are initially still warm from the hiking but it takes only a few moments, especially in a breeze, to become chilled. As a group, try to be disciplined in your timings: when you stop, if everyone has put on their warm jackets, say, 'We will set off in five minutes' time', so that they know when to take them off and are ready to leave exactly on time.

Caring for your feet

The experienced hiker knows the value of taking good care of his or her feet. At the end of a hard day's walking, take off your boots. Leave your socks on for a few extra moments to allow your body heat to drive out some of their accumulated moisture, but then take them off, turn them inside out and air them. Now attend to your feet. If you have enough time, wash them with soap and water so they do not build up bacteria that can cause problems like athlete's foot. Allow them to dry, and as they are drying, massage them. This is important if they have been damp all day or if they have been cold; a massage will help to revitalise them. Dust them with foot powder. If you do this every day or even every other day, your feet will stay in good shape.

Now for fresh socks – in the rainforest I put on waterproof ones which help to dry out my feet. Then if you have with you some lightweight shoes, put them on and leave your boots to air. It is important to take very good care of your socks: try not to drop them into grit, sand or pine needles, which may get into the weave of the sock and later cause a blister.

Blisters

The bane of all foot travellers, they happen all too easily, and can be painful and debilitating. Once they are established they last for several days and are difficult to cure when you are having to hike. As with all things outdoors, prevention is ten times better than cure, so if you detect a hot spot developing within your boot, stop and do something about it. Even a few moments later may be too late.

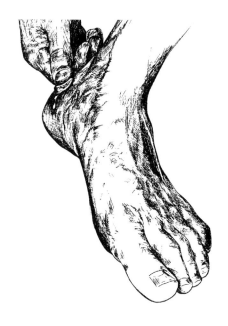

The way to treat a hot spot is to apply some moleskin or mole foam, which provides padding and reduces friction between your foot and your boot. If necessary you can cut out a ring bandage from the mole foam so that the boot is held away from the tender spot on your foot.

Advice with regard to the treatment of blisters varies enormously. Some experienced walkers will say that blisters should be left until they heal, the skin beneath them hardening and gradually taking over, while others believe that they should be drained and injected with friar's balsam to glue the loose skin back to the flesh beneath it – a painful and unnecessary process. Here is a much better approach.

First, assess the position of the blister. If it is on a part of your foot that is likely to be continuously rubbed, like your heel or the ball of your foot, you will need to drain it then pad and dress it. Begin by washing your foot carefully. If this is not possible use an antiseptic wipe from your medical kit around the area of the blister. Then take a needle from your first-aid kit and your lighter. Heat the needle to sterilise it, and when it is cool, carefully pierce the blister bubble close to its edge and gently squeeze out the fluid. Apply a topical antiseptic to the spot where it has been drained then dress the blister with a non-adhesive dressing. This may provide sufficient padding but if not apply a small strip of mole foam over the top.

This treatment will sometimes allow the blister to heal even while you are on the trail, perhaps within three days.

If the blister has burst, you must prevent it becoming infected. It must be kept clean, and if necessary apply some topical antiseptic in the early stages of treatment.

Cover the blister with a non-adhesive dressing then pad it carefully to prevent further abrasion or rubbing. Hydrocolloid dressings are excellent for treating such blisters. If you are carrying an antibacterial ointment use some to facilitate rapid healing – I have had great success with Flamazine.

Toenails

An in-growing toenail may spoil your enjoyment of and hinder your progress down a backcountry trail. An old method of dealing with it is to scrape the top of the nail with the edge of your knife, a file, a piece of emery paper or even a roughened rock like a pumice stone until it can be easily depressed in the middle by your thumbnail. The pressure on the in-growing part of the nail is lessened and your foot will be much more comfortable

Nails should be kept short: if they are too long they will rub against the toe of your boot and cause serious pain at the base of the nail akin to bruising and blistering.

Sprained ankles

Perhaps the most common walking injury, a severely sprained ankle often resembles a fracture, causing lameness, swelling and pain, and may mean two or three days' rest on the trail. It is as well to avoid ankle injuries; one good way to do this is to cut a staff when you are traversing steep, slippery slopes for extra support. An old saying has it that a wise man carries a staff.

If you do sprain your ankle, remember the old medical treatment RICE: it stands for Rest; Ice or cold compress treatment to reduce the swelling; a Compressive bandage – use the cohesive bandage from your medical kit (see page 12); and Elevation of the limb to help reduce inflammation. If you take off

Bandaging an ankle.

your boot straight away with such an injury you may find it impossible to get it back on because your foot has swollen. It may be more appropriate to continue moving with your boot on until you reach a safer and more appropriate place to stop and examine the injury.

Trench foot

Non-freezing cold injuries are associated with backcountry travel after prolonged exposure to moderate or severe cold when the weather is damp and the ground sodden. If your feet have been consistently wet for three days or thereabouts, you are likely to develop trench foot – the term was first used to describe the condition during the trench warfare of the First World War. It may be debilitating in both the short and long term: in severe cases the toes or foot may swell and even blister. Trench foot is serious and the casualty should be taken to hospital.

To prevent it, dry your feet properly at the end of each day, warm them and massage them. Non-freezing cold injuries are more prevalent in people who are undernourished and dehydrated: make sure you eat and drink enough to give yourself the best chance of avoiding trench foot.

Frostbite

Frostbite can occur in temperatures below freezing. It occurs when the tissues of your foot have literally frozen and is usually associated with either footwear which is too tight or a situation where your body as a whole has become chilled. Due to vaso-constriction insufficient blood supply to the extremities has resulted in their freezing. Generally speaking when the thermometer reads −30 degrees Centigrade or below we cannot afford to make a mistake in terms of the care of our feet.

If you find that your foot is becoming cold you can help to rewarm it by shaking it, and the same is true of your hands to increase the blood supply to these. If that fails to work then you must consider asking your teammate to rewarm your foot under his armpit next to his skin, skin-to-skin contact, making sure that you keep your boot off the ground where it will not freeze solid. If you are standing around a lot in very cold conditions put insulation between your feet and the ground. Use spruce boughs or any other such material.

If your foot does freeze you will find that your toes become white and waxy; you must then consider how seriously frostbitten they are. Minor frostbite is only superficial and can be rewarmed very effectively whereas serious deep tissue frostbite where your foot or toes are solidly frozen is a more serious consideration. Generally speaking with serious frostbite it is better to continue travelling with your foot frozen but trying to prevent any further deepening of the freezing rather than to thaw it. Thawing of frostbite is an extremely painful process leading to swelling and usually blisters.

If you have frostbitten feet you will need to seek medical assistance. Under no circumstances should you attempt to amputate any digits, toes or even feet out of fear of gangrene. Today the treatment even in hospital is 90% of the time simply to allow the foot to regenerate and to heal, protecting the foot from infection by the use of antibiotics. It is very unlikely you will need any form of amputation.

At −48°C, to prevent frostbite, students in the arctic learn to rewarm cold feet on the stomach of a team mate. Clothing removed (note glove) should be stuffed inside other clothing, not left to freeze on the ground.

When using a tarp, set your boots on sticks to prevent them filling with rain.

Drying socks and boots

As damp footwear can cause serious problems, consider carefully how you to dry it. If you take with you some waterproof breathable socks, you will always be able to keep your feet dry even if your boots are wet. However, at the end of a day's hiking you should still dry your footwear as best you can. The greatest single mistake beginners make is to place their boots too close to a fire, where the leather dries out, shrinks and cracks. Dry your boots slowly with the opening upward. In the old days hikers filled their boots with oats to absorb the moisture overnight. Today, if you are in a cabin, you may be able to stuff them with newspaper, which will have a similar effect – but is considerably less messy.

In the bush open your boots as wide as possible, scrub away dirt from the outside and leave them in a dry, shady place, off the ground.

In cold weather take them into your sleeping-bag at night to prevent them freezing solid: place them in the sleeping-bag stuff sack first to keep yourself and your sleeping-bag dry. At the end of a trip clean and reproof your boots with Nikwax aqueous wax. Store them in a cool, dry place.

Water obstacles

Water is a powerful natural force in the landscape. Whenever you cross it, pay attention to safety. Drowning accounts for a large number of backcountry deaths – and it is often experienced swimmers who drown.

Water in the wild presents a different set of problems to that of a swimming pool. For a start it may be moving, and although seemingly moving slowly actually moving with immense force. Water in wild areas is often very cold, perhaps even fed by glacial melt waters which can have a shocking effect on a human, causing us to gasp and thereby inhale water. And also water can obscure from view obstacles on the riverbed which could pose a serious threat to our health. So the golden rule when travelling in wild areas is whenever possible to avoid having to directly cross a water hazard. If this is not possible always search for the easiest way of crossing.

River crossing

In wild areas, rivers and other waterways are an essential means of travel for canoeists and even walkers. In rainforests they are a vital navigational aid. As you travel further into the wilderness, bridges, cables or basket crossings are few and far between. Sometimes there may be no alternative but to cross a river as it may be too large to hike round. Remember that after heavy rainfall even small streams turn into raging torrents, and that the force of water must never be underestimated, whether you are trying to cross it or just fall in by accident. Train yourself to deal with it.

Risks

At first glance it is easy to fail to notice the risks associated with water. A calm flowing surface could lull us into a sense of complacency. I like to think of water as a living entity. As it snakes its way across the landscape it has sufficient strength in its nature to shape the land beneath it. Whenever we cross a river we are at risk from the debris being carried within the river, such as trees and branches; in really strong currents, even rocks and giant boulders can be moved along. Sometimes you can even hear the rocks being moved along in the water. When this is the case we certainly should never attempt to cross the water.

But apart from its strength, perhaps the most dangerous aspect of water is the effect of its cold. Many wilderness rivers are fed from glacial melt waters and mountain streams and the temperature may only be a few degrees above freezing point. Certainly more than cold enough to cause us serious problems. It is not uncommon for travellers in the bush to attempt to cross a river, only to decide that the water is actually too cold to be crossed at that point, to come back ashore and then to search for a narrower point to cross the water. Whenever we enter cold water our body suffers cold shock, which causes us to gasp, and if our head is beneath the water this can cause us to inhale water, triggering a panic that results in drowning. Even if we are not overcome by cold shock on first entering the water, there is a great risk that on a long water crossing we may become numbed by the cold of the water sufficiently to make it difficult for us to exit the water at the far bank or in some cases even to reach the far bank.

Added to the risk of things carried in the current and the cold of the water are the more obvious risks; that of being swept away in a strong current, bashed against branches and held against the current, causing us to drown, or being trapped in whirlpools or beneath a stopper at a weir or most commonly caught with our ankle trapped between rocks so that we are bent backwards under the force of the water and thereby drowned.

Perhaps the most dangerous thing of all is overconfidence. Whenever we are involved in crossing water we must pay the greatest attention to safety procedures and plan our crossing with great care. For example, it may be prudent to simply wait for a river in flood to subside, although this may mean waiting longer than we had anticipated and placing a greater strain on our food supplies.

This in many cases would be the preferred option to running the risk of a more serious injury crossing the river in flood. Very often people are caught in flash floods in arid areas where despite the fact that it is not raining locally they are still at risk of floods caused by rains on higher ground, perhaps many miles away where a large massif can act as a huge catchment area for water which suddenly rushes down the riverbed in which they are camped. Usually flash floods, when they first arrive, come as a bubbling mass of muddy water almost like a living creature, but once this has passed through your camp the water levels can rise incredibly swiftly. I have myself seen in Africa, on several occasions, rivers which had only a couple of inches in them rise to twenty feet or more of water in the space of half an hour to forty-five minutes. It can be quite surprising and they can subside just as quickly.

If you are swept off your feet, keep your head out of the water, with your feet raised and pointing downstream.

Crossing water

When confronted with a water obstacle, evaluate the level of risk, decide whether the crossing is feasible, find the most suitable place to cross and organise it. Remember

W	**Water**
A	**Assess**
S	**Search**
P	**Plan**
T	**Technique**
A	**Anticipate**
R	**Rewarm.**

Begin by considering the type of water that confronts you. Is it tidal? Is it cold? Is it deep or shallow? Consider any hazards that might lurk within it, particularly animals like crocodiles. Now you will know whether it is feasible or not to cross it. If it is:

Assess the crossing. Look for the run-out of the river: in other words, what is downstream of where you may cross? Notice hazards, such as trees, branches or snags, either natural or man-made: swept away, you might end up hanging on these. Are there rapids or, worse, waterfalls below your current location? If so, it would be foolhardy to cross at that point. What about whirlpools? Judge the speed of the river by throwing a stick into the flow and walking along beside it. Assess the nature of the riverbed. Is it muddy? If so, you may get stuck. Are there slippery boulders that might trap a foot? Assess the depth of the water: is it deep all the way across or is there a point at which the depth is more contained?

Perhaps there is a sandbar half-way. Assess the human aspect of the crossing. Are the members of your party strong swimmers? If you are going into the wild you should be able to swim. Lastly, consider any alternatives: consult your map or send someone on a scouting reconnaissance; you may discover a point further upstream where the river is braided and you can wade over through shallows from sandbar to sandbar.

Search for the ideal place to cross. Avoid crossing a stream just up from where it joins a river: the speed of the water is faster here and anyone who is swept away may end up swept beyond rescue. Avoid bends in the river and look for a straight section between bends to cross with a gentle bend below your crossing point. The current moves fastest on the outside of a bend so don't aim to complete your crossing here. Arrange your crossing so that the far bank is just upstream of the inside of a bend: you will find that if someone is swept away, they will be able to swim more easily in the slower-moving water or even find a safe eddy to exit from. Consider carefully your potential entry and exit points: find an easy place to enter, not a steep-sided slippery or rocky bank where someone may fall and bang their head.

Plan the river crossing. This must involve the whole team so that everyone understands what is going to happen: the order in which the team will cross, the technique to be employed and any contingency plans – you may need to take into account someone's nervousness. It is sometimes a good idea to team weaker people with stronger ones. Remember that when you are dealing with a moving body of water it can be impossible to hear someone on the far side of the river or even if they are beside you.

Your technique is all important: select one that is appropriate, simple and safe. Don't incorporate rope unless this is absolutely necessary. A simple method of crossing a river, such as wading side by side, providing each other with support, is usually easier to carry through. Rehearse on dry land before you enter the water.

Anticipate problems – and ask for help in this. Here two experienced minds are always better than one. You may come up with simple things, like being unable to communicate verbally above the din of the river: be prepared to use hand signals. Have a rescue procedure in place in case anyone is swept downstream. Consider the consequences for each individual of crossing the water: after heavy rainfall river water may be full of bacteria and anyone with an open wound will need to wash it afterwards. Also, if the water is cold you must be prepared to produce hot drinks: pack kindling and timber or a stove, drink ingredients and mugs in a dry bag close to the top of the first rucksack to go across.

Rewarm after crossing, and allow at least an hour for this. You will be much colder than you anticipate, unless you are in the tropics. Make sure that everyone changes into dry clothes, then gathers together around a fire or hiking stove, and has a warming, calorie rich drink.

Dressing to cross a river

Some hikers prefer to remove most of their clothing before crossing water. However, in cold conditions it is wise to keep some on. I usually opt to wear lightweight, fast-drying spare clothing, and pack my sleeping equipment and everyday clothes carefully to stop them from getting wet. It is amazing how water finds its way into the driest spot in your rucksack. When wading across a slow-flowing stream, tote your rucksack high up on your shoulders if you can.

At other times you will have to rely on dry bags, which will make your rucksack more buoyant in water. Some suggest making your rucksack into a buoyancy aid by attaching your sleeping mat to the top and wearing both shoulder straps. I don't recommend this: there have been accidents where people have been trapped by their rucksack on a snag or between rocks and drowned. It is wiser to rely on the old-fashioned method of wearing your rucksack over one shoulder. In this way, if you fall in, you can easily let go of your rucksack. If you are strapped into it and it fills with water, it may drag and hold you under water.

While crossing water, keep with you your most important items of survival equipment: your knife and a means of starting a fire. Keep your boots on: if you cross a stream barefoot you may slip on slimy rocks, slide into the crevices between them and end up with severe bruising, twisted or fractured ankles – or, worse still, trapped. I take off my socks and, once I'm back on dry land, I put on waterproof socks between dry socks and the wet boots.

To cross shallow water

Perhaps surprisingly even the smallest brook can be a safety hazard. While most people will stride or leap across, others are less confident, especially when they are carrying a rucksack. In rainforests you can often cross streams on fallen trees, which act as natural bridges. But this requires nerve and a good sense of balance. Make sure to watch weaker members of a party and encourage them to cross boldly. Sometimes it's easier for them to sit astride the log and ease their way across; someone more confident can carry over their rucksack. If you plan to travel regularly in the rainforest it is a good idea to train yourself to walk with a rucksack across such obstacles: often the tops of these logs are slippery, especially when you're wearing boots – and the water may be six or seven metres below.

A common way for a party to cross a stream is hopping from rock to rock – natural stepping stones. However, not everyone is nimble-footed, especially if they aren't used to wearing hiking boots. Beware of slips, which may result in ankle injuries and distress from the shock of falling into water, soaked equipment and clothing. You can vault over some small rivers with a stout walking staff, a fun and efficient way to do it that ensures your feet stay dry. The staff must be strong enough to support your body weight plus your loaded rucksack. Don't attempt it with a collapsible walking staff.

Unless the current is very strong, you can wade through rivers that come up to your knees. But there are still a few things to keep in mind. Whenever you wade across a stream, face upstream so that you will see any objects being carried towards you in the water and be able to avoid them. Also if the water is deeper than you thought and you are facing upstream, the force of the water locks your knees so that you stay upright.

Take great care in placing your feet: move sideways gradually in short steps and wait until you are balanced after one step before trying to take the next – you can't walk across a stream in the same way that you would across paving stones. Don't try to hurry it.

When the water reaches above the knee, perhaps to waist height, I like to take a stout staff with me. It acts as a third leg, giving me a wider, more stable base for support. If you do this face upstream and place the staff well ahead of you, keeping your legs wide apart to create a triangular base for your body. Keep two points of support in contact with the riverbed at all times.

If there are several people in your party you can wade across a river providing each other with support. Link arms, grasp clothing or each other's rucksack straps. If there are three of you, face inwards towards each other, then take hold to form a human tripod. Another method involves supporting each other as in a queue, one person behind the other. When using this method the fourth person uses a staff and faces upstream.

A stout staff gives strong triangular support.

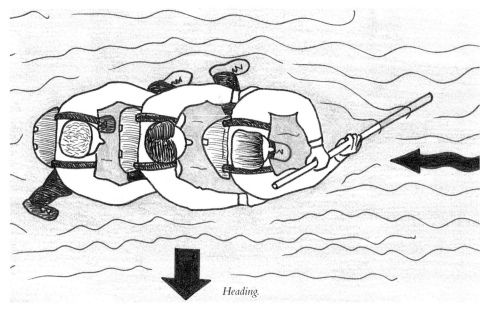

Current.

Heading.

Good support but difficult to co-ordinate.

Students crossing water with improvised flotation aid. Only R for Rewarm is still to go.

Current.

Heading.

Excellent triangular support, excellent co-ordination. Remember to watch upstream.

Trousers can be used as a buoyancy aid - knot the ends of the legs and draw them quickly over your head to fill with air. Passed under your armpits, they function as very effective water wings.

To cross deep water

When crossing deeper water you won't be able to remain in contact with the riverbed, so consider making flotation aids, particularly if the water is very cold.

For example, if you remove your trousers, knot them at the bottom of each leg, draw them over the top of your head to fill with air and then tuck them under your armpits they may act as water wings; or inflate your therma-rest mattress; empty your water bottles and tie them together. Or put the contents of your rucksack into a dry bag, then into a stuff sack. Wrap the whole thing in a lightweight shelter sheet to make an effective float. The last option is perhaps the most efficient of all: the Archimedes principle says that an item floats because it is lighter than the weight of the volume of water it displaces, and one rucksack so wrapped will help two people stay afloat. If you tie several together you can improvise a crude raft so that it supports your chests with your legs kicking to propel you along.

When you enter cold, deep water you will experience the cold-shock reaction. You can reduce its severity with training, for example by taking a cold shower each day before you set off. Royal Navy helicopter pilots are encouraged to do this in case they have to ditch in cold water. When you experience cold shock, keep calm, hang on to your flotation aid and stay close to the shore. After a few moments it will wear off as you get used to the water temperature. Then strike out for the opposite shore. But the cold will sap your energy: before you reach the half-way point decide whether or not you have energy left to make it all the way. Cross in pairs, if possible, and encourage each other on the way.

To cross a large body of slow or still water

If you have to cross a large body of slow-moving water or a lake, the water may be too cold to swim across, even with a flotation aid. Instead, you will have to improvise a boat. This can be done in a variety of ways; usually the safest and easiest is the improvised tarpaulin dinghy.

Make two oval rings of 60cm stakes.

Fill between the stakes with brushwood.

Bind around the brushwood to complete oval facine.

Remove stakes and fit deck.

Lay down tarp and grass or bracken padding.

Place facine on tarp deck-side down.

Tie tarp over facine. Improvise a paddle.

Away you go.

A very stable platform with which to reach the best fishing spots.

Snow obstacles

In the far north, you will probably travel by snowmobile. These machines enable you to travel great distances swiftly and are made to be reliable.

However, operating in some of the most hostile conditions on Earth, they occasionally break down and you will have to be able to walk on deep snow. Also, snowmobile travel gives you a false impression of how far you have come in walking terms. The rule is that if you travel for fifteen minutes on a snowmobile it will take you twenty-four hours without snowshoes. So always carry with you a pair of snowshoes which fit conveniently on a snowmobile – and can be used to dig a track if it gets bogged down in snow – or skis. But what if you forget them? If you're in forested country, you can improvise snowshoes. They won't be as effective as the real thing, but they're better than nothing.

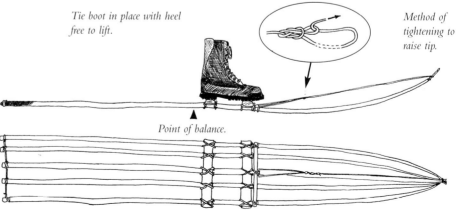

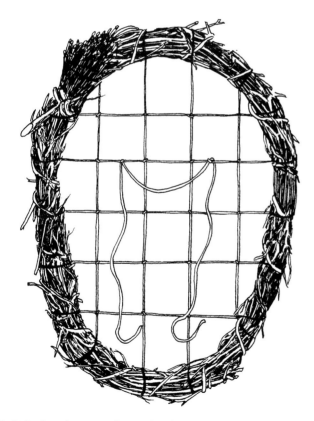

In higher latitudes, use small wispy branches and cord to form a snow shoe like this.

Tie boot in place with heel free to lift.

Method of tightening to raise tip.

Point of balance.

Navigation

The most important bushcraft skill of all. You must be able to navigate to find your way safely through remote areas. Today navigation is easier than ever before: we have accurate topographical mapping of most areas, well-made compasses and satellite-aided navigation. Yet although many people carry the appropriate tools few are skilled bush navigators.

So, how do you become competent? Well, for a start you must be familiar with the use of maps, compasses and GPS in their basic operation and the techniques associated with them. Then, learn to emphasise certain aspects of those techniques: you train yourself to think in navigational terms, to recognise signs in the landscape to keep you on your path. Navigation is a holistic process: a good navigator doesn't slavishly follow map and compass. As you gain experience you will acquire the ability to correct mistakes in estimation and direction swiftly. Most important of all, when your map, compass and conventional navigation equipment fail you, you will be able to find your way.

Map work

Whenever we navigate with a map or compass, we have to work with a degree of inaccuracy: map-makers often have to compromise on position, perhaps to reduce crowding on a small-scale map. Compass accuracy depends on the movement and mechanics of the instrument. When we are navigating we must avoid introducing further inaccuracy into the equation. If you ask someone to show you on a map where you are, they normally point their finger at the area where they think they are and say, 'Here, somewhere.' That won't do. Instead they should be able to reply, 'We are 100m east of this fenced junction,' or 'You're 250m north of the river junction indicated here,' and point at the map with the corner of a compass, the tip of a knife or a pine needle. All it takes is a little practice.

A few things are worth bearing in mind here. You normally march on a 1:50,000 or 1:25,000 scale map. If you are using a 1:50,000 scale map, 1km is represented by 2cm, therefore 1cm = 500m, 2mm = 100m, so when you are working on a 1:50,000 scale map you can estimate hundreds of metres easily. The same is true for a 1:25,000 where 1km is represented by 4cm, 500m = 2cm and 100m = 4mm.

To estimate distances travelled across land you can use a timing chart: with this you time your travel across a known distance measured from your map then relate that to the chart to find your speed. It's especially useful in open terrain,

particularly when travelling at night or in poor visibility. I have one taped to the lid of my compass.

In close cover it is easier to use pacing to estimate distances covered; here you will need to establish how many steps you take to cover 100m. Count the pacing of one foot only. You will find that your pacing varies according to the ground state and your load, so will need to pace yourself over 100m in varying terrains and conditions to find an average. Some people carry a string of beads to count out the paces they take and from that work out the kilometres covered. Others use a mechanical counter. With practice you can become more accurate than a GPS or at least equal to it.

Contours

The undulation of the terrain affects our ability to judge distance. In learning map-reading we are taught that the map is a two-dimensional representation of a three-dimensional land surface, and that contour lines indicate the rise and fall of a slope: the tighter together the contour lines, the steeper the ground; the wider apart, the more level. From studying contour lines, you will be able to build an accurate representation of how the going will be when you travel across the landscape. Again experience helps, and the only way to learn to relate contour lines to land surfaces is to get out on the ground with a map. There is no other way. Experience on the ground is vital in learning to navigate.

Consider buying an altimeter in the form of a wristwatch; Sunto make an excellent one. Altimeters indicate altitude accurately as long as you follow the manufacturers' instructions and re-zero it regularly at known points of altitude taken from your map: atmospheric pressure may cause it to give a false reading.

When you are working with contour lines, watch for an increase in the contour interval. Usually it is 5m but in mountainous terrain cartographers often use a 20m interval so that the lines do not become too complicated on the map. Also in some parts of the world no symbols are used to indicate a cliff face: you will see tightly packed contours of a large interval – stay alert to this and check the map's legend. In some countries it's wise to check the reliability of the local mapping: you can't always rely on it!

River direction

When travelling in wild areas it's important to know in which direction rivers flow. Work this out before you go and if you feel it will help put an arrow on the map to indicate it.

(left) Namib desert, not a place to be lost in.

LIVING FROM THE LAND

In most survival episodes shelter, water, fire and signalling must be attended to before food needs. But when lack of food does become an issue, it becomes the major issue, the key obstacle to human survival. The very fear of starvation can weigh so heavily on our minds as to be in itself overwhelming. At the onset of winter 1981, having neglected to arrange to be collected from a remote wilderness lake in Alaska's Brooks range, Carl McCunn lay back in his tent and shot himself rather than starve to death. Even for those not forced by circumstances to forage for wild foods the question of whether they can themselves find food to keep body and soul together periodically lures adventurers from the urban jungle to pit their wits against the wild.

Sometime around 18 August 1992 in an abandoned bus in the Alaskan bush close to the Denali park boundary 24-year-old Chris McCandless wrote 'I HAVE HAD A HAPPY LIFE AND THANK THE LORD. GOODBYE AND MAY GOD BLESS ALL!' Shortly afterwards he died. Having successfully lived from the land for 112 days, far longer than most if not all of those who criticised him after the event, his adventure was brought to its sad and lonely end by a lack of detailed knowledge. Knowledge of a plant toxin which in his weakened state proved fatal. A detail that perhaps was known only to the local Dena'ina Indians who had in their cultural past faced the same challenge as McCandless. A detailed account can be read in *Into the Wild* by Jon Krakauer.

Living from the land is not easy. Even the most experienced guides and indigenous hunters can at times struggle to find food, particularly in the colder latitudes. Those who are able to do so usually rely, as did McCandless, upon a weapon of some description. Even then this weapon must be used with skill, patience and knowledge of the land. When unsuccessful the empty stomach must be borne with a stoic fortitude and the promise of a new day and a new hunt. Detail and an opportunistic outlook are everything in the bush, most particularly with regard to finding food.

Foraging skills have traditionally been an important part of the outfit of wilderness professionals. If you intend to step or paddle out of the far side of a national park you will need to become acquainted with these skills. Bear in mind that successful foraging is not a process of ruthless exploitation, but one of respect. Prerequisite is an empathy for and understanding of the wild land and its creatures.

(left) All the food on this table was obtained from the land.

Calories

To live we burn food as fuel to generate energy, usually measured in terms of joules or kcal of energy. Before we begin to collect calories we must take steps to reduce any unnecessary wastage of energy, particularly in cold climates; this means that our clothing and shelter must be adequate or improved so as to provide a warm, dry calorie trapping environment. Otherwise our food gathering efforts will be no better than dropping food into a basket that has a hole in it.

Every environment provides its own problems from the point of view of foraging, but perhaps the most difficult of all are those of extreme cold, or damp cold where our calorific requirement is higher and where calories are difficult to obtain, there being fewer plant sources available. As we move towards the tropics more energy rich plant foods become available, although meat still plays a very important role in a survival diet. This statement is of course a generalisation; there are many places where foraging may be futile, for example high in mountain environments or in places where the food resources are out of season. Nomadic groups travel more by necessity than choice.

The effects of food deprivation

If you are not familiar with the effects of food deprivation, being without food is a frightening and stressful experience, intensified by a confusing cocktail of debilitating symptoms. If, however, we understand the way in which our body responds to being without food, we can learn to recognise and understand these symptoms of food depletion. This in turn can help us to reduce the psychological stress and to fine tune our food gathering strategy. The good news is that times of hunger have been a common human experience for millennia, the result of which is that we are born with a physiology that is evolutionarily well adapted to coping with episodes of famine. The annals of human survival are full to the brim with tales of people who have survived for astonishingly long periods on reduced diets.

The first few days without food are a critical time for anyone trying to make the step from surviving to living in the wilderness. It is in this period that we exhaust our body's store of carbohydrate.

Long after the flesh of the marula fruit has rotted away the seeds can be smashed open to obtain an edible kernel.

Because carbohydrates such as starches and sugars are composed of very simple, easily digested molecules, they are an efficient food source that can be digested with little waste. Quickly and easily converted to energy, carbohydrates are vital in the supply of energy to our brain and nervous system and are consequently utilised before the other food sources of fat and protein.

We are able to store carbohydrate in our muscles, the liver and a small amount in our blood. For use this is converted to glucose then transported to wherever it is needed, particularly the brain and nervous system, by our blood system. The rate at which we exhaust our store of carbohydrate depends on how hard we are working, but can be as little as 3 or 4 hours when working hard in a cold environment. When our reserve of carbohydrate is exhausted our blood sugar level drops, resulting in a reduced supply of energy to the brain. Because the brain is unable to store energy for itself it demands a continuous supply; when there is a reduction in this supply a range of symptoms are triggered.

Tiredness
Headache
Easy irritation
Loss of concentration
Reduced ability to make decisions
Depression
Increased susceptibility to cold
Increased concern with oneself

As time goes on fast intensive work becomes very difficult; even walking up a moderate slope becomes very difficult. Tasks which at other times would be straightforward, such as crossing bodies of water, now become extremely hazardous as we become more susceptible to cold and hypothermia. There is danger here if we fail to recognise that our body is no longer able to withstand conditions that would otherwise pose little risk.

Adjusting to the exhaustion of carbohydrate

When our reserves of carbohydrate have been exhausted our body makes adjustments to mobilise fats and proteins to ensure a continuing supply of energy to the brain, fat being the more important of these food resources.

Fats are found in butter, cheese, oils, nuts, egg yolks, animal fats and vegetable oils. They are more complex foods than carbohydrates, consequently the energy in fat is more slowly released than that in carbohydrate, providing a longer lasting form of energy. This is particularly well suited to slow monotonous work, but provides a poor source of energy for fast intensive activity. A fat rich diet increases the need for water. In extremely cold climates a lower carbohydrate intake (40%) and a higher fat intake should be eaten to help maintain body warmth.

If we eat fat rich food before sleeping, we sleep warmer.

Ketone toxicity

One of the by-products of carbohydrate depletion is an increase in the use of fatty acids within our muscles as our activity levels increase. Remember that fat burns in a carbohydrate flame; when we are low on carbohydrate we are unable to burn body fat efficiently. In these circumstances too large a consumption of fat results in the production of waste products called ketones. These can lead to headaches, nausea, difficulty in drinking, the loss of body salts and energy.

Ketones are excreted in our urine and breath where they can be identified by a characteristic acetone scent. If you overexert yourself under such circumstances you can be overwhelmed by the build up of ketones in your blood, leading to a coma state similar to that experienced by a diabetic.

Hunting provides an essential contribution to the hunter-gatherer diet, even in rainforests.

Protein

Proteins have the most complex molecules of any food type; this means that they are the most inefficient food for the production of energy. The digestive process breaks proteins down into various amino acids, which are converted into new body tissue proteins such as muscle.

Complete proteins provide the body with the exact balance of amino acids it requires to rebuild itself; some of these amino acids are essential and vital for the body to function. Examples of complete protein sources are:

fish
meat
poultry
blood

Incomplete proteins are lacking one or more of the amino acids. Examples of incomplete proteins are:

cheese
milk
cereal
grains
legume seeds

Ideally a survival diet should contain 75 to 80 grams of complete proteins each day.

However, if only incomplete proteins are available two or more types of food may need to be eaten in combination to provide complete protein. Grains and legume seeds eaten in combination contain all of the essential amino acids.

Because proteins are the most complex type of food they supply energy after our carbohydrate and fat reserves have been used up. Lack of protein results in malnutrition, skin and hair disorders as well as muscle atrophy.

The average body contains approximately six kilograms of protein in the muscles. As a source of energy it is less important; its prime function is as the building material for cells and stomach enzymes. Without protein the body cannot repair itself; a high protein intake increases our need for water.

In the face of starvation our body is adapted to consume the least important protein first. The first proteins consumed in this way are the stomach enzymes responsible for breaking down food in the stomach. Once these have been consumed the body uses protein from the muscles. With increasing activity muscle consumption increases; after the second day without food up to half a kilogram of muscle tissue may have been consumed to cover the loss of carbohydrate. When food does again become available recovery from the period of starvation is prolonged due to the body's difficulty in digesting food and the muscle tissue damage.

The poisonous puff-adder may seem a threat to some; to others, it is a meal.

Vitamins

Vitamins carry out important work in different body processes, for example:
– vitamin B is involved in energy conversion
– vitamin C is important in the intake of iron within the intestine; it also assists cells and tissues in holding together and is important in maintaining a healthy immune system
– vitamins A, D and K assist eyesight, our intake of calcium and the coagulation of our blood

Vitamins B and C cannot be stored within the body; ideally they should be sought in the survival diet. Vitamin C is found in many plants while vitamin B is found in some plants and the liver of animals. Vitamin deficiencies and their related medical conditions, such as scurvy, are considerations only for a long-term survival situation.

It is worth bearing in mind that some plants can contain toxins that reduce the effect of vitamin B within our body.

Fibre

Fibre aids the efficient functioning of the stomach and intestine. If eating again after a period of starvation, only small amounts of fibre, gradually increasing, should be attempted.

A foraging strategy

Calories

The requirement of an average person doing an average job is approximately 3,000 calories per day. Experiments show that a healthy person can subsist for a considerable period of time on 500 calories of carbohydrate a day without harmful effect. For this reason we should strive to attain this each day, bearing in mind that in colder weather or when working hard this will need to increase. This requirement is also increased in the presence of infection or injury. So in cold, when working hard, or when infected or injured, we must strive to provide ourselves with more than 500 calories of carbohydrate per day, and fat.

Types of food

Carbohydrate, found in plants, is easier to obtain than meat; this will require us to learn to recognise and process local food plants. So we shall search for edible plants before meat.

Overall we learn from this that we must strive to find some carbohydrate to maintain the ability to respond to demands for fast intensive work and to be able to efficiently metabolise our body's store of fat. We should also understand that proteins which provide a complete balance of amino acids are highly desirable.

Minerals

Minerals (salts) are needed so the range of different chemical processes can work within our body. For example, iron binds oxygen within our blood, potassium and sodium aid nerve function, while calcium is the building block of our skeleton. Problems associated with mineral deficiency are only likely to occur in prolonged circumstances where a balanced diet has not been obtained over several weeks.

If game is readily obtained it is possible to subsist indefinitely in good health on a diet of meat, fat and water. So we shall maintain an effort to procure game. Flesh is the most reliable source of amino acids. Complete protein is important to healthy body function. So we shall consider all options for obtaining this, including insect larvae, which may be very easy to obtain.

Methods of obtaining food

Nothing ventured; nothing gained

When it comes to finding food we need to be very open minded; many sources of nutrition will be strange to us, some may even seem repugnant. But if it is a matter of survival we must not allow our prejudice to deter us from obtaining nourishment. It is important to note that many of the best techniques for obtaining food in the wild are now regulated or banned. In a real emergency no one is going to quibble over the way you find food, but if you wish to travel and supplement your rations with wild food you must stay within the law, restricting yourself to the foods and techniques permissible.

Sadly regulations are sweeping over many wild plant foods which do not need saving from foragers', hands in the cause of preservation. As you will discover, the most important wild foods are the most common and readily available plants. In my experience people who have learned to utilise wild foods are more in tune with the natural environment, as they understand intimately the growth cycle of the plants and are more alert to the effects of the local weather, geology and geography on those species. In the longer term I fervently believe that the most effective route to the preservation of wilderness is by teaching the youth of today to recognise, touch, feel and taste it so that they become a part of the natural world rather than passing observers.

Plants

Plants are an important wild food resource, providing carbohydrate, vitamins and minerals. Although widespread across our planet, there are regions of the Earth where for practical purposes there are no vegetable food sources which we can utilise, most particularly in the subarctic forests and northern lands beyond. Here, before the arrival of trade goods, the indigenous population would eat the fermented contents of reindeer or caribou paunches to obtain vitamins C, B and K.

Today in the far north this practice has all but disappeared with the availability of processed foods.

Learning to recognise edible plants is a rewarding study that greatly improves our appreciation and understanding of wild places. Even if you are no amateur botanist you can learn to recognise a few important edible species of plant. While the expert forager will utilise a wide range of plant foods, for the purpose of survival we need only learn a handful of plants for each region we find ourselves in.

For survival use a plant should be common, provide carbohydrate, ideally for a prolonged period of the year, be easily used without the need for complicated processing and be easily recognised. If it can be confused for a toxic species you must know how to differentiate between them. Try always to learn to recognise the habitat in which the plant grows; this will enable you to more easily find food in the landscape as a whole.

Bear in mind that the most energy rich plant foods are those with edible roots, seeds (including nuts), or fruits. Of lesser survival value are the greens, which contain less nourishment but which will supply a ready source of vitamins and minerals.

Once you can correctly identify an edible plant you must also know how to process it. Plants have a wide range of defence mechanisms from thorns to a complex array of toxins that can kill quickly, cause serious dermatitis and blister the predator's mouth, interfere with the predator's ability to reproduce, or even cause slow starvation by preventing the conversion of carbohydrate to energy. You will therefore not be surprised to learn that many humans have fallen victim to plant toxins, particularly the more subtle ones which act slowly. Perhaps the most famous example was the death of Burke and Wills, who were poisoned in Australia by failing to correctly process a plant called Nardoo.

Energy equation

Almost nothing about foraging is straightforward. Novices are often under the impression that you simply walk along picking the odd leaf here or there. In fact the process is far more difficult as you are expending considerable amounts of energy to obtain energy. Obviously it is important to maximise your return while reducing your expenditure. This means being able to prioritise your locally available food sources and having the right knowledge to obtain them easily. For example, roots growing in sandy soils are frequently larger than those in clay and are considerably easier to extract. Bear in mind that it may be better to collect several small roots that are easily dug up than to struggle excavating one large root from difficult soil. These are considerations that our ancestors would have been keenly aware of. Also bear in mind that there are techniques that will maximise the collection and processing of wild foods; for example, beech nuts open when warmed by the fire, saving tedious work splitting open the cases. Acorns can be winnowed from leaf litter or put into a slow flowing stream where they sink while the leaf litter floats away.

Roots

Cat-tail Typha *spp*

Cat-tail roots

Cat-tail *Typha spp*

This plant is often described as the supermarket of survival. There are so many parts of the plant that can be used for food that it must be top of our list. The real magic of Cat-tail, or as it is otherwise known Greater Reedmace, is that it can provide carbohydrate at just about any season of the year. It is also very easily identified and grows in a very predictable location. Cat-tail is the plant that we will probably be most familiar with, having seen it in flower arrangements inside a church at Harvest Festival season. It's the plant that has a seed head which looks like a sausage on a stick and grows in ditches at the margins of ponds and in areas of very slow flowing water.

It is the root that provides the most use in this plant. If you reach down underneath the plant into the ooze in which it grows you will find rope-like rhizomes stretching sideways as a subterranean mat intertwining and interlocking with each other. If you pull these up carefully they are a creamy yellow colour with lots of small rootlets on the outside. They feel somewhat leathery and a little hollow. If you cut one through you will find a spongy layer just underneath the outer surface enclosing a tightly compressed bundle of long fibres covered in a starchy substance.

This is the most important part of the plant and has a very high food value. The easiest way to use this is simply to harvest these roots and then to break them into lengths of about 30–40cm and throw them on to the embers of a fire until they are charred black all over. This done, remove them from the fire, break the outer surface and pull the central fibres free with your teeth and suck the starchy pulp from them, spitting the fibres out. Cooked correctly they taste like warm sweet chestnut and are quite delicious. They can also be eaten raw but they don't taste anywhere near as good and you may run the risk of picking up a parasite from the water.

Other parts of the Cat-tail are also edible. The young shoots or corms emerging from the base of the central flowering stem of the plant can be collected and stir-fried. The central starchy core at the base of the flowering stem, which is very hard and white, can be diced and added to stews for long slow cooking or can even be sliced thinly and deep fried to make an improvised form of potato chip. As the flowering shoot emerges from a new plant the base of the plant in the early summer and late spring can be cut free from the root and you will see that it resembles a leek, often referred to as Cossack Asparagus. The white tip to this part of the plant is frequently eaten raw or sliced and added to salads and is quite delicious. As the flower head begins to develop you will find that, like an ear of sweetcorn, it will be encased in folded leaves and a light emerald green in colour. This provides a good mid-season snack and can be collected and steamed lightly and served with butter just like corn on the cob. As the flower head emerges the upper part of the plant will develop a strong cone of brilliant chrome yellow pollen and this can be collected and was a traditional favourite ingredient added to conventional flour to improve the nutritional value of bannocks and other improvised trail breads and biscuits.

The plant has quite a few other uses: the leaves can be used to improvise rope and other cordage and woven into mats for cooking and other purposes. The dried flowering stalk from the previous year makes very good hand drill, although somewhat delicate, and the seed head can be used for tinder. The seed heads can also be collected and used to stuff clothing to improvise a duvet by placing the broken open seed heads in between the lining and outer layer of a jacket.

Burdock *Arctium spp*

Burdock is a wonderful wild food and it has to be one of my favourites. It occurs at the edge of woodland and in disturbed open ground. It comprises a large heart-shaped leaf with a very distinctive rich, musty odour. You will probably recognise this plant as in its second year it grows with a flowering stalk on which are spiky round seed heads which attach themselves very effectively to woollen clothing as we brush past this plant.

Burdock is a biennial, which means it completes its life cycle over a period of two years. In the first year it grows from a seed, puts up leaves and by the magic of photosynthesis uses the leaves as solar panels to collect sunlight and convert that into starch which it stores within its ever swelling root. At the end of the first year's growth the plant dies back and over winter the starches in the root turn to sugar so that come spring in the second year of the plant it can put up leaves more swiftly, collect more sunlight and then use this energy to create its flowering stalk. which then grows to a height of a metre, sometimes even a metre and a half, where it sets seeds and eventually dies.

For food we must collect the root of burdock from the completion of its first year's growth to the beginning of its second year's growth. Only then is the root full of carbohydrate and succulent. Spring roots are sweeter than autumn gathered roots and can be eaten raw, while autumn and winter gathered roots are best roasted in hot ashes or diced into stews. If roasting the root in ashes roast it in its rind. otherwise the 5mm thick rind should be peeled away before cooking. The only difficulty with collecting burdock is its preference for growing in hard ground; roots collected in soft ground are not only a more efficient return for your labour they are also frequently larger in size.

These related plants are very widespread, considered today to be weeds of arable land. Once they may have been important edible plants. Despite giving milky sap their roots can be eaten after first scraping away the outer rind, slicing and soaking in plenty of water for an hour or more. Then they can be added to stews or roasted as a parsnip-like vegetable. Dandelion and Sow Thistle can be rather bitter, but much less so the Bristly Ox Tongue. These roots are far less bitter when collected before the plant flowers.

Burdock *Arctium spp*

The root of a burdock after a year's growth is swollen with starchy goodness.

Dandelion *Taraxacum officinale*

Sow Thistle *Sonchus oleraceus*

Bristly Ox Tongue
Picris echioides

Pig Nut *Conopodium majus –
likes shady woods.*

Pig Nut *Conopodium majus –
note the 90° turn in the stem.*

Pig Nut *Conopodium majus*

Pig Nut *Conopodium majus*

Pig Nut is a true wild delicacy. Its delicate leaves can be found by the observant forager from May to July. It is the raw radish-like root that is eaten, which can range in size from marble to golfball. Fresh and crunchy, it is a favourite spring nibble or salad plant. The plant defends itself from foragers by means of a thread-thin attachment between the stem and tuber, which turns through ninety degrees just as it leaves the tuber. Consequently these tubers can only be harvested by carefully following the stem down to the tuber. The tuber has a thin brown skin which can easily be squeezed off before eating.

Lesser Celandine *Ranunculus ficaria in flower.*

Lesser Celandine
Ranunculus ficaria

Lesser Celandine *Ranunculus ficaria*

Lesser Celandine is an early spring flower that exploits the light of the forest floor prior to the growth of leaves in the forest canopy. It has small flask shaped tubers up to two centimetres in length which can be harvested in large quantities in the late spring after the flower has begun to die back and the leaves have turned yellow. These must be cooked before eating; they can be boiled in two changes of water or roasted in hot ashes. No other parts of this plant should be eaten.

Ramsons *Allium ursinum*

Ramsons *Allium ursinum*

Ramsons are wild onions and frequently announce their presence to the nose before the eye. They can be collected and used like spring onions, although eaten raw their onion flavour is overpowering and long lasting. Better to collect the tubers and roast them gently in hot embers until golden brown, after which they taste like shallots. Or try braising them in a beef or vegetable stock. Used sparingly they can be an adventurous ingredient in our outdoors kitchen.

Rosebay Willowherb *Epilobium angustifolium*

The roots of Rosebay Willowherb can be used for food; however, without careful preparation they will be disappointingly bitter. Collect the roots before the plant flowers, scrape the outside of the root and remove the central brown thread in the root before roasting the roots in hot ashes.

Thistles *Cirsium sp*

All thistles are edible, despite their prickles. Some thistles are perennial, others biennial; whichever, the secret to harvesting succulent roots is to collect them at the completion of their first year's growth. Cook them by roasting in hot ashes.

Water Plantain *Alisma plantago-aquatica*

Water Plantain has always struck me as a plant with a noble bearing. Its very distinctive leaf emerges from mud beside slow flowing water. The root can be gathered and eaten after boiling with two changes of water.

True Bulrush *Scirpus lacustris*
Club Rush *Scirpus maritimus*

Both these water plants have edible underground parts which can be eaten after roasting in hot ashes. They pose a forager the problem of how to access them as the most productive part of the plant needs to be harvested from the deepest water. However, they have been an important food resource for many native peoples due to the great quantity that can be harvested.

Rosebay Willowherb
Epilobium angustifolium

Thistles *Cirsium sp*

Water Plantain
Alisma plantago-aquatica

True Bulrush *Scirpus lacustris*

Seeds

Next in importance to carbohydrates found in roots and inner bark is that found in the seeds of trees, plants and grasses. Here we will concentrate on the most useful, starting with the fat hens and melds. These are particularly heavily endowed with seeds which can be collected and added simply to stews or soups as a thickening, or they can be dried and ground up with a small amount of water and dribbled on to a hot rock or hot ashes to form a very simple native bannock. The seeds of Greater Plantain can also be used in this way; they can often be collected in large quantities and are rich in mucilage. They can be ground up or used as is in soups as a thickening agent or to make a simple bannock again. Delicious used in this way, giving a rye-flavoured biscuit.

Acorns *Quercus spp*

Acorns *Quercus spp*
One of the most important of all seeds throughout the temperate and semi-arid areas is that from the oak tree. Acorns can be collected by gathering them with leaf litter from underneath the tree. Place this into slow flowing water where the acorns sink and the leaves are carried away. They can then be dried in front of the fire, which will open the shell, and they are then removed laboriously from the shells. The dried and roasted acorn can be used to make coffee, or if you boil the acorn in many changes of water to remove the tannins that turn the water brown they can then be ground up to make a flour substitute which can be used to make a warming mush cooked with a hot rock or cooked into a bannock in hot ashes.

Sweet Chestnut *Castanea sativa*
Much more palatable than acorns are sweet chestnuts, and these wonderful, very spiny nutcases can be broken open to reveal the fruit. This is a nut which is sold at Christmas time on the streets of northern cities and can be eaten raw, although I think they are at their best once cooked. I like particularly to add them to a bannock recipe with crab apple and cook them in that way. Quite delicious.

Hazelnuts *Corylus avellana*
Hazelnuts, again, are a wonderful food, particularly popular in the south east of the United Kingdom where we call them cob nuts or filberts. These are usually collected from low bushes, which are heavily laden with them. They are at their best when they are just ripe, but you have to beat the squirrels to them which is not always easy! Unfortunately hazelnuts do not keep particularly well, and so perhaps in the past they were used less as a storage food and more of a food of the moment. They are delicious raw, and you just need to improvise a nutcracker from a fork of a hazel branch and crack the nuts to extract the meat.

Sweet Chestnut *Castanea sativa*

Walnuts *Juglans regia*

Walnuts, now much less common than they were in the past, are a familiar food and can be collected where there are plenty of walnut trees.

Beechnuts *Fagus sylvatica*

Beechnuts, or beech mast to use the traditional name, are one of my favourite foods. They are very high in oil but the trees do not always produce good kernels. You have to keep an eye on the trees as the season goes by, and if you find them laden with productive beech mast you will notice this at a distance because the branches will droop more heavily as they are weighed down by the weight of the seeds. These can then be collected and the seed cases held in front of the fire where they warm and burst open to reveal the three-sided nut. This has a brown outer layer which must be broken open to reveal the meat inside. They are absolutely delicious and energy-rich.

Grass and Sedge Seeds

Some grasses can be used to produce good seed but you must take care here to ensure there is no black Ergot fungus growing in the seed heads. Take time to learn to recognise this infestation because it is potentially lethal. Akin to grasses are sedges and all sedges are edible. Perhaps the most useful of these is the Pendulous Sedge, which grows in a very majestic way in the open shade of temperate woodland, the seed heads bowing over heavily laden with seeds which can be very easily collected and dried, ground with a small amount of water to a paste, dribbled on to hot ashes or rock and cooked as a simple damper.

Walnuts *Juglans regia*

Beechnuts *Fagus sylvatica*

Grass and Sedge Seeds

Nettle *Urtica spp*

Mallow *Malva sylvestris*

Hedge Garlic *Alliaria petiolata*

Greens

Nettle *Urtica spp*

The prime green food of the northern temperate zone has to be the stinging nettle. Very easily identified and recognised, the nettle, when used with seasonings and other ingredients, can produce one of the most healthful and delicious foods. It is also an extremely abundant plant. The secret is to use the young leaf tops at the top of the nettle stem; never use old or nasty looking nettle leaves, simply go for the tenderest looking leaves. Once cooked or parboiled they lose their stinging property and are quite delicious incorporated in other foods. They can be bitter if you don't have any other ingredients to add to them, but used in a small quantity in a survival stew they will prove effective.

Mallow *Malva sylvestris*

Next in importance to nettle is mallow. Mallow leaves make some of the best soup of all the wild greens, very popular in the Middle East and quite delicious. Unfortunately today we only see mallow growing alongside roads and motorways; it is a great indictment of the way we manage our landscape that there are fewer habitats to be found away from roads and sources of pollution where these wild foods grow.

Rosebay Willowherb *Epilobium angustifolium*

Fire Weed or Rosebay Willowherb is a popular green. The young leaves can be used as a potherb or they can be dried and used to produce a tea; the very young shoots can be steamed and peeled as an asparagus–like food. The pith can be removed from the mature growing stalks and used to thicken soups. You need quite a lot to act as a thickening agent but it does work effectively. Rosebay Willowherb is also used to produce cordage and tinder (see relevant sections earlier in the book).

Hedge Garlic *Alliaria petiolata*

Hedge Garlic or Jack by the Hedge grows as its name suggests in the dark shade beside hedgerows and country lanes. It is a quite wonderful plant with a very strong garlic flavour and can be used in small quantities added to salads or to stuff food steamed underneath the fire. It is a very useful plant.

Sorrels *Oxalis acetosella, Rumex acetosa, Rumex acetosella*
Wood sorrel, common sorrel and sheep sorrel have a very acidic flavour somewhat akin to apple peel and can be used raw in small quantities to remove the flavour of less palatable wild foods or stuffed into fish steamed underground. Particularly good is sorrel sliced very fine and stuffed inside a trout for steaming.

Sea Beat *Beta vulgaris*
Sea Beat is often mistaken for spinach, so closely does it resemble it and it can be used in exactly the same way. It is a very good alternative to spinach and found very commonly along rivers close to estuaries and along the coastal shoreline.

Sea Purslane *Halimione portulacoides*
Sea Purslane inhabits the salty margins of estuarine rivers, estuaries and mud flats. These fleshy salty leaves can be a wonderful addition to a wild meal if lightly steamed first; a particularly good accompaniment to fish caught on the coast such as sea bass.

Oxalis acetosella.

Rumex acetosa

Sea Purslane *Halimione portulacoides*

Fruit

Fruits are a seasonal glut which should not be ignored and here there are many wonderful offerings to be had in the wild. Some indigenous people would collect their fruits and mash them into a pulp on a finely woven mat, which could then be held over warm, dry, smoky air to create what's called a fruit leather as a means of preservation. These can then be rolled up and stored in the winter months. Today, with refrigeration available in even remote rural communities, this is seldom done.

Bilberry *Vaccinium myrtillus*

Elderberry Sambucus nigra.

Wild Apples *Malus sylvestris*

Bilberries *Vaccinium myrtillus*
The bilberry grows on low bushes in much of the temperate zone, and in Siberia these berries are collected by the use of quite a unique birch bark basket designed to be swept through the bush, dislodging the berries and then collecting them at the end of the sweep. Bilberries and blueberries for that matter are not really good food to be nibbling on in a survival situation as they have a tendency to lower our blood sugar level, but used with other ingredients, such as added to breads and bannock mixtures with a little touch of sugar, they are a wonderful flavouring that really shouldn't be passed up.

Elderberries *Sambucus nigra*
Elderberries can prove to be emetic if eaten in large quantities from the bush, and we must take care not to confuse the ordinary elderberry with the poisonous dwarf elderberry. But elderberries can be dried and then added to breads and bannocks as flavouring or cooked and added to stews even. They are often found in great abundance and they have various other uses, including the manufacture of hand drill sticks.

Wild Apples *Malus sylvestris*
Crab apples are an astonishing wild food. They are the ancestor of all of our domestic apples, yet because of their crabbiness or bitter taste they are very often completely disregarded by people today, yet once cooked they lose that property and work just as well as any ordinary apple. Certainly if I am cooking a wild pie I would much rather use crab apples than conventional apples, and they can be collected in large quantities quite easily in the autumn, shaking them down from the bush. Consider them not just as a survival source of sugar but even a potential addition to some savoury dishes, particularly in risottos with wild mushrooms. The crab apple can be just toasted over a fire until the skin is soft and loosened so it can be squeezed off easily and eaten just as it is. This is a very good way of using them in the wild, providing a sugary delicacy.

Rosehips *Rosa canina*

Rosehips are well known for their vitamin C content, partly because during the Second World War large quantities of rosehips were collected and used in the home to provide vitamin rich rosehip syrup. The important thing to remember about rosehips is that they contain small seeds covered in tiny hairs, which can irritate our gut, so they must first be cleaned of these seeds. They way I like to use them in the wild is, having cleaned them to take the bright orange seed cases and infuse them for ten or fifteen minutes, drink the liquid as an impromptu rosehip tea, and then to eat the seed cases themselves. Having infused them, the cell walls will burst and the flavour is greatly improved. The other advantage of rosehips is that they can be found throughout the winter.

Sloes *Prunus spinosa*

Sloe berries are blue, round berries about the size of a marble that grow on the blackthorn bush. They are very tart and have a high tannin content but this can be greatly reduced by cooking, and in fact we know from large quantities of the seeds found at prehistoric sites that they were once a very popular food. A good way of using them is to deseed and dry them and then add them to other things such as breads and bannocks.

Bullace

This is related to the sloe but suffers from none of the sloe's tartness. Bullace is the wild plum and more plum shaped but still only quite small. It is a delicious wild food, a real gem when you find it and something well worth looking out for.

Blackberries *Rubus fruticosus*

Blackberries need very little introduction. They are one of the most common and popular wild foods. Few children haven't discovered the joys of the blackberry, and absolutely brilliant eating they are too. Dried leaves from blackberry can be used as a tea substitute.

Rosehips *Rosa canina*

Sloes *Prunus spinosa*

Bullace

Blackberries Rubus fruticosus

Raspberry *Rubus idaeus*

Raspberry *Rubus idaeus*

Wild raspberries are also to be found in many woodland edges and hedgerows and they are quite delicious. Raspberry has to be my favourite fruit, and the leaves of raspberry mixed with the dried leaves of blackberry, make a very acceptable tea substitute.

Cloudberries *Rubus chamaemorus*

Cloudberries are found mainly in mountainous and moorland regions or in the forests of the very far north. They are a very rich flavoured, wonderful orange looking raspberry growing on a very low shrub, more of an Arctic berry, but found sometimes on the edge of the temperate zone.

Cherries *Prunus avium, Prunus padus*

Wild cherries can also be found. They are only very small and have a large pit in the middle which must be removed because it contains cyanide, but the cherry flesh itself is every bit as good in the wild fruit as in the cultivated, it's just much smaller. The problem is getting to the cherry before the birds get to them, and for this reason few people have eaten wild cherries. The wild cherry, *Prunus avium*, occurs quite high up in the forest canopy and is difficult to reach, whereas the Bird Cherry. which is more common towards the west of the UK, is more of a shrub, allowing the cherries to be more easily collected.

Fungi

Around the world edible fungi are collected in the wild; many are highly prized. In terms of survival education they are frequently ignored, it being suggested that the poor calorific return from fungi does not compensate for to the potential risk of collecting a poisonous fungus. Certainly there is risk associated with collecting toxic fungi, which in certain cases can cause irreversible and fatal poisoning, yet in a remote situation the same risk exists for the gathering of edible berries and roots. As for the food value of fungi, this should not necessarily be measured in calories alone. Fungi are rich in minerals, are filling food and above all can transform bland dishes into cordon bleu feasts.

The forager of any wild food must be well able to differentiate edible from poisonous. The real problem with fungi is that they can pose more subtle problems in identification than plants. While it is perfectly feasible for a novice to teach themselves to identify plants by the sole use of a field guide, it is not wise to attempt this for fungi. If you are interested in eating wild mushrooms you should attend a field study course where you will be able to study the fungi you are interested in with confirmed identification. After such training field guides become infinitely more useful. Bear always in mind that the only true way to differentiate between poisonous and edible fungi is by the acquisition of knowledge and by learning to recognise specific species. Do not eat any fungus unless you are certain of its identification. For all practical purposes poisonous fungi are not rendered safe by cooking. Indeed the testimony of victims reveals that many of the most lethal species actually taste pleasant before and after cooking, including the aptly named Death Cap, *Amanita phalloides*. Lethal fungi are also frequently consumed by animals and invertebrates, but this is not an indication that we can eat them.

IF IN DOUBT - LEAVE IT OUT

This fungus, the Death Cap, is absolutely fatal. Victims have reported that it is delicious.

Know your poisonous fungi

The most poisonous fungi belong to the Death Cap family *Amanitaceae,* of which there are over 20 species to be found within the United Kingdom. Not all members of the family are poisonous, Caesars Mushroom, *Amanita caesarea* (not found in the UK) is one of the most sought after edible mushrooms. However, for survival purposes we err on the side of caution, considering all members of this family to be poisonous. Members of this family possess the characteristic features that you should learn to recognise. (see page 192).

191

Death Cap *(Amanita phalloides): note the basal sac reaching up the stem, the white skirt beneath the cap and the olive green colour of the cap.*

How to recognise the *Amanita* family

(1) A universal veil which encloses the immature fruit body.
In some species (such as the Fly Agaric *Amanita muscaria* and Panther Cap*Amanita pantherina*) remnants of this remain as white spots/scales on the cap surface of the mature fungus. These spots/scales can be easily brushed off or washed away by rain.

(2) A skirt or ring under the cap.
In other species (such as the Death Cap *Amanita phalloides,* and Grisette *Amanita vaginata*) remnants of the universal veil remain as a basal sac or volva.
A skirt is commonly found around the stem beneath the cap, although it is sometimes absent

(3) All members of this family have white spores.
These can sometimes be seen in the characteristic gill pattern coating leaves beneath the toadstool. If not they can be observed by placing the cap on to a smooth dark surface overnight. The spores of poisonous *Amanitas* are also extremely poisonous.

(4) All British species have white/cream gills, free of the stem.

(5) Cap colour varies
Olive-green cap for the Death Cap *Amanita phalloides*.
White for Destroying Angel *Amanita virosa*.
Red for Fly Agaric *Amanita muscaria*.
Brown for Panther Cap *Amanita pantherina*.

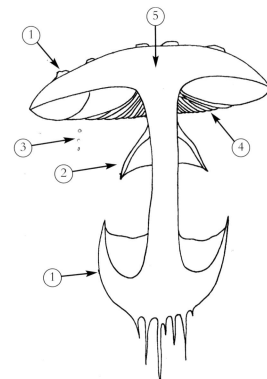

POISONOUS AMANITAS

- The Death Cap *Amanita phalloides*
- Destroying Angel *Amanita virosa*
- Fly Agaric *Amanita muscaria*
- Panther Cap *Amanita pantherina*
- The Blusher *Amanita rubescens*
- Grisette *Amanita vaginata*
- Tawny Grisette *Amanita fulva*
- The Spring Amanita *Amanita verna*
- *Amanita echinocephala*
- *Amanita gemmata*

OTHER POISONOUS FAMILIES

Apart from the Death Cap family there are many other poisonous fungi to be avoided. Certain other families pose a threat to the unwary forager, most notably the:
- Cortinarius family *Cortiariaceae* (particularly *Cortinarius speciosissimus* and *Cortinarius orellanus*)

Also included in the family are:
- The Inocybe family (particularly the Red Staining Inocybe *Inocybe patouillardii*)
- The Hebeloma family

In addition to these families the following species have been mistaken for edible species:
- False Morel *Gyromitra esculenta*
- *Entoloma sinuatum*
- Yellow Stainer *Agaricus xanthoderma*
- Brown Roll-rim *Paxillus involutus*
- Satan's Boletus *Boletus satanus*
- *Boletus erythropus*
- *Boletus luridus*
- Woolly Milk Cap *Lactarius torminosus*
- *Lactarius pubescens*
- Common Earthball *Scleroderma citrinum*
- *Scleroderma verrucosum*
- Sulphur Tuft *Hypholoma fasiculare*
- False Chanterelle *Hygrophoropsis aurantiaca*
- The Sickener *Russula emetica*
- Beechwood Sickener *Russula mairei*

The Death Cap *Amanita phalloides*

Boletus erythropus

Fly Agaric *Amanita muscaria*

Common Earthball *Scleroderma citrinum*

Panther Cap *Amanita pantherina*

Beechwood Sickener *Russula mairei*

Most cases of poisoning occur when toxic species are confused with edible species, and a useful question to ask of the victims or their mushroom-picking benefactors is the identity of the mushroom they thought they were picking. In the absence of a well-preserved specimen, the answer to this question could narrow the possible suspects considerably.

SENSITIVITY: some people are undoubtedly sensitive to some kinds of mushrooms, especially if eaten raw, e.g. the Wood Blewit *Lepista nuda,* and Chicken of the Woods *Laetiporus sulpureus.*

Collecting fungi for food

Many fungi are good eating, and if care and caution is exercised a large proportion of them can be identified in the field by eye.

When you are collecting fungi for eating follow these rules to avoid making unnecessary mistakes in identification:

1. Do not collect baby/button stage fungi. It can be difficult to positively identify immature fungi.

2. Handle the fungus carefully to prevent damage that may impair its identification.

3. Make certain that you have all of the fungus; the base of the stem can be vital to correct identification.

4. Do not collect old or decaying fungi. Fungi that are old can be difficult to identify correctly because their colours change and their distinguishing features become damaged.

5. Do not eat any fungus unless you are 100% certain of its identification.

6. When collecting do not mix poisonous with edible species.

7. Having positively identified an edible fungus always cook it before eating.

IF IN DOUBT - LEAVE IT OUT

FUNGI GROWING FROM THE GROUND

WITH A SPONGY LAYER UNDER THE CAP

These fungi are generally referred to as 'Boletus' fungi. They are very prized and collected in many countries in large numbers. They are one of the safest forms of fungi for beginners. If you cut the cap in half you will see that the sponge-like layer is comprised of many parallel tubes. Some of these fungi will exhibit a rapid colour change to blue on cutting or bruising; this is not an indicator of the edibility of the fungus.

– Penny Bun *Boletus edulis*
– Bitter Bolete *Tylopilus felleus*
– Bay Boletus *Xerocomus badius*
– Summer Boletus *Boletus aereus*
– Brown Birch Boletus *Leccinum scabrum*
– Orange Birch Boletus *Leccinum versipelle*
– Oak Boletus *Leccinum quercinum*
– Aspen Boletus *Leccinum aurantiacum*
– Slippery Jack *Suillus luteus*
– Larch Bolete *Suillus bovinus*

Penny Bun *Boletus edulis*

Penny Bun (alternative form).

Bitter Bolete
Tylopilus felleus

Bay Boletus
Xerocomus badiu

Brown Birch Boletus
Leccinum scabrum

Oak Boletus
Leccinum quercinum

Slippery Jack
Suillus luteus

WITH SPINES UNDER THE CAP

These fungi are generally referred to as 'Hedgehog' fungi. Within the UK none is poisonous although some are too tough to eat.

Hedgehog Fungus *Hydnum repandum*
Yellowish with pale flesh coloured cap. Can grow in large numbers. Deciduous and coniferous woodland. Excellent eating.

Hedgehog Fungus *Hydnum rufescens*
Salmony orange–brown cap. Can grow in large numbers. Deciduous and coniferous woodland. Excellent eating.

Sarcodon imbricatum
Velvety reddish–purplish brown cap, cracking into overlapping scales (not removable). Pale flesh coloured background. Most frequent in Scottish pine forests.

Hedgehog Fungus *Hydnum repandum*

TRUMPET SHAPED WITHOUT GILLS, SPONGE OR SPINES

Horn of Plenty *Craterellus cornucopides*
Blacket trumpet-like fungus fading grey with age. Often found in large groups in leaf litter. They dry well and are good flavouring for a survival stew.

Horn of Plenty
Craterellus cornucopides

Giant Puffball
Langermannia gigantea

Calvatia utriformis

The Common Puffball
Lycoperdon perlatum

BALL SHAPED FUNGI

Ball shaped fungi are called puffballs because of the way they disperse their spores. Before they mature to this puffing stage they can be collected for food.

PUFFBALL GUIDELINES
The flesh of a puffball must be pure white when cut through without any signs of the development of other features.

> AVOID:
> - Puffballs that have a yellow or purple colour inside or that have turned to spores.
> - Earthballs which can be mistaken for puffballs. These have a rubbery outer layer and a rich cream interior when very young which turns deep purple to black inside as the fungus matures.
> Button stage fungi that show the shape of the developing toadstool.

Giant Puff Ball *Langermannia gigantea*
The Giant puffball is difficult to mistake, a large round white fungus most often about the size of a football. When cut through it should exhibit smooth, firm, textured, creamy white flesh with no signs of any features such as stem or gills developing internally.

Calvatia utriformis
A white ball-shaped fungus about the size of a tennis ball with a short stubby stem.

The Common Puffball *Lycoperdon perlatum*
A white puffball about the size of a ping-pong ball, with a short stem. Its outer surface is covered with tiny spines that brush off easily.

The Stump Puffball *Lycoperdon pyriforme*
A beige to brown coloured puffball slightly smaller than a ping-pong ball with a short stem. This puffball only grows on wood which may be buried in leaf litter.

FUNGI WITH GILLS
(LIKE THE COMMON/TRUE MUSHROOM)

Most poisonings occur with gill bearing fungi. Particularly when confused for the true mushroom or the chanterelle.

IF IN DOUBT – LEAVE THE GILLED FUNGI OUT

True Mushrooms

The true mushroom MUST have a ring round the stem and MUST have gills turning pink to chocolate.

One member of the mushroom family can give alarming symptoms of sweating and stomach cramps –Yellow Stainer *Agaricus xanthoderma*. This is a true mushroom but when handled or bruised it turns a very bright yellow and has an unpleasant smell of carbolic. It does not affect everyone, but it is best avoided. It is frequently found on the margin of deciduous woodland.

Judge's Wig/Shaggy Ink Cap *Coprinus comatus*
A very distinctive fungus like its common name. Also known as Shaggy Ink Cap because of the large white scales with brownish tips. This fungus is upright and all white in colour. (Do not confuse it with the black and white capped Magpie Ink Cap *Coprinus picaceus*.) Eat only young specimens, before the gills have started to dissolve into the inky spore-bearing liquid.

Judge's Wig/Shaggy Inkcap *Coprinus comatus*.

Magpie Inkcap – not edible.

Parasol Mushroom
Lepiota procera

A very large fungus with an excellent taste. Sometimes almost as big as a dinner plate. Cream coloured gills and cap with shaggy scales (scales cannot be brushed off). The stem has a large double 'sliding' ring and snake-like markings.

Shaggy Parasol
Lepiota rhacodes

A similar fungus to *L.procera,* cream coloured gills, cap with very shaggy scales (scales cannot be brushed off). The stem has a large double 'sliding' ring but without the snake-like markings. Flesh turns red on cutting. Although also edible it can cause stomach upsets in some people.

Chanterelle
Cantharellus cibarius

A wonderful fungus to find which is seldom wormy and one of the best edible species. It can grow in large numbers in woodland, often near pine. It is a wavy edged trumpet-shaped fungus with egg-yellow gills, which more resemble veins running down the stem. Smells of apricots. The stem is robust and tends to snap cleanly when bent.

Honey Fungus *Armillaria mellea*

This fungus can be found in large areas of woodland and can grow in dense clusters at the base of trees. Although edible, honey fungus can be mildly toxic if eaten raw, so it must be cooked, even if only boiled up for a few minutes (the water then discarded). Honey fungus is very varied in form but generally speaking, as the name suggests, is honey-coloured and has gills off-white to dark brown. The stem has a ring. Several other fungus species grow in groups in this manner and can be harmful (in particular the toxic Sulphur Tuft *Hypholoma fasiculare,* which has sulphur-coloured gills) so care must be taken in the identification of this species.
IF IN DOUBT LEAVE HONEY FUNGUS OUT

RISKS OF CONFUSION

Chanterelle is one of the most sought after of edible fungi; inevitably their have been deaths and serious poisonings when the unwary have mistaken it for other species. Particularly *Cortinarius speciosissimus, Cortinarius orellanus,* neither of which has gills running down the stem and have a distinctive radishy scent.

More easily mistaken for Chanterelle is the False Chanterelle, *Hygrophoropsis aurantiaca,* which can grow near to the true chanterelle. This has a more red-orange colour, more blade like gills which do run down the stem. The stem is more flexible and tends to green-stick fracture when bent. The scent of apricots is absent.

In the USA Chanterelle can be confused with Jack O'Lantern *Omphalotus illudens.* This has crowded bright orange blade-like gills that run down the stem, but lacks the distinctive apricot odour of Chanterelle. An unusual feature of this fungus is that fresh the gills glow a bright greenish yellow in the dark.

Fungi growing on trees

AT THE BASE OF MATURE SCOTS PINE TREES

The Cauliflower Fungus *Sparassis crispa*
20–50cm across. Found usually in a large clump at the base of mature Scots pines or nearby. This soft, rubbery, brain-like fungus is very distinctive and large specimens will last for days. Portions dry well hung up on strings. Excellent eating.

The Cauliflower Fungus *Sparassis crispa*

ON THE TRUNKS OF STANDING MATURE TREES ABOVE WAIST HEIGHT

Chicken of the Woods *Laetiporus sulphureus*
15–50cm across. A spectacular fungus growing mostly on yew, cherry, sweet chestnut, oak and mature willow. Brilliant yellow to orange with a velvet-like texture, it usually grows in tiers and resembles polystyrene pouring out of the tree. It darkens with age before eventually fading white when it dries. Best sliced finely and fried or added to a survival stew.

Ox Tongue or Beef Steak Fungus *Fistulina hepatica*
As its name suggests it resembles a large liver or tongue. It usually grows above shoulder height on oak and sweet chestnut trees, large logs and stumps. When cut through it looks like steak and has a blood-like sap. Bitter to taste, it is best sliced into chunks soaked in salt water for at least two hours before kebabing with other wild foods. Eaten hot it resembles steak.

Oyster Fungus *Pleurotus ostreatus*
6–14cm across. Blue-grey shell shaped fungus growing in clusters, one on top of the other. Found on the trunks and stumps of dead or decaying trees, particularly beech, often in large masses.

Pleurotus cornucopiae
Similar to *P. ostreatus* but with a cream colour and growing usually on oak, beech and elm.

Chicken of the Woods
Laetiporus sulphureus

Ox Tongue or Beef Steak
Fungus *Fistulina hepatica*

Oyster Fungus *Pleurotus ostreatus*

Pleurotus cornucopiae

GROWING ON THE STEMS AND BRANCHES OF ELDER

Jew's Ear *Auricularia auricula judae*
2–4 cm across. This brown ear-like fungus is easily recognised, particularly when growing on elder. Rubbery and elastic, its outer surface is velvety. In dry weather it shrinks and dries hard, in which state it can be picked and stored for rehydrating by soaking in warm water or dropping into the survival stew at a later time.

Jew's Ear *Auricularia auricula judae*

Lichen

This is perhaps one of the most unlikely food resources. In biological terms lichen are distinct organisms, based on a symbiotic relationship between fungi and algae. Some lichen are edible and have been used as food in times of famine, while others are eaten as a rare delicacy. They can sometimes be found in great quantity, but you will use a lot of energy in cleaning them. Only a few species of lichen are toxic, such as wolf lichen, *Letharia vulpina*.

Slow-growing edible lichen should be collected for food only in times of extreme shortage and where they grow in abundance. They contain acids which make them unpalatable and, more seriously, can cause an emetic reaction. The acids can be neutralised by boiling them in a solution of bicarbonate of soda or, if this is not available, an alkaline solution made by boiling wood ash in water. Strain the lichen, then boil again in fresh water. They are an unappealing foodstuff with little flavour, but can be added to other wild foods for their carbohydrate.

Iceland Moss *Cetraria islandica*
This lichen is common in Arctic and sub-Arctic regions. Boil the lichen in several changes of water then dry it to reduce the bitterness. Powder it and boil it again. Skim off any scum before consumption. Flavour is decidedly lacking, so use the lichen broth as the base of a soup made with other more flavourful ingredients.

Lichen has to be one of the most unlikely sources of food.

Old Man's Beard *Lichen Alectoria sp* and *Bryoria sp*
Like cotton wool, these lichen festoon trees in the far north. They are commonly used as tinder but can also be eaten. Collect the lichen and pick out as many needles and twigs as possible, then boil in a solution of bicarbonate of soda or wood ash. In British Columbia these lichen were cooked in ground ovens in layers with wild onion bulbs.

Rock Tripe *Umbillicaria*
The most unlikely-looking edible lichen. Dark greeny grey, it covers rocky surfaces in the north. Leathery when moist, it is brittle when dry and the most acidic of the edible lichens. After collecting the lichen wash out the grit and dry it, then boil in a solution of bicarbonate of soda or wood ash.

Reindeer Moss *Cladonia sp*
This lichen thrives in sandy conditions, particularly on the tundra. Grey-green in colour it is multi-branched, growing in tufts, which can be extensive. As its name suggests, it is the food of reindeer, which dig down and graze it from under snow in the winter. Wash and boil or fry it.

Seaweed

'Weed' suggests a nuisance plant, a sad term, because many of the finest edible herbs are considered weeds by gardeners. When it comes to the seaweeds we dismiss too easily a rich harvest that many island nations cherish. In fact most of us are unwitting daily users of products containing seaweed extracts: alginates, carrageen, agar and furcellaran are all seaweed extracts and are used in the manufacture of many popular food products such as milk shakes, ice cream, yogurt, instant desserts, fruit juices, soft drinks, wine and beer, bread, cakes, pies, salad dressings, jams and cereals. Seaweed extracts are used in the preparation of some toothpastes and in the dissolving of sutures.

The majority of us have direct contact with seaweed only when walking on the shoreline, or delving into rock pools. Usually it appears lifeless and rubbery in unappealing colours. When it rots, seaweed attracts clouds of flies and gives off a repellent odour. To appreciate seaweed, we must get into the water with it. The best time to do this is in the warm summer months, when seaweed growth is at its height. Arrange to be on a beach at low water of a spring tide: spring tides occur fortnightly throughout the year in the UK but are most extreme in March and September. At these times more of the seabed is exposed than at other times in the year.

I like to search rock pools as the tide goes out, and look for seaweed as it comes back in. Seaweed species prefer different zones of the shore: some, such as *Chorda filum,* thrive in areas of permanent water while others. like *Enteromorpha intestinalis,* tolerate exposure at low tide and therefore proliferate on the upper part of a beach. Choose an area that will not be cut off by the rising tide and snorkel with the seaweeds as the tide rises. In this way you will be able to explore the seaweed profile of your beach and, most importantly, come to appreciate the majesty and grace of these remarkable plants. Also, if you are a keen naturalist you will discover that seaweed provides habitat for a wide range of other wildlife.

It has been stated that all species of seaweed are edible, but this is not strictly true: while the majority are edible some are not worth eating and a few, notably the *Desmarestia aculeata* and *Desmarestia lingulata* species (sometimes referred to as sea sorrels), are too acidic. However, the best and most common edible seaweeds are very easily recognised.

As a source of food seaweed has traditionally been used as a substitute for other forms of agriculture, particularly where conventional farming was difficult – it plays a significant role in the Japanese diet. Seaweeds are rich in minerals, particularly iodine: in some cases, a thousand times more iodine is found in seaweed than in other vegetables. They also contain notable amounts of protein and carbohydrate. In most cases 10 per cent or more, of the dried weight of seaweed is comprised of protein and over 50 per cent carbohydrate. However, only a small proportion of the carbohydrate is digestible – in fact unless one is accustomed to eating seaweeds it is wise at first to only eat small amounts as they have a well-established reputation as a purgative. They are also quite filling.

The vitamin content of seaweeds is quite astonishing: 100g of an average seaweed can provide over half your daily requirement of vitamin C, and more than the daily requirement of vitamins A, B2, B12, sodium, potassium and magnesium. They also contains chlorine, calcium and vitamin D. Tests have shown that a diet that includes seaweed can help to prevent goitres.

So, which seaweeds are good to eat, and how do we prepare them?

Sea Lettuce *Ulva lactuca*
Without a doubt, Sea Lettuce is the most appetising seaweed to look at: its bright emerald green is somewhat reminiscent of lettuce leaves. Its other common name is green laver. I like to eat it raw, cut up into small segments and included in seafood salads. Dried and chopped up finely it is a pleasing addition to seafood soup.

Dulse *Palmaria palmata*

Dulse has beautiful translucent red fronds, a treat added to a wild salad. Well washed dulse is exceptionally good eaten raw. It is crispy-textured with a wonderful ocean flavour. Dried, it has been ground to a powder and used as a salt substitute. It has a high protein content and contains all of the trace elements we need. Rolled into tight tubes and dried, dulse make an excellent savoury trail snack for hikers. Indeed, in some parts of Peru, travellers valued it as a means of restoring energy to tired legs. Surprisingly it is excellent deep-fried like potato crisps.

Irish Moss/Carrageen *Chondrus crispus; Gigartina stellata*

Irish moss releases gelatine when boiled, as does the similar seaweed *Gigartina stellata*. They can be used to produce nourishing if bland tasting jelly. I use them as a thickening agent in soup.

The classic use for these seaweeds is to produce blancmange. Wash a good handful of the seaweed in clean water, tie it into a cheesecloth with a vanilla pod and cook it for 30 minutes with 1 litre of milk in a bain-marie. Remove the cheesecloth, sweeten, and chill.

Enteromorpha intestinalis

A delicate emerald green seaweed that floats in the high-water region of a beach; it can be easily found and used as Sea Lettuce.

Sweet Oarweed *Laminaria saccharina*

Common, and good eating, particularly the fresh young stipes cooked in a little water or steamed. As its name suggests it contains a sugar, mannitol, which crystallises when the seaweed

Laver *Porphyra umbilicaris*

Egg Wrack *Ascophyllum*

Sweet Oarweed *Laminaria saccharina*

Laver *Porphyra umbilicaris*

Laver resembles a piece of old polythene more than an edible food, but it is widely considered excellent eating, and is cultivated in Japan. It is the best known of our edible seaweeds. Laver bread takes time and effort to produce and I prefer to dry laver and eat it like dulse or diced in soups as for sea lettuce.

Egg Wrack *Ascophyllum nodosum*

The Egg or Knotted Wrack is an unlikely looking food: tough rubbery fronds with large egg-shaped flotation chambers. With a high fat and oil content, it has a delicate flavour after cooking in a little water or steaming. I like to cook this seaweed in ground ovens where it helps to protect other foods from the hot rocks. Only use the tenderest young samples.

Gathering Seaweed

Don't just empty the shore: cut young healthy specimens leaving the holdfast attached to the rock with plenty of frond still attached. Then the seaweed will continue to grow.

Shellfish

Shellfish provide rich and easily collected food and can be found in fresh and salt-water environments.

SHRIMPS

Marine shrimps are traditionally collected by either scooping them from the sea at low tide using hand nets, or further out to sea using trammel nets. On remote shorelines it is possible to improvise a shrimping net from a mosquito net attached to an H-shaped frame of light wood which can be towed through the surf.

Freshwater shrimps are mostly found in a useful size in warm tropical waters: most shallow streams in rainforests contain them. They can be collected with a mosquito headnet converted into a dip net or stretched taut in a frame. Disturb the leaf litter in the stream to flush out the shrimps, then scoop them up with your net a little way downstream.

Many shellfish can be cooked simply in the embers of your campfire.

Large jungle crayfish. One of the joys of remote wilderness can be an abundance of wild food, a lesson in conservation.

CRABS, LOBSTERS, SQUAT LOBSTERS AND CRAYFISH

Crabs, lobsters and crayfish provide some of the tastiest wild food. However, without access to a boat and crab or lobster pots, it is unlikely that you will find large crabs or lobsters, although in tropical regions large mud crabs can be speared in rock pools at low tide. Even so it is well worth searching rock pools for smaller crabs, and at very low tide turning over rocks in search of squat lobsters. A hooked stick or crooked piece of metal rod can be a great help in hooking them out of their retreats. You can improvise a trap for crab and lobster from strong fishing line and saplings. Make a hoop of flexible sapling or vines and reinforce it with two spokes crossing at its centre. Knot nooses made from fishing line around the circumference, then attach a weight and bait – dead rotting oily fish is ideal – at the centre. Lower this from rocks at high tide or anchor it to the seabed at low tide and recover it at the next low tide. In trying to reach the bait, the crabs and lobsters become entangled in the snares. In clear water it may be possible to collect crabs by improvising a drop net, baited in the same way. Attach a mosquito net or a piece of old fishing net to a weighted frame. Lower it on to the seabed, watch it, and when crabs scramble over it, lift it. In England the same method has been used in less clear water using an old bicycle wheel as the frame for the drop net. Bait and lower it into a likely spot for 10–20 minutes then haul it up swiftly to the surface.

In the tropics crabs are frequently to be found in freshwater streams. In the head-waters of the Orinoco I watched as women deftly hooked small crabs out of logs – hollowed out for the purpose, rather like a nesting box for birds.

Crayfish are highly prized as a delicacy, wherever they occur. In Aboriginal Arnhemland in the tropical north of Australia I have speared crayfish spotlighted at night with torches. In Indonesia you can catch them with shrimps. In Honduras I have seen giant crayfish taken with hook and line, while in Europe they are caught with drop nets and more elaborate crayfish traps. The classic method for catching crayfish is to take an old bucket or large tin can and punch pencil-diameter holes into the sides and bottom so that it will sink, or use a chicken-wire mesh drum. Bait it with old meat, the smellier the better, and submerge it close to a river bank. Crayfish are skilled trap robbers: to foil them remove the trap before daylight.

Wild crayfish caught with a headnet in a small stream.

Bivalves

Bivalve shellfish include some of the most popular *fruits de mer*, like mussels, oysters and clams. However, you must exercise caution in eating them. Bivalvular shellfish are filter feeders: they strain nutrients from water passed through a siphon organ, and may contain pollutants themselves, especially mussels, which live in open water, so filter more than clams, which live in nutrient-rich silt and sand. For the most part pathogenic bacteria are destroyed in cooking as long as the shellfish are cooked at 100 degrees Celsius for longer than 20 minutes, or for a shorter time in the much hotter embers of an open fire.

The toxin most responsible for shellfish poisoning is a marine algae of the *Gonyaulax* genus. When prevalent in large numbers, the algae become visible, turning the coastal water a reddish brown. Hence the term applied to their presence, 'red tides'. Unfortunately, they can be present in sufficient quantity to pose a serious threat to our health yet not be visible to the naked eye. Red tides cause two forms of poisoning: diarrhoetic shellfish poisoning (DSP), which causes serious illness , and paralytic shellfish poisoning (PSP), which is life threatening and leads to paralysis and the ultimate failure of our vital organs. Local knowledge of seasons when these tides occur is the only way to predict them. Hikers foraging along shorelines should stay alert to fishery authorities' advice and warnings. Bivalve shellfish also concentrate chemical pollutants after shipwrecks.

In the urban world we are far removed from the reality of the life of hunter-gatherers. Consider the demands of raising children. In the billy can is a meal of freshwater crabs collected in the headwaters of the Orinoco River.

Mussels

Marine mussels are easily collected from rocks at low tide. They should be cleaned up and kept overnight in fresh water. The next day check that they are still healthy before you cook them. Squeeze the shell slightly open: healthy mussels will close again, tight shut. Discard any mussels that remain closed after cooking by steaming or boiling for at least 20 minutes, or for less time in the embers of an open fire. Discard any which do not open up through the heat of the cooking.

FRESHWATER MUSSELS

Found in rivers with silty beds – look for old shells washed up on sandbars along the river. You will frequently encounter them when searching for aquatic food plants, such as the tubers of arrowhead *Sagittaria*.

Spend enough time in the company of hunter-gatherers and you become alert to a wealth of potential food sources, such as these freshwater mussels.

Clams

Clams and cockles can be raked or dug from sand or silt at low tide depending upon the species. They can be treated in the same way as mussels.

Razor-shells are only available at the lowest tides and they can dig themselves rapidly into the sand to evade you; you must employ special means to capture them. My favourite method is to approach their distinctive keyhole-shaped opening in the sand stealthily and sprinkle salt, or squirt a concentrated salt-water solution, into the hole. After a few seconds the razor-shell will project upwards through the hole by a couple of centimetres. Grasp it with your thumb and index finger, but do not pull. You will feel the razor-shell attempt to escape but soon it will exhaust itself and relax. Then you can draw it out easily.

These clams, called 'white mussels' in Namibia, are arranged for cooking. Hot ashes and embers are laid over them; as they cook the meat shrinks back towards the hinge and away from the sand.

Univalve shellfish

Includes whelks, limpets and winkles. Whelks are usually trapped in baited basket traps and, with the exception of the occasional whelk trapped in rock pools at extreme low tide, are usually beyond the reach of foragers. They may be affected by the red-tide organism (see page 206) as they eat filter feeders.

Limpets are one of the most reliable survival foods. As grazers, they are less prone to pollutants than filter feeders. They are not collected commercially because they are difficult to harvest and their texture is rough and chewy. However, neither is reason enough for a forager to discard them. To collect limpets, strike them swiftly and firmly with a rock to dislodge them. Use stealth and surprise: if you are unsuccessful on your first attempt they will clamp down extra hard.

To cook them, either place them upside down in a shallow bed of embers or allow them to clamp down on to a flat rock or metal sheet over which you ignite a rapid hot fire of dry grass or small twigs. When they are cooked the shell will easily lift free. Cut away the black blister, which contains the internal organs, and eat the orange mussel-like meat. They can be made into kebabs or even diced and used in a chowder.

Winkles are still a treat in coastal Britain. Boil them for 20–30 minutes and then use a pin to lift off their watertight seal and extract the spirally body. The same process is used elsewhere with mangrove snails and telescopium snails.

Sea urchins

Sea urchins are frequently a thorn in the forager's foot, but a popular seafood, particularly in the Mediterranean. Here they are boiled or steamed then broken open to reveal the soft edible interior.

Octopus

Octopus are usually harvested by spear fishermen, although occasionally they can be found in rock pools. Turn them inside out to kill them. To cook, boil or stew them in marinades made from fruit or coconut cream.

Limpets are an undervalued source of food.

209

Insects

Today the idea of eating an insect is utterly repulsive to many people, yet historically insects have been an important source of human nutrition. Indeed, in many tropical countries indigenous peoples still relish insect foods. High in nutritional content, insects are an easily digested source of protein.

Caterpillars

Generally, caterpillars are toxic, which is recognisable from their bright colour or irritant hairs. Never handle hairy caterpillars: they can cause serious, long-lasting skin rashes. In Africa the mopane caterpillar, the larval stage of the mopane moth, *Gonimbrasia belina*, is spiny, hairless, yellow, red and black, 6-8cm long and found in large numbers on the mopane tree. They can be eaten raw, sun-dried or cooked. Discard the head before eating.

Witchetty grubs – delicious.

Witchetty grubs

Several different species of witchetty grub are eaten by aboriginal people in Australia. They are found in the roots of the witchetty bush – you will know they're there if you can find the empty cases of emergent moths below it. Excavate the roots of the bush and look for 15mm diameter holes in them. Break open the roots and collect the grubs. They can be eaten raw or cooked quickly in hot ashes. They taste of scrambled eggs.

Palm grubs

Large white palm grubs are found in the trunks of fallen sago and other palms. They are such an important food source that some peoples deliberately fell palm trees to create a habitat for them. When you cut into the soft palm wood, look for 2–3cm diameter holes, which betray their presence. They can be eaten raw or cooked and have a pleasant palm oil flavour.

Palm grubs are even tastier than witchetty grubs.

Teredo worms

The Teredo, mangrove or ship worm inhabits dead timber in the marine environment, particularly mangrove wood. They are easily found by chopping into dead mangrove wood beside any 8–10cm diameter holes. A mollusc, this borer is one of the least appealing of all edible grubs but tastes good. Eaten raw it is rather like crab.

Teredo worms were a bane to ancient mariners, boring through ships' timbers.

Despite their appearance they taste fine…really.

211

Ants

Ants are eaten in many parts of the world, particularly the green ant in Australia which tastes of lemon and has antibiotic properties. During summer in the northern temperate zone wood ant larvae will make an emergency meal. Fried gently they taste of shrimp. To collect them trick the ants into doing the work. Lay your tarp next to the ants' nest and break open the nest, casting the larvae, nest material and ants on to the centre of the tarp. Lay some sticks around the edge of the tarp and fold over the sides to create shade. The ants will collect up the larvae and deposit them in the shade. After 20 minutes fold back the tarp edges and scoop up the larvae, which look like puffed rice.

Wood ants' nests are a lesson in shelter building.

1. Cast nest and larvae on to tarp – do not use all of the nest.
2. Fold over the tarp edge to create shade.
3. The ants do the work for you – after 20–30 minutes open up the shade and hey presto.

Honey ants taste like barley sugar.

Earthworms

In dire emergency the humble earthworm has been used as a source of protein. British POWs used them to supplement their meagre rations while forced to labour on the Burma railroad. They kept the worms in salt water, massaging them until they had purged and were pink in colour. Then they were added to the ordinary ration. They can also be sun-dried and powdered for use in bouillon.

Slugs and snails

Slugs are generally best avoided as they feed on poisonous fungi and may also become toxic.

Snails are widely eaten. In the tropics giant land snails are sold in the markets in bundles of five with a liana tie passed through holes in the shells. In Europe, the giant Roman snail, commonly found on chalky downs, and the smaller common grey snail are edible. It is best to purge them by keeping them for several days and feeding them only dandelion or wild garlic leaves. If you are confident that they have not been feeding on toxic plants, you can cook them immediately. Cooked Aboriginal style in hot embers until their juices boil over they are a tasty if chewy delicacy.

Amphibians and reptiles

A wide range of amphibians are eaten, from crocodiles to frogs. In an emergency, frogs are easy to catch but only the hind legs are worth eating. All members of the *Rana* genus are edible. Beware of tropical frogs, which may be highly toxic, such as arrow-poison frogs. Toads are toxic, although they were used as food in Britain's rural past. Remove the dangerous paratoid glands, situated behind the eyes, and gut them before cooking. Today, with ever-disappearing wetland habitats, many amphibians are protected by law – and I would far rather watch them than eat them!

Lizards and snakes are eaten in many parts of the world, caught either by snare or spear. They are white-fleshed and good eating.

Happy with this meal, the San bushman heads home to share this lizard with his family.

Respect must be accorded to the spirits of the animals which the Sanema hunt. Failure to do so can result in illness or even death.

Birds

One of the most delightful aspects of outdoors life is the constant presence of our feathered cousins, but of course in an emergency they may also be an important food source. The most important food species are ducks, geese, grouse, pheasants and pigeons, although many smaller birds are eaten by indigenous peoples. Eggs can also be collected, most easily found in wetland habitats. Birds are protected by law from poaching, but in a true emergency these traps from our pre-industrial past may save the day.

When using birds as food, do not drink their blood or eat raw flesh: they are prone to parasitic infestation.

Old English bird trap.

In Namibia a San bushman sets a snare for a Koran bird.

In Lapland a Sami man sets a snare for Ptarmigan.

Detail of the bushman Koran trap –
note tree gum used as bait.

Bats

In many tropical areas bats are considered a delicacy, hunted with throwing sticks or by collection from caves.

In Indonesia bats are considered a delicacy amongst the Nuaulu.

Old English cribbett trap – catches ground birds alive.

Fishing

Many a skilled fisherman has used rod and line to feed a party in the wilds after the food stocks have been damaged or lost. Conventional fishing techniques are a useful and important aspect of wilderness travel. In my experience lure and worm fishing are the most widely successful techniques: a good reel, a good-quality line, a carriage rod (in several sections) and a selection of hooks and lures need not be heavy and bulky. Make sure that you have the required licence and that you follow the authorities' guidelines on species and size. The rules are intended to safeguard the river ecology, which is, after all, what we are there to enjoy.

Here are some techniques commonly employed in the wilderness when fishing for food and not sport. On civilised waters they may be considered bad practice or be prohibited. However, in remote areas where pressure on fish stocks is virtually non-existent they remain an appropriate means of fishing for food.

Where to look for fish

Before considering the fishing method, you must look for the most productive water in your vicinity. Finding fish is essentially a commonsense process: if it is hot and sunny look for cool shady pools; if it is cold, seek warm, sunny spots. Check deep eddies on fast-moving streams, particularly where insects falling from overhanging vegetation may offer a popular feeding place. When water babbles or gushes over rocks it becomes oxygenated: the oxygen-rich water below can provide first-rate fishing opportunities, as can nutrient-rich areas of rivers, such as where a stream joins a river. On wide open water look for narrows – for example, between islands or between an island and the shore where the fish will be funnelled into a smaller area. Observe the behaviour and movements of other wildlife: herons, pelicans, otters and many other expert fisher creatures may point the way to your own success.

INDICATORS OF FISH FEEDING

The most obvious sign is fish breaking the surface to take insects. However, many species stay close to the bottom, grazing on vegetation and molluscs, disturbing vegetation, which rises to the water surface.

WHEN TO FISH

Generally, early morning, late afternoon, twilight and at night are the most productive times, but here experimentation will be your best guide.

Wild brown trout are a delicious meal, a gift of nature to the respectful fisherman.

TICKLING

Tickling, or guddling as it is known in Scotland, is a widely prohibited method of fishing. In the past, tickling was the high art of non-commercial poaching, and no other method of fishing is so primal or as satisfying. Not even fly fishing! Tickling was employed in two types of water: the first in shallow water to take fish almost beached on their way to spawn, the easiest method, and still used on the Falkland Islands; the second in rivers with clear water, shady pools and overhanging banks. Classically the fish is gently encouraged into a shady pool where it takes refuge under a bank. Then, wading slowly and gently, with your hands submerged in front of you, palms up, reach under the bank, exploring with your fingertips. Amazingly, you will eventually discover the gentle flick of a fin and the belly of the fish. The first time you do this you will certainly flinch and scare the fish away. The second time, however, you will be ready. Having found the fish, the secret is to move your palms under its belly, then swiftly and without hesitation snatch it with an enfolding grip that bends it, preventing its escape. Draw the fish towards your stomach and cast it well up on to the bank. Many a fish has escaped by wriggling back into the water.

Strangely enough trout taste best poached.

BALING

A technique I have seen employed in tropical Africa. A section of small slow-flowing stream is dammed off in two places and the water between the dams bailed out to reveal the bed. As the water level drops, the fish take refuge under stones, logs and any crevice they can find. They must be winkled out from their hidey-holes, which is surprisingly difficult. It must be the least skilful fishing technique, but effective none the less.

DRIVING - *LAU*

In Western Samoa I had the opportunity to take part in a *lau*. This involves a group effort. Before low tide people gather on the beach and make a long rope of vines and coconut-palm leaves to use as a corral: the palm leaves are spliced in so that they will hang down in the water like a screen. When it is ready the *lau* is taken out into the water at low tide, held by people 4–5 metres apart. The party gradually creates a circle at least 100 metres in diameter. The reef fish are trapped inside the corral as they are not prepared to pass the leaf screen. When the circle is complete, spear fishermen enter it and catch the trapped fish. Afterwards the catch is divided between the participants, and with the wisdom of generations, the reef just fished is left until the stocks have recovered.

POISONING

A controversial method of fishing. When employed by small extended families in the wilderness it is of little concern. Today, however, it is a cause for great concern. In remote rainforests large mission-station-based communities carry out fish poisoning on a larger scale than was traditionally the case. In the Philippines skin-divers stun reef fish with poison to supply an illicit trade in aquarium fish. Fish collected in this way soon die from the effects of the poisoning. Increasingly the poisons used are modern synthesised toxins. Traditionally, plant poisons were used, such as barringtonia, virolla vine or the less harmful saponins available in a wide range of plants.

In South America poisoning is still widely practised - but to fill stomachs, not for trade.

SPEARING

Today spearing survives only in remote communities where fishing is solely a matter of food collecting. Of the many methods I have encountered the technique that most impresses me is that of the Aboriginal peoples of northern Australia, who use a long, light spear with four splayed metal tines 40cm long. Traditionally made from hardwood bound with banyan fibre and beeswax, metal and copper wire or strong mono-filament fishing lines are now the norm. This easily made hunting tool is used to catch fish, rays, crabs, longnecked turtles, lizards, birds, crayfish. It is enhanced by the use of a *woomera* (spear-thrower) which increases the speed of throwing, aids accuracy and, if necessary, can impart greater force to the spear. To use this weapon requires considerably more skill than a modern hunting tool. For example, when hunting rays you learn quickly that tidal conditions must be in your favour, just on the ebb so that the water is clear with good visibility and not sandy. Then you have to move slowly with stealth and recognise the subtlest disturbance in the pattern of the seabed that betrays the presence of the ray. Once they are seen, you must throw with accuracy and without hesitation. The *woomera* serves as the club to dispatch the prey. When hunting among Aboriginal people, you will not easily detect any

obvious process of conservation, but each hunter's hand is guided by ancient wisdom, a process of conservation enshrined in strictly observed Aboriginal law that dictates which species each hunter may or may not hunt.

In the far north the Inuit still employ leister spears to catch the delicious Arctic char. To do this they cut a hole through the ice of a frozen lake, a difficult task as the ice can be two metres thick. The narwhal ivory lure attracts the char to the hole where they are speared. It is a process that requires skill, endurance and patience.

In the tropics, on reefs and in forest streams, simple harpoons are put to great use. To succeed with them you need swimming goggles or a diving mask. In many places goggles are still carved from wood then fitted with glass lenses – traditionally they were fashioned from thinly scraped translucent sea-turtle shell. Today harpoons are usually powered by rubber, either with a spear and catapult-like arrangement or, more commonly, with a loop of rubber attached to the tail of a spear with several tines. To fire it the thumb is passed through the loop of rubber, which is stretched, and the spear grasped well up its shaft. Releasing the shaft causes the harpoon to shoot forward. A simple and effective fishing method.

221

Angling

Angling or fishing with a hook and line is the most widespread fishing method, and if you are travelling on water you should consider taking a rod and lures with you, or improvising a simple rod from a thin stiff sapling: remove the bark and allow the wood to dry and stiffen for a couple of days . Attach a stretch of line the same length as the rod to the tip. Or improvise rings from wire and cast a longer line like a fly line.

Fish species and techniques vary widely around the globe. Before you enter any wild area ask local fishermen what tackle and bait they would use. If you cannot afford the weight of a rod in your outfit, try one of the following techniques.

HAND-LINE HOBO FISHING

Hand-line fishing offers less control than rod fishing, but it is rewarding in its simplicity. Many different sizes of fish can be caught in this way in both marine and inland waters. All manner of lures can be fished from a hand-line, but with a slower retrieve than that provided by geared lure fishing reels. I find that modern silicon-bodied jigs work best: they behave in a convincing way, even when retrieved slowly. But don't confine yourself to artificial lures: worm and hook are particularly effective on a hand-line when set as a simple fixed paternoster, or running leger. Let the line run over an outstretched finger to detect a bite.

One of the joys of hand-lining is its compactness: you do not need a purpose-made reel – virtually any smooth cylinder can be converted into a hand-line reel, and discarded beer cans or plastic drinks bottles are ideal. The latter provide a receptacle for tackle storage. I have even pressed a mosquito-repellent bottle into service as a hand-line reel. Attach the end of your line to your improvised reel then wind on the line by hand. Hold the reel securely in one hand, pointing it to where you intend the lure to fall. Cast the lure with the other hand in one smooth underhand swing, releasing it at just above waist height. With a few minutes' practice you will discover how economical a cast this is, and that you can place the lure with great accuracy. Retrieve the lure by winding the line on to the reel, staying alert to the vibrations caused by fish nibbling it. When a fish strikes, play him from the reel rather than your hand as you reel in.

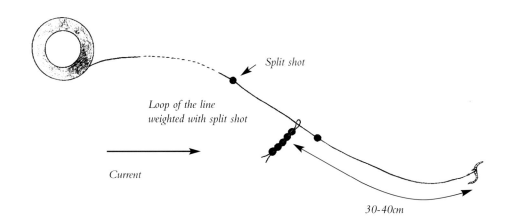

Split shot

Loop of the line weighted with split shot

Current

30-40cm

Hand line and running ledger rig.

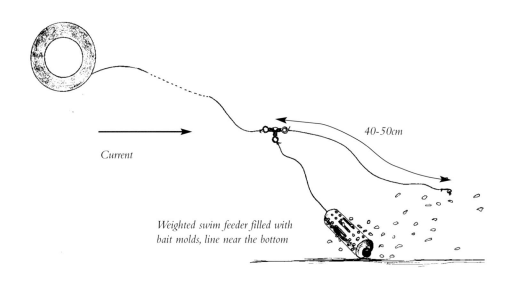

Current

40-50cm

Weighted swim feeder filled with bait molds, line near the bottom

Hand line with fixed paternoster and swim feeder.

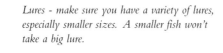

Lures - make sure you have a variety of lures, especially smaller sizes. A smaller fish won't take a big lure.

A small rod like this is ideal for wilderness travel.

NIGHT-LINES AND TROT-LINES

Night-lines are strictly prohibited in most circumstances, but in the wild they remain an effective emergency fishing method. Take a long length of heavy fishing line or thin nylon cord, attach dropper loops 30cm apart, and to each loop a leader of nylon line 40–50cm long. Tie on the hooks and bait them with thick leathery-skinned grubs and slugs rather than worms, which many fish can remove from the hook. Attach a rock at one end of the line and tie the other end to a thin flexible sapling or overhanging branch on shore. Lay the hooks and line into the water then cast out the rock from the bank. This will prevent tangling – and you hooking yourself. Once set, the night-line will fish many levels within the water. Check morning and evening, rebaiting and setting as necessary. Night-lines need not be large and cumbersome: 4–5-hook lines are fine.

In marine environments you can make a similar arrangement, but peg it to the seabed at low tide and retrieve it at the next low tide. Sandy areas among rock outcrops can be excellent places to catch flounders, dabs or plaice – bait with lugworm, limpet or fish.

Metal fish hooks are difficult to replace, but you can make do without them. Until the turn of the century trot-lines were set on sandbars in the Thames estuary with hooks made from hawthorn. Perhaps the most commonly employed alternative is the gorge hook, a toggle that turns side on and embeds itself in the throat or mouth of the fish. These can be made from bone, antler or even hard wood. Hooks almost identical to modern metal hooks were once carved from bone, and perhaps the most cunning hook I have ever seen was fashioned by Stone Age fishermen in what is now France from a wild-boar tusk which, in cross-section, has a perfect hook shape. In the far north of Europe a three-pronged Y-shaped gorge was still commonly used for catching burbot until recent times.

On the Pacific coast of British Columbia and Alaska, the first nations fashioned a wide variety of specialised hooks from wood and bone. Their steam-bent and halibut hooks were works of art, but the trolling hook, made from wood, bone and lashed with a split root, is easily made and can be used to great effect in place of metal hooks.

Snaring

In clear water poachers snared fish. They cut a hazel or alder sapling to the required length, leaving the bark on, and attached a single strand of snare wire to the point with a noose 15cm in diameter. Often the wire was blackened with soot from a candle flame or a piece of birch bark. Then they lowered the snare into the water and carefully manoeuvred it over the fish's head and back behind the gill flap. Then they lifted it smartly upwards, bringing the fish into the air and to shore.

In the wilderness a gill net is a useful survival tool for emergencies.

Netting

Unsporting and outlawed in managed waterways, the most important of all fishing techniques for survival in a remote land is the use of a gill net. Using this technique, you can take fish that are difficult to hook. A gill net is not heavy and takes up little space, so it is easy to bury one in your outfit. Traditionally native people used natural fibre nets dyed red, a tradition that survives today among northern net fishermen because red is difficult to see under water. I have set a gill net several times to discover it had caught fish before I had finished laying it.

Ice fishing

In winter, lakes and rivers in the far north freeze and the ice thickens progressively as the season deepens. Despite its apparent beauty, water in its frozen forms of snow and ice must at all times be considered treacherous. Moving on frozen water is hazardous at the beginning and end of winter and wherever the water is travelling fast over rapids or through narrows. I remember travelling one February for several hours by snowmobile over frozen lakes in Labrador when my guide stopped to show me fast-moving water boiling up from an area clear of ice. In darkness or poor visibility and without his expert local knowledge, it would have been easy to drive straight into the water. Generally, the minimum thickness of freshwater ice that will support a single person on skis is 5cm, and it is as well to avoid moving on such thin ice. Bear in mind that a heavy snowfall on ice will load and stress it, as will a drop of the supporting water level below it. With ice 20cm thick, fishing is a far safer proposition. Frequently in midwinter ice can be a metre thick or more.

To break through ice, you will need either an ice chisel or an ice auger. With both tools, you must take great care not to injure your feet when using them.

Ice chisels are heavy and long-handled. The tip is either chisel-shaped, about 5cm wide, or triangularly pointed. The chisel-ended ones cut more efficiently but are more difficult to keep sharp and in good order than the triangular type. Widely used in Canada, they have no moving part to malfunction and will cut through very thick ice or cut very wide holes. On Baffin Island I have helped Inuit fishermen cut two holes through 2.5 metres of ice to set a net for Arctic char. It was a long and labour-intensive process.

In northern Europe, and increasingly elsewhere, rotary ice augers are preferred. Sometimes these are motorised and wide-bladed, but more commonly hand-powered. Fitted with two simple cutting blades they drill neatly through ice up to a metre thick. They are prone to damage from misuse, particularly if they are banged down on the ice, which blunts the blades. Like all sharp tools, ice chisels and augers should be either masked or set into the ice when not in use.

To cut through the ice, first clear an area of snow to expose the ice surface, then cut the hole. Once cut, the water will gush up so beware of soaking your feet. Clear any lumps of ice from the hole and shovel them away. Almost as soon as you have done this the surface of the water will begin to freeze over – keep it clear by scooping away the ice. Ice fishermen use special scoops but the tip of a snow shovel does equally well.

Indigenous people usually fish through ice with a short stick or rod, and metal lures. They place spruce boughs, a reindeer or caribou pelt beneath their knees for insulation. However, I opt for a set-line left overnight. In this hooks can be baited, increasing the prospect of a catch. Ensure that your line is in the centre of the hole to prevent it being frozen in as the hole will refreeze inwards from the edge. Then plug the hole opening with some spruce-bough tips and cover it well with snow as insulation to slow the freezing process. If you attach the line to an anchor stick longer than your knife blade you will be able to reopen the hole, should it freeze, by chipping without fear of cutting the line.

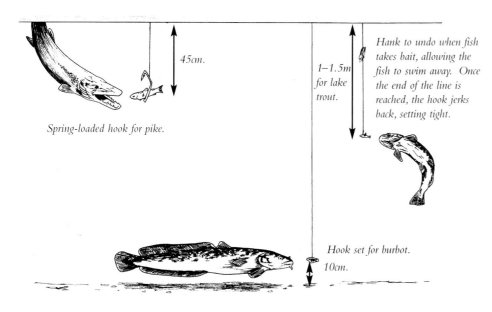

45cm.

Spring-loaded hook for pike.

1–1.5m for lake trout.

Hook set for burbot. 10cm.

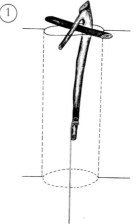

Hank to undo when fish takes bait, allowing the fish to swim away. Once the end of the line is reached, the hook jerks back, setting tight.

Using a stick will enable you to chip out the line if the hole freezes closed, without fear of cutting the line and losing both fish and tackle.

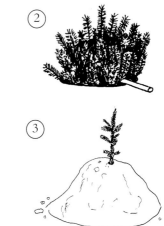

Mark the location of the hole, so that it can be found after snowfall.

Eels

Eels were once caught widely for food by workers in the British countryside, and to this day eels and liquor – a type of gravy – are a popular food in the East End of London. (The eel's extremely tough leathery skin was once used to fashion the universal joint of threshing flails, and makeshift hinges.) Both freshwater and marine eels are edible but avoid the large tropical marine eels found in coral reefs as they may be toxic due to the coral component in their diet.

Eel grabbing

The simplest method of catching eels is to pluck them from clear, shallow water. As with all things bushcraft, simple is not necessarily easy – rare indeed is the countryman who is well accomplished in this technique. To grasp an eel, lock it in a scissor grip between your middle, index and third fingers, hooking the middle finger over the eel.

Eel line

Eels can be caught with hook and line, and commonly with a night-line anchored at the bank to a thin sapling or, more traditionally, a tied-back branch that acted as a shock absorber, preventing the eel breaking the line.

Babbing, freshwater and marine eels

For freshwater eels: thread a length of wool through a mass of worms and tie it into a loop so that the worms are squeezed together. Attach the loop to a stronger line, then to a sapling rod. Let the worms drift down with the current in a stream or ditch towards where you have seen an eel or suspect it to be. When the eel takes the bait the wool becomes entangled in its needle-like teeth. Pull the eel upward – steadily so it cannot escape and will be brought to the surface. In New Zealand this technique was employed by the Maori, using fibres from flax leaves.

An alternative method involves placing the bait – rank-smelling animal intestine is ideal – in a small bag woven from thin fibrous material; onion sacks and hairnets are popular

Eel bag

A reliable means of taking eels. You will need a cloth sack and some suitable bait, such as high-smelling intestine. Weight the sack with a small rock, half fill it with dry grass or similar and place the bait in the middle. Close the bag and cut some small slits in its side. These should be large enough only to encourage the eel to bite its way into the sack. Attach a line to the sack and throw it into a deep pool. Leave it overnight and retrieve it early in the morning. With luck you will find one or more eels inside.

Eel gaffs and spears

Perhaps the most widespread means of taking eels.

Eel traps and boxes, freshwater and marine

Traps range from simple bamboo tubes to elegantly woven wicker baskets, but today eel baskets are made from wire mesh. An interesting marine eel trap I saw in Western Samoa consisted of a wooden box with a round opening. On the inside a tin fitted with a cloth sleeve formed a tunnel entrance. When the eel entered the box through the sleeve it could not find the way out again. The trap was baited with a dead fish then buried in the side of a coral head and left overnight. The tin-can/sleeve tunnel can also be used with a sack instead of a box.

Mammals

Trapping prompted some of the earliest human attempts at mechanics and engineering. In our pre-farming past, trapping was the easiest way to secure meat. It is an important and effective survival skill. Unfortunately, in the past we have allowed indiscriminate trapping skills to bring some species to the brink of extinction or beyond it. For traditional trappers, respect and wisdom of generations dictate the method and quota to be taken on trap lines. Families that have hunted and trapped in their territory for centuries know that their own welfare is bound up with that of their prey, that they cannot live without it.

If we are travelling in really wild regions and find ourselves without food we may find ourselves facing starvation. Experienced backwoods travellers are always equipped to hunt and fish and know how to catch animals for meat by trapping. I believe that the skill of trapping is akin to firelighting in its contribution to our self-reliance in the wilderness, but that we must respect our prey: we should employ techniques that are effective yet minimise suffering, and only employ them in times of need.

Modern British rabbit snare.

Rabbit snares

An ancient means of trapping, which is still in relatively widespread usage today. The traditional British rabbit snare comprised four parts: the snare itself, ideally made from six–eight strands of thin brass wire with a free running eyelet twisted in; the cord; the teeler stick and the peg or stake. The snares are placed on a rabbit trail over the low place where the rabbit lands when moving down the trail. Snares can also be placed on the rabbits' look-out post, but never at a burrow entrance. Traditionally the snare was set with a noose of fist size diameter held four fingers high by a teeler stick made from a short cleft of hazel wand. The cord was then staked firmly to the ground. Today a modified snare is more commonly employed incorporating a teeler of fencing wire to which the wire is firmly anchored, the cord and peg being made fast to a loop in the wire teeler. The wire of these newer snares is set at the same height but with a larger diameter loop.

The same arrangement is frequently used for taking hares but the noose is pear-shaped and set hand-high on the run.

Rabbits and hares taken by these means are usually alive when the snares are checked, sitting quietly. The trapper dispatches the rabbit without fuss or alarm by gently grasping its neck between two fingers of one hand and the hind feet with the other. Then, with a smart, firm, stretching action, he breaks its neck with a simultaneous deft lifting of the rabbit's chin. Done correctly, this is the most humane and certain way to dispatch a rabbit.

Hare snare set in the Arctic.

227

Acknowledgements

A dear friend once told me that writing a book is like being pregnant, and this book has been no exception. While publishers paced the corridors of Hodder & Stoughton eager for news of the expected arrival, friends and colleagues proffered advice and support; they are owed the greatest debt of gratitude. Thanks then to the Woodlore team, particularly Ben McNutt who has provided all of the illustrations for *Bushcraft*. Also to Juha Rankinen and James Lock for demonstrating for the camera. To Tom Lutyens, the ablest of US Survival Instructors, for demonstrating banana craft, and to Eleanor Dunn for helping with setting up photos and carrying camera bags. Also to Ian Palmer, whose hands make a brief appearance in Fire.

Special thanks must go to: Gordon Hillman for his unflinching support and advice, Rob and Barbara Newington for providing locations for much of the photography, Lord and Lady Selborne and Viscount Chelsea for believing in the value of bushcraft.

To true friends and men who really know the woods – Lars Fält, Robert Colin-Stokes, George Neal and Peter Nicol, and to the many different indigenous peoples who have invited me to their firesides and showed me the way that they employ bushcraft.

To Jane Brown for typing the manuscript, and the greatest thanks of all to Rachel, without whose strength this book would never have been completed.

All photographs by the author, except: page 38 right Tom Lutyens; page 52 left and bottom right Danny Cane; pages 82 and 119 right Alan Duxbury; pages 123 and 141 Barrie Foster; page 143 Matt Brandon; page 224 Lars Fält. From Oxford Scientific Films (OSF): page 182 bottom left Bob Gibbons; pages 184 top, 185 top right, 198 top left and centre left and bottom G.A. Maclean; pages 185 bottom right, 194 bottom right Barrie E. Watts; page 186 top Mike Slater; pages 186 bottom right, 187 bottom Ian West; page 188 top left Niall Benvie, top right LSF; page 189 bottom left Faithjof Skibbe, bottom middle Tim Shepherd; page 194 middle right H.L. Fox; page 198 top right Robin Redfern; page 199 bottom centre Sinclair Stammers, bottom right Bob Fredrick; page 202 Laurence Gould; page 203 top right and bottom G.I. Bernard, top centre Fredrick Ehrenstrom; page 201 top left C.W. Helliwell. From Garden Picture Library (GPL): page 191 top right Geoff Dann/GPL.

Photography

Throughout *Bushcraft* the photographs were taken using Fuji film. For the most part they have been taken on Provia 100 or 100F although, where practical, Velvia has been used and, where necessary, Provia 400 and 400F.

All of the 35mm images were captured with Nikon cameras and lenses, mostly using a FM2 or F5.

Panoramic images were taken on a Hasselblad X-Pan, and medium format images on a Hasselblad 203FE.

www.fco.gov.uk/knowbeforeyougo

Index